Essays on Individualism

Essays on Individualism

Modern Ideology in Anthropological Perspective

Louis Dumont

The University of Chicago Press

Chicago and London

The University of Chicago Press, Chicago 60637
The University of Chicago Press, Ltd., London
© 1986 by The University of Chicago
All rights reserved. Published in 1986
Paperback edition 1992
Printed in the United States of America

95 94 93 92   5 4 3 2

An earlier version of this book was published in 1983 by Editions du Seuil, under the title *Essais sur l'individualisme: Une perspective anthropologique sur l'idéologie moderne.*

Library of Congress Cataloging-in-Publication Data

Dumont, Louis, 1911–
    Essays on individualism.

    Enl. translation of: Essais sur l'individualisme.
    Bibliography: p.
    Includes index.
    1. Individualism—History. I. Title.
JC571.D913 1986   302.5′4   86-1477
ISBN 0-226-16956-1 (cloth)
ISBN 0-226-16958-8 (paperback)

♾ The paper used in this publication meets the minimum requirements of the American National Standard for Information Sciences—Permanence of Paper for Printed Library Materials, ANSI Z39.48-1984.

To Jenny's memory

Contents

Preface to the English Edition

On the publication of an English version of my *Essais sur l'indivi-dualisme* (1983) I have seized the opportunity to add two more chapters (3 and 5). I am thankful to the American publishers who have allowed me to thus make the book more complete. Most of the constituent parts had already been published in English.

The Introduction and chapters 5 and 6 have been translated by Paul Hockings, whom I thank for his cooperation, and the author. I have pleasure in recording my gratitude to Joseph Erhardy, whose expertise in the English language made his help invaluable to me from the time of the *Contributions to Indian Sociology* to the present, and particularly, here, for the texts that have become chapters 1, 2, and 9. More circumscribed assistance is recorded in the relevant chapter openings.

The book is very much a halfway report. I have been engaged for some twenty years in a study of modern ideology, which has resulted in a series of essays of restricted scope bearing on different periods and on various aspects of that vast topic. A friend, Paul Thibaud, director of the periodical *Esprit*, suggested collecting those essays along with a few others of a more distinctly anthropological cast. He thought the general social-anthropological perspective of the latter would throw light on the former and help the reader to reach the global point of view that has led to the study of modernity and might otherwise appear arbitrary—even if it does not evoke the "intellectual effrontery" of Parisian hue that a British critic once laid at my door.

I followed Paul Thibaud's advice that the time had come to provide some general idea of my research on modern ideology, given the limited future with which I must henceforth reckon for its pursuit. As to the social-anthropological background, I had already sketched the transition from the anthropology of India to the present study in the introduction of my book *From Mandeville to Marx*. But that left out of account the very conception of anthropology that I hold, which is far from being common among specialists or familiar to the general public.

In the following introduction, therefore, I had to go back into my own experience, back to the very origin of the conception of anthropology. It was not difficult, for the general orientation has not varied. Yet it meant retracing my steps mentally forty years back, in an area in which personal and professional concerns can hardly be separated. The memory of the companion of all those years, who left me in 1978, is inseparable from such a journey. That is why the book is dedicated to her memory.

I wish also to extend my thanks to all those who have encouraged me in the past few years, in diverse ways, to persevere in an endeavor which might have been deemed futile. They helped me carry on, and are still helping me, more than I can say. The thought of them indwells this volume.

Louis Dumont

Introduction

This Introduction has two aims: first, it attempts to tie the two parts of the book together, straddling the academic distance between on one side social anthropology as a speciality within social science, and, on the other, the history of ideas—or rather the intellectual history of our modern civilization. It needs to be shown here that a study of the set of ideas and values characteristic of modern times can be justified and even commended from a social-anthropological viewpoint. Yet, if I understand aright the wish of Paul Thibaud that is mentioned in the Preface, this will not be quite enough, for the viewpoint or orientation of the ideological study—we might say its very spirit—should be made to appear not as something arbitrarily imposed but as the natural result of an anthropological perspective.

In a sense, of course, everything that follows in this book, especially in part 2, will have to answer those needs. This Introduction will serve to direct the reader's attention immediately to principles, to bring into relief the dominant lines that run through the different chapters, and to recover the inspiration behind it all. The task is not difficult, since at the outset this inspiration has both a face and a name, those of Marcel Mauss. Just as his teaching was the source of my own efforts, so this Introduction has to start from his views.

Before coming to Mauss himself, however, we have to recall that there are two kinds of sociology distinguished by their starting point and their global approach. In the first kind, one begins, as is natural for modern scholars, by positing individual human beings, who are then seen as living in society; sometimes one even attempts to show society as arising from the interaction of individuals. In the other kind of sociology, one starts from the fact that men are social beings, that is, one takes society as a global fact irreducible to its parts—and here it is not a matter of "Society" in the abstract but always of a particular, concrete society with all its specific institutions and representations. Since one speaks of methodological individualism in the first case, one might speak of methodological holism in the second. In fact, every time we confront a foreign society the holistic approach is called for, and the ethnologist or anthropologist cannot do without it: he will only be able to communicate with the people he wants to study when he has mastered the language they have in common, for that is the vehicle of their ideas and values, of the ideology through which they think of everything, including themselves. At bottom, that is why British and American anthropologists, for all the inclination toward individualism and nominalism they derive from their culture, have been unable to do quite without the sociology of Durkheim and his nephew Marcel Mauss.

There is one point in Mauss's teaching that is essential to what has just been said: the stress on *difference*. First, on differences in general. For Mauss, confining oneself to what societies have in common and neglecting their differences, in the manner of Frazer and the first British school of anthropology, was out of the question.[1] His favorite theme, the "total social fact," is by definition a *specific* complex of a particular society (or type of society), which cannot be made to coincide with any other. To interpret this in some measure: there is no sociological fact apart from the reference to the global society it concerns.

There is a second point, even more important than the first if that is possible: among differences there is one that dominates all others. It is the difference that separates the observer, as a bearer of modern ideas and values, from those observed. Mauss was thinking mainly of tribal societies, but what he says is basically true of large societies of the traditional type. Every anthropologist is confronted by this difference between *us* and *them*; it is omnipresent in his practice. Let us suppose he has become familiar with the culture he studies. Then his problem will be, as Evans-Pritchard used to say, "translating" that culture into the language of our own culture and

---

1. Cf. *Homo Hierarchicus* (1980; henceforth *HH*), p. 425, n. 1. Similarly my book *From Mandeville to Marx* (1977), will be designated throughout as *MM*.

of anthropology which is a part of it. I might add that the operation is even more complex than translation. Mauss mentions again and again the pitfalls awaiting us here, the difficulties and precautions resulting from that basic difference. Among other things, our most general rubrics, such as ethics, politics, economics, are not easily applied to other societies: they can be resorted to only warily and temporarily. In the last analysis, in order to truly *understand* we must be able on occasion to ignore this partitioning and to search, in the whole field, for what corresponds on *their* side to what *we* acknowledge, and for what corresponds on *our* side to what *they* acknowledge. In other words, we must strive to construct on both sides comparable facts.

It is perhaps worth stating what happens here in general terms. From the viewpoint that is most immediately relevant to the study, that is, with regard to the social representations he shares, the "observer" is unavoidably present in "the observed"; he plays, so to speak, an obbligato part in it. The picture he delivers is not an objective picture in the sense that the subject is absent from it: it is a picture of something seen by someone. That is an all-important circumstance from the viewpoint of the philosophy of science, which begins just at the point where the "objective" picture is referred to the subject who produces it. In the kind of anthropology we have in view here (as in nuclear physics), we stand from the outset on that more radical level where the observer cannot be abstracted. Admittedly, this is not quite explicit in Mauss. In the study of religion, when he draws our attention to the question, "Who are the people who have such and such a belief?" he does not add "as compared with us, who have this other belief"; instead, *we* add it on the strength of numerous other passages where Mauss emphasizes the particular, more or less exceptional character of our modern ideas.[2] The value of this perspective is seen from the fact that, all considered, it embraces everything essential that social and cultural anthropology has ever done. True, it entails increased complication and intimidating constraints, which may be the reason it is not more widespread. To mention only two points: (1) the jargon of established sociology is cut out; (2) the prospect of laying hold of universals recedes to the horizon: one can speak of "the human mind" only when two different forms of it are subsumed under a single formula, when two distinct ideologies appear as two

2. See Mauss 1968–69, 3: 178–79, 202–4.

variants of a single broader ideology. This process of subsumption, ever in need of renewal, designates the human mind both as its principle and as its asymptote.

Save for this final digression, I have tried here to schematize as little as possible the great principle which arises from Mauss's teaching and which has directed all my work. If there was need for external confirmation of that principle, it could be found in the resounding demonstration by Karl Polanyi of the exceptional nature of our modern conception of economics: everywhere else what we call economic facts are embedded in the social tissue, and it is only we, the moderns, who have singled them out so as to build them into a distinct system. There is, however, a shade—perhaps more than that?—of difference between Mauss and Polanyi. For Polanyi, modernity, in the form of economic liberalism, lies at the very opposite pole from everything else; while for Mauss it is sometimes as though everything else were leading up to modernity: there are moments when a remnant of evolutionary thought comes along to cover up the discontinuities, no matter how steadfastly they are recognized. This is so when he refers to the grand Durkheimian project of "a social history of the categories of the human mind," which evokes a linear development of mankind as well as a sociological causalism,* which Mauss had not come to abandon completely either. Polanyi's radical critique of economic liberalism and of the primacy of the economic dimension shows the gap that has opened up between Mauss's generation and ours. Yet that distance by no means endangers the basic conception of comparison and of anthropology which we are here taking up as Mauss's bequest. Moreover, he himself had already discreetly distanced himself from what scientism and sociological hubris there was in Durkheim. Besides, in a broad sense "the social history of the categories of the human mind" is still the order of the day for us, only it seems infinitely more complex, more multiplex and arduous to us than it did to the Durkheimian enthusiasts at the beginning of the century; and if we read closely what Mauss said in 1938 about the results of their research, we shall see that his claims were after all modest.[3]

*The author uses the word *causalisme* in the French version to mean the belief that causality has the same place in sociology as elsewhere, and that social facts are eminent causal factors.—Trans.

3. See the beginning of the lecture "La notion de personne," in Mauss 1950: 333–34.

Let us be quite clear that the portrait I offered of Mauss in 1952 (reproduced below as chapter 7) as presenting what is essential for us is in no way the critical appraisal of him that one would hope for today. At that earlier time my intention was simply to introduce him to British colleagues and students who knew little about him and might be misled, or repelled, by a brilliant but overly abstract recent interpretation. Today the situation is altogether different, for Mauss now enjoys worldwide a great prestige among anthropologists, even, I might say, a kind of reverence that is quite rare, transitory perhaps, but nonetheless elating for those who knew him. However difficult the task may be, the time has certainly come for a discussion of Mauss's theoretical views and the interpretations they have received, a discussion that should be at the same time wary and thorough. This is not, however, our object here, where only the very basics are called for.

Practically, or methodologically, Mauss teaches us always to maintain a double reference—a reference to the global society on the one hand and, on the other, a reciprocal reference of comparison between observer and observed. In the pages that follow I have been led to schematize or objectify the opposition between observer and observed as an opposition between modern and traditional or, more broadly, between modern and nonmodern. Admittedly this kind of distinction is hardly welcome today. Someone might ironically suggest that such binary oppositions have a sort of nineteenth-century flavor, or state with Mary Douglas that "binary distinctions are an analytic procedure, but their usefulness does not guarantee that existence divides like that. We should look with suspicion on anyone who declared that there are two kinds of people, or two kinds of reality or process" (Douglas 1978, 161).

To this we shall quietly respond that there are two ways of looking at any piece of knowledge, a superficial one that leaves the knowing subject out of account, and a deeper one that includes him. At a pinch, this will be enough to justify our distinction.

Nonetheless, the reader who is not a specialist may well be surprised, for here we are probably far from the image of social science that public opinion is encouraged to harbor. Let me then explain bluntly how anthropology has diverged from that image, especially in the past few decades. As soon as one abandons the damaging partitions I have mentioned, as well as naive ideas about one part of social life being determined by another ("infrastructure and superstructure"), one loses interest in developing taxonomies like those of the natural species for social systems or subsystems. Some time ago Sir Edmund Leach derided such "butterfly collecting" (1961: 5). And the more we stress—beyond social organization alone—facts of consciousness, ideas and values, what Durkheim called collective representations, in other words, the keener we are to carry out a "comprehensive" anthropology, the more difficult it becomes to compare different societies.[4] Let me add that the few theories we have (if the term is not too ambitious) apply best to just one type of society or one region of the world, one "culture area"; the fact can be deplored, but if it betokens a kind of servitude it also marks the eminent dignity of anthropology: the several social varieties of man that we concern ourselves with thrust themselves upon us in their infinite and irreducible complexity, as brothers, we might say, rather than as objects.

In fact, the title I gave to my summary presentation of Mauss is still topical. We are a "science in process of becoming." The conceptual apparatus at our disposal is far from meeting the exigencies of a genuine social anthropology. Progress for us consists in replacing our concepts by more adequate ones, little by little, one by one if need be, by concepts that are increasingly free from their modern origins and better able to grasp the data that we earlier distorted. Such is my belief: our conceptual framework is to this day not only inadequate and rudimentary; it is often deceptive or false. Descriptions and analyses of particular societies, ethnographic monographs, are the most valuable part of anthropology. Comparison between these monographs is often extremely difficult. Fortunately, each of them already enshrines to some extent a comparison—a comparison of the most basic sort, between "them" and "us," the ones who speak about them—and thus modifies our conceptual framework to a variable extent. This comparison is radical, for it brings into play the observer's own ideas, and in my view it governs everything else. Now from this point of view, the way we conceive of ourselves is obviously not irrelevant; whence it follows that a comparative study of modern ideology does not lie beyond the concern of anthropology.

To be complete, I must add to the above, which comes straight from Mauss, an element or principle that arose in the course of the research and, in combination with the principles we have already

4. For the attempt of Clyde Kluckhohn and his team to do this, see chap. 9 below.

reviewed allowed for its development. Looking at their systems of ideas and values, we can take the different types of society as representing so many different choices among all possible choices. But such a view is not enough to set comparison on a firm foundation and give it a modicum of form. To do that we must take into account the relative importance, in every society or culture, of the levels in experience and in thought that society acknowledges; in other words, we must consider values more systematically than has usually been done in the past. That our system of values determines our entire mental landscape can be readily realized from the simplest possible example. Let us suppose that our society and the society under study both show in their system of ideas the same two elements A and B. That one society should subordinate A to B and the other B to A is enough for considerable differences to occur in all their conceptions. In other words, the *hierarchy* present in a culture is essential for comparison.[5]

Let us take note of the close union, the unity of this principle with the ones discussed earlier: an emphasis on difference, i.e. on the specificity of each instance; an emphasis on the difference—among all other differences—separating "them" from "us," i.e. modern from nonmodern, which is fundamental epistemologically; and finally within each culture an emphasis on the hierarchical levels it shows, i.e. an emphasis on values as essential to differences and comparison. It all hangs together. Granted, it was Indian society, on which I was working, that so to speak compelled me to rediscover the idea of hierarchy; yet looking back it is clear that without that idea comparison could not have been furthered and deepened. Here, incidentally, is an example of how a monograph, the study of a single society, contributes to the general theoretical framework. I do believe that the introduction of hierarchy allows one to develop Mauss's basic insights. In retrospect, it would seem that the Durkheimians suffered grievously from missing it. The idea may look awkward, my discourse about it may still be halting. Yet it is indispensable because it restores a neglected and important dimension of the given.

If this is so, it will be asked, why does hierarchy enter the scene so late? First, anthropological studies are so difficult and complex that the discipline is actually still in its beginnings—this point was

5. See *HH*, sec. 118, for a schematic idea of such a comparison.

alluded to above. Second, the very word "hierarchy" commands profound aversion in our societies. Third, we notice that there is only one circumstance or situation in which we are forced to acknowledge the hierarchical principle: it is when comparison shows discord between two different hierarchies. Now in these systems of representations there is much that is *implicit*, and *what is implicit in our case is fairly transparent to us*, so that the fact that *we* stand at one of the poles of comparison is not without its use in clarifying the whole comparative set. Maybe this is the main point: we are back to what we called radical comparison, a comparison in which we ourselves are involved.

The last two essays in this volume explain and articulate the conception of anthropology that has just been outlined. Both are recent, for they could not have been written until the study of modern ideology was sufficiently advanced. The first, "The Anthropological Community and Ideology" (chap. 8) was primarily intended for use only within the profession: it attempts to draw the consequences of this theoretical orientation with respect to the present state of the discipline and its place in our present-day world. At the same time it is an effort to deepen the Maussian perspective, and in this latter regard it certainly deserves a place here.

The last essay (chap. 9) takes the opportunity to present the idea of hierarchy in a language more familiar to anthropologists, that of "values." Going straight for the contrast between modern and nonmodern, it suggests a format for the anthropology of modernity. As such it serves as a conclusion to this collection, it being understood that the research itself allows only a provisional conclusion at this stage.

It will be readily seen from the foregoing that, if anthropology is thought of as we do here, the modern ideas and values that are familiar to us as moderns are not alien to anthropology but, quite to the contrary, are part of its very constitution. Whatever steps we make toward knowing them better will be steps forward for anthropology, in regard not only to its object of study but also to its actual operation and its body of theory. A complementary thesis remains to be demonstrated or at least defended: an anthropological perspective, inversely, will allow us better to understand the modern system of ideas and values that we think we know all about simply because we think and live in the system. This is apparently a very ambitious claim, and I shall have to exert myself to justify it with the help of chapters 1 through 6.

A system of ideas and values current in a given social milieu I call an ideology. I am calling the system of ideas and values that *characterizes* modern societies modern ideology. (The formulation differs from the preceding one, a point I shall return to in my conclusion.)

In the first place, the anthropological or comparative approach has an inestimable advantage: it allows us to see modern culture in its unity. As long as we remain within this culture we seem condemned, both by its richness and its particular form, to cut it up into pieces according to the layout of our disciplines and specializations, and then to place ourselves in one or another of the resulting compartments (see chap. 9). Acquiring an external vantage point, setting our culture in perspective—and perhaps that alone—allows for a global view, which will not be an arbitrary one. That is of the essence.

The study of modern ideology began in 1964. The conceptual grid of the research issued quite naturally from an inversion of the approach that had been needed for a sociological understanding of India. Analysis of the Indian material had called for freeing oneself from our modern individualistic ideas so as to be able to grasp sets or wholes and, ultimately, the society as a whole (Dumont 1975a: 25). Reversing the movement, one can see modern society against the background of nonmodern societies in general. It will be the major viewpoint here, though with notable qualifications, limitations, and complications. Modern ideology is individualistic—individualism being defined sociologically in relation to global values.[6] But we are dealing not with one isolated feature, however important, but with a *configuration* of features. As a value, the individual has certain attributes—such as equality—and some implications or concomitants of which comparison has made the researcher aware.

---

6. For a definition of "individualism," "holism," and other basic terms as used here see the Glossary.

The limited but sometimes "prescribed" place of "individuality" in different societies is discussed by my colleague Kenelm Burridge in a book of distinguished quality, *Someone, No one: An Essay in Individuality*, (Princeton 1979). The approach is passably different from the present (see e.g. p. 30).

Let us take an example to show the difference between ordinary discourse and the sociological discourse we have in mind. Without explanation, someone contrasts individualism to nationalism. He probably means that nationalism evokes a group sentiment that is generally contrasted to "individualistic" sentiment. The basic sociological fact, however, is that nation, in the precise modern sense of the term, and nationalism, as distinct from mere patriotism, are historically conjoined with individualism as a value. The nation is precisely the type of global society which corresponds to the paramountcy of the individual as value. Not only does the one historically accompany the other, but the interdependence between them is clear, so that we may say that the nation is a global society composed of people who think of themselves as individuals (*HH*, app. D, p. 317). There is a series of linkages of this sort which allows for labeling the modern ideological configuration with the word "individualism." This is how comparison—more precisely the movement of turning back from India to ourselves—provides the vantage point or so to speak the conceptual grid to be applied to the data (see Glossary, s.v. "Individualism").

What data? Texts, at least in the main, and for two reasons. First, for convenience. Our civilization is to an unprecedented extent a written civilization, and we can scarcely think of another way of bringing together a comparable mass of data. And, second, because the historical dimension is essential: the individualistic configuration of ideas and values we are familiar with has not always been there, and it did not emerge in one day. Previous authors have seen the origin of "individualism" nearer or farther back in time, no doubt according to the idea they held and the definition they gave of it. If we look closely enough we should be able, in a historical perspective, to bring to light the genesis of the configuration in its main connections. All that is needed is a broad but precise study gathering the best fruits produced in the various disciplines, with no slavish respect for disciplinary boundaries; for it is easy to see, by way of example, that the "political" treatises of Locke register the baptism of private property, while the "political" philosophy of Hegel bestows the form of the State on the *community* as opposed to (civil) society.

Against an endeavor of this kind all sorts of objections can be raised. In the first place, the immensity of the field and the complexity of the object under study may be objected to. At this point I would like to take the time to clarify things and set aside misconceptions. Let us grant that the job is not plain sailing. It demands a lot of care, rigor, and wariness, and consequently it will also require much of the reader, who cannot be provided with the continuous and seamless presentation, the broad, overall picture our statement of the task seemed to promise him. Let us even admit that, in its very vastness, the task is out of proportion to the powers of the researcher who started work on it.

All that being granted, let us add at once that in our view the results obtained so far suffice to justify the enterprise against the radical objection that it is impossible in principle. To consider awhile this kind of objection: it is argued that we cannot in practice grasp an object that is as complex and vague as the configuration of ideas and values we are envisioning, that such a configuration does not really exist and is nothing but an arbitrary construct of the mind. Just as there is really no such thing as a people's mind, or spirit, it will be said, so there can be no such thing as a common configuration of ideas and values beyond all the differences between individuals, social milieux, epochs, schools of thought, different languages, and distinct national cultures. Experience, however, teaches us to the contrary, since on the one hand there has been and there is historical continuity and intercommunication, and on the other—as Mauss and especially Karl Polanyi have ascertained—modern civilization differs radically from other civilizations and cultures. The truth is that our culture is permeated by nominalism, which grants real existence only to individuals and not to relations, to elements and not to sets of elements. Nominalism, in fact, is just another name for individualism, or rather one of its facets. What we propose is to analyze it, but it refuses to be analyzed: in this sense there is no way out of the disagreement. Nominalism will know only John, Peter, and Paul. But John, Peter, and Paul are men only by virtue of the relations that exist between them. So, to go back to our own problem: in a given text, or in such-and-such an author, there are ideas linked by certain relations, and without these relations the ideas will not exist. In every case the relations form a configuration, and these configurations vary from text to text, from author to author, from one milieu to another, but they do not vary as chalk does from cheese, and we can try to see what they have in common at each level of generalization.

In social science in general, it is a fallacy to claim, as is often done, that traits, elements, or individuals are more tangible than sets or wholes. Let us consider, rather, how we may be able to grasp such complex objects as global configurations of ideas and values. They can be apprehended through contrast with others and under certain aspects only. *In contrast with others*: India, and in a less precise way traditional societies in general, form the backdrop against which the modern innovation can be seen as a figure. *Under certain aspects only*: Is not arbitrariness raising its head again here? Not at all. I said earlier that specifically modern ideas or categories of thought fit other societies badly; it is therefore interesting to study the emergence, and the position or function, of these categories. For example, we find that the economic category has first appeared among modern people: we can follow its genesis as is done in a book cited above (*MM*). The work consisted in making the most complete inventory possible of the relations between this category and the other elements of the global configuration (the individual, politics, morality), in seeing how the economic category becomes differentiated and ultimately what role it plays in the global makeup. In the final analysis we found that the configuration is made up of necessary linkages and that the economic view is a thoroughgoing expression of individualism. In this search for relations it is possible that we have only found a part of them and that others have eluded us. If so, it was involuntary, and not because we deliberately rejected them. In any case those relations we have brought to light are reasonably certain.

There is a seeming paradox in what I just said: a consideration intended as global is recognized as incomplete, hence partial. In effect, all discourse is partial, as the nominalists would have it, though it may have a bearing on the whole, as it does here, or it may not. It may be that our discourse remains most often incomplete, but it does relate to a *given* global object. It is the reverse of a discourse that would aim at completeness and would deal with arbitrarily *proposed*, selected objects.[7] It would be wrong to conclude from the breadth of the object of study that the researcher's ambition is excessive, for the ambition remains ultimately descriptive, bound to the given. If there is hubris somewhere, it does not lie here but, rather, in the intention of other writers to construct a closed system, or else to attribute no meaning to the given except through its critique.

7. In a discussion of an essay reprinted here (chap. 1), Roland Robertson (1982) wanted me to answer all the questions considered in the sociology of Max Weber. In fact, this research lies quite outside the Weberian paradigm.

A little should be said about the devices used to avoid error and ensure rigor. We are far from an anthropological investigation in the strict sense, and yet I have tried to retain some of the virtues of anthropology. We are studying texts and not living people, and as a result we cannot supplement the conscious aspect with the aspect observed from the outside, the ideological with the "behavioral." In this sense the research remains incomplete anthropologically or sociologically, as I explained elsewhere (*MM*, 27–29), observing that this absent dimension has been in some fashion made up for by the systematic introduction of a comparative dimension. Anthropology is also marked by the combination of a permanent focus on ensembles* and meticulous care for details, all the details. Hence the preference for monographic, intensive studies of sets of limited scope; hence also the punctilious avoidance of any intrusion or presupposition, any ready-made idea, any recourse to the facile blanket term, the rough summary, the personal paraphrase. The history of ideas is obviously a fertile field for those devices, which are difficult to avoid and threaten to mask certain problems by letting the writer's own view gain the upper hand. Therefore we turn as often as we can to small monographs, as for example, in the work cited (*MM*), the chapter on Mandeville's *Fable of the Bees*, or the word-by-word exegesis of passages from Adam Smith on the labor theory of value. This procedure is not always possible, or sufficient, in which case we shall have to make do with compromises. Nor can we do entirely without summaries; but their wording will have to be strictly controlled. The casual reader may only notice a part of these precautions; a more attentive reading or a close study will reveal them. Anyway, this is perhaps enough to let the reader understand why we can smooth the way for him only to a degree, and why the happy short-cut he might hope for will most often be avoided.

I still have to introduce briefly the first six studies (chaps. 1–6). So far as their form is concerned, the reader might no doubt wish for something better. He has before him a series of discontinuous essays, of various dates, each one of which was originally intended to stand by itself; for this reason there are repetitions, especially of basic definitions. I have changed or extended their titles so as to

---

*The French word *ensemble*, profusely used by the author, is here often translated as "whole," which says a little more, or as "set," which says a little less.—Trans.

signal their position in the overall work, but have refrained from altering their wording (in the few cases where wording has been changed, the change is mentioned in a note); this out of inability to do otherwise as well as out of principle. Each of these papers in fact condenses extensive work; thus collected, they present the precipitate or report of the research, and the author is fully responsible for them as they are. Perhaps the repetitions themselves are not useless: unfamiliar ideas and definitions gain something by being recalled each time they are put to work.

As for the substance, let me now place these papers in the research that is going on. From the beginning I have tried to put the method to the test on several levels, or in several directions. First, there is the overall framework, that is to say the comparative anthropological view of modernity, the placing of individualistic ideology into a hierarchical perspective. That is the point of chapter 9, as I have mentioned. Then a primary axis of research proved mandatory, the chronological axis: the *genesis* and development of modern ideology had to be followed through history. On this level, three studies have been completed. They bear on different epochs—not without some overlap—and even more on different aspects of ideology. The first paper (chapter 1) looks at the Church during its early centuries, with an extrapolation about the Reformation, and shows how the Christian individual, at the beginning a stranger to the world, found himself more and more involved in it. The second (chapter 2) shows the progress of individualism since the thirteenth century through the emancipation of a category, the *political*, and the birth of an institution, the *State*. (This is the first study in terms of date, hence its very general presentation and somewhat archaic look in the light of recent developments). Then a third study traces the emancipation of the *economic* category, beginning in the seventeenth century, which in its turn represents some progress of individualism in relation to religious and political matters, Church and State. This particular study has become a book, *From Mandeville to Marx* (*MM*), and therefore cannot be reproduced here. To give an idea of its approach, however, one short and central chapter from that work is included here (chap. 3), thus ensuring that this section of the research project is represented alongside the others. In this way, we offer, if not a complete picture, at least three major aspects of the genesis of modern ideology.

A second axis was chosen for the research from the outset: the comparison of national cultures in Europe. It is a fact that modern ideology takes notably different forms in the different languages or nations or, more accurately, in the different subcultures that more or less correspond to these languages and nations. Considering each of these more or less national ideologies as a variant of modern ideology, it should be possible for the first time to offer the beginnings of a systematic comparison and thus of a true intercomprehension between these variant forms—be they French, German or English—which have until now remained somewhat opaque to each other. In practice the work bore mainly on the German variant as compared, more or less explicitly, with the French. The research is well advanced, though for the most part still unpublished: it is represented here by two essays (chaps. 4 and 5).[8] The first, "*Volk* and Nation in Herder and Fichte,*" is brief, but the theme is absolutely central for the social philosophy of German idealism and also represents an important step in the constitution of the modern idea of nation. The second piece, published here for the first time, uses a text from Troeltsch on "the German idea of liberty" to throw light on another essential aspect of German ideology, the concept of *Bildung* or self-education, which dominated the intellectual world in the nineteenth century and the beginning of the twentieth, and the corresponding attitude toward the State and sociopolitical questions, including foreign policy.

There is a third axis to the research, or rather a third perspective, which is to a great extent compounded of the first two. What happened to modern ideology once it came into operation? Does a comparative view allow us to illuminate the problems posed by the political history of the past two centuries, and especially totalitarianism seen as a disease of modern society? Chapter 6 is a contribution to the study of National Socialism, viewed here on two levels— a general or intercultural level of the contemporary world and, at the same time, the level of German ideology. Nazism was linked to the latter in the sense that German ideology had entered a historical crisis which Nazism exploited. The study enlarges on the place of anti-Semitic racism in the set of representations which Hitler himself presented as being his own in his book *Mein Kampf.*

On this particularly sensitive point of totalitarianism I would like to add a brief discussion. Vincent Descombes, in a long article largely devoted to a favorable and penetrating consideration of *MM*

---

8. An article on K. P. Moritz and the transition from pietism to aesthetics (Dumont 1982) is not reproduced here.

(Descombes 1977), touched on the relation between the sociology of Durkheim and Mauss and totalitarianism. He asked what connection there is between the Durkheimians' holism and totalitarianism. Had not Durkheim unknowingly idealized the Nazism to come when he wished in 1912 that our societies might have "hours of creative effervescence," and did not Mauss confess his embarrassment when faced with the event (ibid.: 1023–26)? Moreover, Descombes seems to suggest that I, in turn, am reproducing Durkheim's "misadventure," the "catastrophe of the Durkheimian school" in the face of totalitarianism. Now there is a great distance between the definition I give of totalitarianism as inherently contradictory (cited by the critic, p. 1026) and the common view of it as a simple return to primitive or medieval communion, which Mauss implies in the letter referred to by Descombes. There would seem to be some misapprehension. It happens that on a precise and basic point I had noted that Durkheimian formulations were transcended in my own. At the very beginning of *HH*, when distinguishing between the two meanings of "the individual" (the particular, empirical man and man as the bearer of value; cf. Glossary), I showed in a note (3a) that the distinction is needed by using a passage from Mauss himself as an example. Once this distinction is established, the confusion Descombes attributes to the Durkheimians is impossible. It is something the critic failed to take sufficiently into consideration. Certainly, Durkheim saw individualism quite clearly as a value (Lukes 1973: 338 ff.), but he did not work it indelibly into his vocabulary: he did not adequately emphasize the distance created by this value between modern man and all others;[9] only by failing to do so could he come, in the passage from *The Elementary Forms* that Descombes pinpoints, to imagine that modern societies might go through a communal "effervescence" similar to that of Australian tribes.

The situation is different once the two senses of "the individual" are distinguished, and when, on this basis, the incompatibility between individualism and holism is established (*HH*, sec. 3). This done, any pretended return to holism at the level of the modern nation is revealed as an enterprise of fallacy and oppression, and Nazism is shown to be a masquerade. Individualism is the cardinal value of modern societies. Hitler could escape it no more

---

9. We noted above how the distance became more marked in Polanyi as compared with Mauss.

than anyone else, and the essay dealing with him here attempts to show precisely that a deep individualism underlies his racist rationalization of anti-Semitism.

Indeed, totalitarianism expresses in a dramatic way something we keep running into in the contemporary world: individualism is all-powerful on the one hand and, on the other, is perpetually and irremediably haunted by its opposite.

This is quite a vague formulation, and it is difficult to be more precise when speaking generally. Yet this coexistence in the contemporary ideology of individualism and its opposite comes forth more forcefully than ever at the present stage of research. In this sense, the individualistic configuration of ideas and values *characterizes* modernity, but it is by no means coextensive with it.

If nonindividualistic elements, aspects, or factors are present in contemporary ideology and in society at large, where do they come from? They derive in the first instance from the permanence or "survival" of premodern and more or less general elements—such as the family. But they also derive from the very operation of individualistic values, which has let loose a complex dialectic resulting in combinations where they blend subtly with their opposites—in diverse domains, and for some of them as early as the end of the eighteenth and the beginning of the nineteenth centuries.[10]

The issue is relatively simple and, thanks to Karl Polanyi, clear in socioeconomic matters. There the application of the individualistic principle, "liberalism," has made it necessary to introduce measures for social safeguarding leading finally to what might be called contemporary "postliberalism."

A more complex process, a very important one even though it has hardly been detected to date, is found in the domain of cultures and results from their interaction. To the extent that the individualistic ideas and values of the dominant culture are spreading worldwide, they undergo modifications locally and engender new forms. Now—and this has escaped notice—the new, modified forms can pass back into the dominant culture and operate there as modern elements in their own right. In that way the acculturation of each particular culture to modernity can leave a lasting precipitate

---

10. Starting from Karl Polanyi's historical critique of economic liberalism, I sketched a generalization at the end of Dumont 1983c.

in the heritage of global modernity. Further, the process is sometimes cumulative inasmuch as this precipitate can in turn be transformed on the occasion of a subsequent acculturation.

Let no one think for a moment that modern ideology is being diluted or weakened through these adaptations. Quite to the contrary, the remarkable and engrossing fact is that the combination of heterogeneous elements, the absorption by individualism of foreign and more or less opposed elements, results in an intensification, a rise in the ideological power of the corresponding representations. This is the ground on which totalitarianism grows as an involuntary, unconscious, and hypertensive combination of individualism and holism.

It was the brief study of Hitler that prompted this digression, which will also serve as a conclusion. The contemporary ideological world is like a fabric woven by the continuing interaction of cultures at least since the end of the eighteenth century; it is made up of the actions and reactions of individualism and its opposite. This is not the place to develop such a view and it is too soon to do so; the view is just the general result of the research done so far or, better, it is the perspective that opens up at this point, a new slope of the mountain waiting to be explored. There follows from this a shift in perspective, as compared with the one I started with, and even a certain uneasiness at the level of vocabulary—the toll of the route covered. To begin with, I had tried to isolate what is *characteristic* of modernity in contrast with what preceded it and still coexists with it, and to describe the origin of this something, which we have here called individualism. At that stage I tended quite broadly to identify individualism with modernity. But now a substantial fact demands to be acknowledged, namely, that in the contemporary world we find something other than what had differentially been defined as modern. This is true even in that part of the world considered "advanced," "developed," or "modern" *par excellence*, and even on the level of the ideology itself. Furthermore, it is found on close examination that some ideas and values or, I should prefer to say, some value-ideas that might be taken as most intensely modern are actually the result of a historical process in the course of which modernity and nonmodernity or, more precisely, individualistic value-ideas and their opposites, have combined intimately.[11]

11. See now, for some development, Dumont 1985a (in French; to appear in English as my contribution to *The Case of the Humanities: Questionable References*, a colloquium held at Johns Hopkins University in November 1984).

So we might speak of "postmodernity" for the contemporary world, but our job is rather to analyze these more or less hybrid representations, to follow concretely the interactions from which they sprang and their subsequent destiny; in brief, to study the history of the ideology of the past two centuries in an intercultural perspective.

Part 1

On Modern Ideology

1 Genesis, I

The Christian Beginnings: From the Outworldly Individual to the Individual-in-the world

This study is in two parts. The main part bears on the first centuries of Christianity, when the first stages of an evolution are perceived. A complement, or epilogue, shows the evolution coming to a conclusion, long afterwards, with Calvin.

The First Centuries

In the last decades, some of us have become increasingly aware that modern individualism, when seen against the background of the other great civilizations that the world has known, is an exceptional phenomenon. Now, if the idea of the individual as a value is as idiosyncratic as it is fundamental, there is by no means agreement on its origins. For some scholars, especially in countries where nominalism is strong, it has always been everywhere; for others it

The first part of this chapter is a slightly expanded version of the 1980 Deneke Lecture given at Lady Margaret Hall, Oxford. I am thankful to the College for the opportunity to return to a previous study which had remained uncompleted (see *Annuaire de l'Ecole pratique des Hautes Etudes, 6e section*, for 1973–74). The general hypothesis presented here was sparked off by a *Daedalus* colloquium on the first millennium B.C., and I am much indebted to the participants—mainly Arnaldo Momigliano, Sally Humphreys, and Peter Brown—for their criticism and some suggestions (see *Daedalus*, Spring 1975, for the first and restricted form of the hypothesis, which the criticisms have contributed to modifying and widening).

The complement on Calvin was proposed in a seminar on the category of person (Oxford, Wolfson College, May 1980).

The present text reproduces that of the first English publication in *Religion* 12 (1982): 1–27, "A Modified View of our Origins: The Christian Beginnings of Modern Individualism"), with the addition of a short section on Saint Augustine which originated with the Renaissance or with the rise of the bourgeoisie. Most commonly perhaps, and according to tradition, the roots of the idea are thought to lie in our classical as well as in our Judeo-Christian heritage, in varying proportions. For some classicists, the discovery in Greece of "consistent discourse" was the deed of men who saw themselves as individuals. The mists of confused thinking have dissipated under the Athenian sun. Then and there myth surrendered to reason, and the event marks the beginning of history proper. There is undoubtedly some truth in such a statement, but it is so narrow as to appear parochial in today's world and surely it needs, at the least, some modification. To begin with, the sociologist would tend to give prominence to religion as against philosophy, because religion encompasses the whole of society and relates immediately to action. Max Weber did this.

As for us, let us leave aside all considerations of cause and effect and consider only configurations of ideas and values, ideological networks, to try and reach the basic relations on which they are built. To state the thesis in approximate terms, I submit that something of modern individualism is present with the first Christians and in the surrounding world, but that it is not exactly individualism as we know it. Actually, the old form and the new are separated by a transformation so radical and so complex that it took at least seventeen centuries of Christian history to be completed, if indeed it is not still continuing in our times. In the generalization of the pattern in the first place, and in its subsequent evolution, religion has been the cardinal element. Within our chronological limits, the pedigree of modern individualism is, so to speak, double: an origin or accession of one sort, *and* a slow transformation into another. Within the confines of this lecture I must be content to characterize the origin and to point out a few of the earliest steps in the transformation. Let me apologize at the outset for the condensed abstraction of what follows.

---

had been initially left out. The paper was briefly discussed by R. Bellah, K. Burridge, and R. Robertson, ibid.: 83–91. A subsequent article by S. N. Eisenstadt, "Transcendental Visions, Otherworldliness and its Transformations: Some More Comments on L. Dumont" (*Religion* 13 [1983]: 1–17), is actually an original contribution, which cannot be discussed here as it would deserve (but see note 13 below). Thanks are due to T. N. Madan, in his careful reprinting of the paper in *Contributions to Indian Sociology*, 17 1 (1983), for material improvements that are taken up here.

To see our culture in its unity and specificity we must set it in perspective by contrasting it with other cultures. Only so can we gain an awareness of what otherwise goes without saying: the familiar and implicit basis of our common discourse. Thus, when we speak of man as an individual, we designate two concepts at once: an object out there, and a value. Comparison obliges us to distinguish analytically these two aspects: one, the *empirical* subject of speech, thought, and will, the individual sample of mankind, as found in all societies; and, two, the independent, autonomous, and thus essentially nonsocial moral being, who carries our paramount values and is found primarily in our modern ideology of man and society. From that point of view, there emerge two kinds of societies. Where the individual is a paramount value I speak of individualism. In the opposite case, where the paramount value lies in society as a whole, I speak of holism.

In rough and ready terms, the problem of the origins of individualism is very much how, starting from the common type of holistic societies, a new type has evolved that basically contradicts the common conception. How has the transition been possible, how can we conceive a transition between those two antithetic universes of thought, those two mutually irreconcilable ideologies?

Comparison, in the instance of India, offers a clue. For more than two millennia Indian society has been characterized by two complementary features: society imposes upon every person a tight interdependence which substitutes constraining relationships for the individual as we know him, but, on the other hand, there is the institution of world-renunciation which allows for the full independence of the man who chooses it.[1] Incidentally, this man, the renouncer, is responsible for all the innovations in religion that India has seen. Moreover, we see clearly in early texts the origin of the institution, and we understand it easily: the man who is after ultimate truth forgoes social life and its constraints to devote himself to his own progress and destiny. When he looks back at the social world, he sees it from a distance, as something devoid of reality, and the discovery of the self is for him coterminous, not with salvation in the Christian sense, but with liberation from the fetters of life as commonly experienced in this world.

---

1. Cf. my essay "World Renunciation in Indian Religions," first published in French in 1959, now reprinted as appendix B in Dumont 1980 (*HH*).

The renouncer is self-sufficient, concerned only with himself. His thought is similar to that of the modern individual, but for one basic difference: we live in the social world, he lives outside it. I therefore called the Indian renouncer an individual-outside-the-world. Comparatively, we are individuals-in-the-world, *inworldly* individuals, while he is an *outworldly* individual. I shall use this notion of the outworldly individual extensively, and I beg to draw your full attention to that strange creature and its characteristic relation to society. The renouncer may live in solitude as a hermit or may join a group of fellow-renouncers under a master-renouncer, who propounds a particular discipline of liberation. The similarity with Western anchorites and between, say, Buddhist and Christian monasteries can go very far. As an instance, both congregations invented independently what we call majority rule.

What is essential for us is the yawning gap between the renouncer on the one hand and the social world and the individual-in-the-world on the other. To begin with, the path of liberation is open only to those who leave the world. Distance from the social world is the condition for individual spiritual development. *Relativization* of life in the world results immediately from world renunciation. Only Westerners could mistakenly suppose that some sects of renouncers would have tried to change the social order. The interaction with the social world took other forms. In the first place, the renouncer depends on that world for his subsistence, and would instruct the man-in-the-world. Indeed a whole dialectic, a specifically Indian dialectic, set in, which must be disregarded here. What must be borne in mind is the initial situation as still found in Buddhism. Short of joining the congregation, the layman is taught only a relative ethic: to be generous towards the monks and to avoid deleterious and self-abasing actions.

What is invaluable for us here is that the Indian development is easily understood and indeed seems "natural." On the strength of it we may surmise: if individualism is to appear in a society of the traditional, holistic type, it will be in opposition to society and as a kind of supplement to it, that is, in the form of the outworldly individual. Could we then say that individualism began in the same way in the West?

That is precisely what I shall try to show: that, notwithstanding the differences in the content of representations, the same sociological type that we found in India—the outworldly individual—is unmistakenly present in Christianity and around it at the beginning of our era.

There is no doubt about the fundamental conception of man that flowed from the teaching of Christ: as Troeltsch said, man is an *individual-in-relation-to-God:* for our purposes this means that man is in essence an outworldly individual. Before developing this point let me attempt a more general one. It can be argued that the Hellenistic world itself was so permeated with the same conception among the educated that Christianity could not have succeeded in the long run in that milieu if it had offered an individualism of a different sort. This is admittedly a strong thesis, which seems at first sight to contradict well-established conceptions. Actually, it is a mere modification and allows for bringing together a number of discrete pieces of evidence better than the current view does. It is commonly admitted that the transition in philosophical thought from Plato and Aristotle to the new schools of the Hellenistic period shows a discontinuity, a great gap—the surge of individualism (see Sabine 1963, 143). Self-sufficiency, which Plato and Aristotle regarded as an attribute of the *polis,* becomes an attribute of the individual (ibid.: 125) that is either assumed as a fact or posited as an ideal by Epicureans, Cynics, and Stoics. But I must go straight to my point. It is clear that the first step in Hellenistic thinking has been to leave the social world behind. I could quote at length, for instance, Sabine's standard *History of Political Thought* from which I have already reproduced some formulations, and which characteristically distinguishes the three schools as different varieties of "renunciation" (ibid.: 137). These schools teach widsom, and to become a sage one must first renounce the world. A critical feature runs throughout the period in different forms; it is a thorough dichotomy between wisdom and the world, between the wise man and the unenlightened men who remain in the throes of worldly life. Diogenes opposes the sage and the fools; Chrysippus states that the soul of the sage survives longer after death than that of ordinary mortals. Just as, in India, truth is attainable only by the renouncer, so according to Zeno only the sage knows what is good; worldly actions, even on the part of the sage, cannot be good, but only preferable to others: accommodation to the world is obtained through the relativization of values, the same kind of *relativization* that I underlined in the case of India.

Accommodation to the world characterizes Stoicism from its inception, and increasingly during its middle, and then late phases. It has certainly contributed to blur, in the view of the later interpreters, the outworldly anchorage of the doctrine. The Roman Stoics assumed heavy duties in the world, and a Seneca was felt as a closely related neighbor by medieval minds, as well as by Rousseau, who borrowed extensively from him. Yet, it is not difficult to detect the permanence of the Stoic cleavage: the self-sufficiency of the individual remains the principle, even when he acts in the world. The Stoic must remain detached, he should maintain indifference even to the sorrow he tries to allay. Thus Epictetus: "He may sigh (with the suffering man) provided his sigh does not come from the heart."[2]

This feature, to us so strange, shows that, even if the Stoic has returned to the world in a manner foreign to the Indian renouncer, it represents for him only a secondary accommodation while at bottom he still defines himself as a stranger to the world.

How can we understand the genesis of this philosophical individualism? Individualism is so taken for granted that in this instance it is commonly seen without more ado as a consequence of the ruin of the Greek *polis* and of the unification of the world—Greeks and foreigners or barbarians confounded—under Alexander. Now this tremendous historical event can explain many traits, but not, to me at least, the emergence of the individual as a value, as a creation *ex nihilo*. We should look first of all to philosophy itself. Not only have Hellenistic teachers occasionally lifted out of the Presocratics elements for their own use, not only are they heirs to the Sophists and other currents of thought that appear to us as submerged in the classical period, but philosophical activity, the sustained exercise of rational inquiry carried out by generations of thinkers, must by itself have fostered individualism, because reason, universal in principle, is in practice at work through the particular person who exercises it, and takes precedence, at least implicitly, over everything else. Plato and Aristotle, after Socrates, were able to recognize that man is essentially a social being. What their Hellenistic

2. Quoted in Bevan 1927: 63. The same author has noted the similarity with Indian renunciation. He quotes at length from the *Bhagavad Gita* to show the parallelism with Stoic maxims on detachment (ibid.: 75–79). Actually what the *Gita* exposes is renunciation accommodated to the world; cf. my paper (note 1 above), section 4.

successors essentially did was to set up a superior ideal, that of the wise man detached from social life. Such being the filiation of ideas, the vast political change, the rise of a universal empire opening the gate to the intensification of interrelations, will no doubt have favored the movement. In that environment, direct or indirect influence from the Indian type of renouncer is not entirely to be ruled out, but the data are insufficient.

If a demonstration was needed of the all-pervading pattern of otherworldliness among educated people in the times of Christ, it can be found in the person of the Jew, Philo of Alexandria. Philo showed to the later Christian Apologists the way to accommodate the religious message to an educated pagan audience. He tells in glowing terms of his predilection for the contemplative life of the recluse, to which he yearns to return, having interrupted it to do political service to his community—which he did with distinction. Goodenough has precisely shown how this hierarchy of two modes of life and that of Jewish faith and pagan philosophy are reflected in Philo's double judgment on politics—exoteric and apologetic on the one hand, esoteric and Hebraic on the other (see Goodenough 1940).

Turning now to Christianity, let me first say that my main guide will be the sociological historian of the Church, Ernst Troeltsch. In his extensive work, *The social Teachings of the Christian Churches and Groups*, published in 1911, which I consider to be a master-piece, Troeltsch had already given a relatively unified view, in his own words, of "the whole sweep of the history of the Christian Church" (Troeltsch 1922). While Troeltsch's treatment may of course have to be completed or modified on some points, my effort will be in the main to take advantage of the comparative perspective I have just outlined in order to reach a still more unified and simpler view of the whole, even if we are concerned for the moment with only a fraction of it.[3]

The subject matter is familiar, and I shall only isolate schemati-

3. The distance is small between Troeltsch's inspiration and the present for-mulation. Thus Benjamin Nelson, a perceptive sociologist, noting that the interest not only of Troeltsch but of leading German thinkers in the nineteenth and twentieth centuries, from Hegel onward, had focused on "the institutionalization of primitive Christianity," formulated their problem alternatively as "how the charismatic fel-lowship of the apostolic Church had been bureaucratised" or, "*how an otherworldly 'sect' gave rise to the Roman Church*" (Nelson 1975: 232n; emphasis added).

cally a few critical features. It follows from Christ's and then Paul's teaching that the Christian is an "individual-in-relation-to-God." There is, Troeltsch says, "absolute individualism and absolute universalism" in relation to God. The individual soul receives eternal value from its filial relationship to God, in which relationship is also grounded human fellowship: Christians meet in Christ, whose members they are. This tremendous affirmation takes place on a level that transcends the world of man and of social institutions, although these are also from God. The infinite worth of the individual is at the same time the disparagement, the negation in terms of value, of the world as it is: a dualism is posited, a tension is established that is constitutive of Christianity and will endure throughout history.

Here we must pause and ponder. For the modern man this tension between truth and reality has become most difficult to accept or to value positively. We sometimes speak of "changing the world," and it is clear from his earliest writings that the young Hegel would have preferred Christ to declare war on the world as it is. Yet, in retrospect, we see that had Christ done so as a man, the result would have been poor as compared with the consequences his teachings have led to throughout the centuries. In his maturity Hegel has made amends for the impatience of his youth by fully acknowledging the fecundity of Christian subjectivism, that is, of the congenital Christian tension.[4] Actually, in a comparative perspective the idea of "changing the world" looks so absurd that we come to realize that it could appear only in a civilization which had for long implacably maintained the absolute distinction between the life promised to man and the one he actually lives. This modern folly has its roots in what has been called the absurdity of the cross. I remember Alexandre Koyré opposing in conversation the folly of Christ to the good sense of Buddha. And yet they have something in common, precisely the exclusive concern for the individual coupled with, or rather founded on, a devaluation of the world.[5] That is how

4. Cf. Hegel 1907: 327ff., 221–30; in English translation by Knox 1971: 283ff., 152–65. The young Hegel was carried away by his revolutionary zeal and his fascination with the ideal *polis* (ibid.: 163–64, 297–302, 335; Knox, 81–83, 248–52, 293). Yet he slowly came to a better recognition of Jesus ("The spirit of Christianity"). For his mature views, see Theunissen 1970: 10–11 and *passim*.

5. That the devaluation is relative here, radical there, is another matter. The more restricted parallel set up by Edward Conze between (Mahayana) "Buddhism

both religions are truly universalistic, and therefore missionary, and have spread and endured, how they have brought solace to innumerable men, and how—if I may venture so far—both are true in so much as, for human life to be bearable, especially in a universalist view, values must be maintained well beyond the reach of events.

What no Indian religion has ever fully attained and which was given from the start in Christianity is the brotherhood of love in and through Christ, and the consequent equality of all, "an equality that exists purely," Troeltsch insists, "in the presence of God." Sociologically speaking, the emancipation of the individual through a personal transcendence, and the union of outworldly individuals in a community that treads on earth but has its heart in heaven, may constitute a passable formula for Christianity.

Troeltsch stresses the strange combination of radicalism and conservatism that results. It is advantageous to look at the matter in hierarchical terms. There are a whole series of similar oppositions—between this world and the beyond, body and soul, state and church, the old and the new dispensations—which are the basic framework used by the early Fathers and which Caspary (1979) calls the "Pauline pairs" (see his analysis in a remarkable book on the exegesis of Origen). It is clear that the two poles in such oppositions are ranked, even when it is not obvious on the surface. When Christ teaches to "render unto Caesar the things that are Caesar's, but unto God the things that are God's," the symmetry is only apparent, as it is for the sake of God that we must comply with the legitimate claims of Caesar. In a sense the distance thus stated is greater than if the claims of Caesar were simply denied. The worldly order is relativized, as subordinated to absolute values. There is an ordered dichotomy: outworldly individualism encompasses recognition of and obedience to the powers of this world. If I could draw a figure, it would represent two concentric circles, the larger one representing individualism in relation to God, and within it a smaller circle standing for acceptance of worldly necessities, duties, and allegiances; that is to say, the accommodation to a society, pagan at first and later Christian, which has not ceased to be holistic. This figure—encompassing the antithetical worldly life

---

and Gnosis" clearly rests on the underlying presence on both sides of the outworldly individual (see especially the concluding developments and the last note in Conze 1967: 665ff.).

within the all-embracing primary reference and fundamental definition, and subordinating the normal holism of social life to outworldly individualism—can accommodate economically all major
subsequent changes as formulated by Troeltsch. What will happen
in history is that the paramount value will exert pressure upon the
antithetical worldly element encapsulated within it. By stages
worldly life will thus be contaminated by the outworldly element,
until finally the heterogeneity of the world disappears entirely.
Then the whole field will be unified, holism will have vanished from
ideology, and life in the world will be thought of as entirely con-
formable to the supreme value; the outworldly individual will have
become the modern, inworldly individual. This is the historical
proof of the extraordinary potency of the initial disposition.

If only I had time, I should like to add at least a remark on the
millenarist aspect. The first Christians lived in the expectation of
the imminent "Second Coming" of Christ, who would establish the
Kingdom of God. The belief was probably functional in helping
people to accept at least provisionally the uncomfortable position of
holding a belief which was not immediately relevant to their actual
predicament. It so happens that the world has recently known an
extraordinary proliferation of millenarist movements often called
"cargo cults," in conditions very similar to those prevailing in
Palestine under Roman domination. The main sociological difference lies perhaps precisely in the outworldly climate of the period
and first of all the outworldly orientation of the Christian community, which kept the upper hand against extremist tendencies,
whether of the rebel Jews or of the Apocalyptic writers, of Gnosti-
cism or Manicheism. From that angle, early Christianity would
seem to be characterized by a combination of millenarism and
outworldliness with a relative predominance of the latter over the
former.[6]

Schematic and insufficient as this development has been, I hope
at any rate to have made it likely that the first Christians were, all in
all, nearer to the Indian renouncer than to ourselves, more or less
snugly ensconced in the world which we think to have accommodated to ourselves. In actual fact, we have conversely—also?—
accommodated ourselves to it. This is my second point, which I

---

6. Sir Edmund Leach has drawn attention to the millenarian aspect, but he saw
it unilaterally and somewhat indiscriminately as a model of "subversion" (Leach
1973: 5–14; see also note 14 below).

shall now turn to by singling out some of the early stages of that accommodation.

How was the outworldly message of the Sermon on the Mount brought to bear upon life in the world? The institutional link was the Church, which may be seen as a sort of foothold or bridgehead of the divine, and which spread, unified itself, and extended its sway only slowly and by degrees. But there had to be also a conceptual tool, a way of thinking which concerned earthly institutions in the light of outworldly truth. Ernst Troeltsch laid great stress on the borrowing from the Stoics by the early Fathers of the idea of Natural Law, which was to serve as this indispensable instrument of adaptation. What was this pagan "ethical Law of Nature"? I quote:

> Its leading idea is the idea of God as the universal, spiritual-and-physical, Law of Nature, which rules uniformly over every-thing and as universal law of the world orders nature, produces the different positions of the individual in nature and in society, and becomes in man the law of reason which acknowledges God and is therefore one with him. . . . The Law of Nature thus demands on the one hand submission to the harmonious course of nature and to the role assigned to one in the social system, on the other an inner elevation above all this and the ethico-religious freedom and dignity of reason, that is one with God and therefore not to be disturbed by any external or sensible occurrence (Troeltsch 1922, trans. 1960: 64).

As regards the special relation to the Stoics, it could be objected that by our time such conceptions had become widely diffused, and that Philo and, some two centuries later, the Apologists borrowed as much or perhaps more from other schools of thought. Troeltsch has replied in advance: "The concept of an ethical law of nature from which are derived all juridical rules and social institutions is a creation of the Stoa" (1925a: 173–74). And it is on the level of ethics that the Church will construct her medieval social doctrine: "a doctrine which, albeit imperfect and confused from a scientific viewpoint, was to have practically the utmost cultural and social meaning, was indeed to be something like the Church's dogma of civilisation" (1922: 173). The borrowing appears quite natural once we admit that both Stoicism and Christianity were wedded to out-worldliness, and to the concomitant relativization of the inworldly. After all, the message of Buddha to the man-in-the-world as such was of the same nature: subjective morality and ethics constitute the interface between worldly life and its social commands on the one hand, truth and absolute values on the other.

Let us return to the founder of the Stoa three centuries before Christ, in whose teaching we find the principle of the whole later development. For Zeno of Kition, who was more a prophet than a philosopher according to Edwyn Bevan,[7] the good is what makes man independent of all external circumstances. The only good is internal to man. The will of the individual is the source of his dignity and self-containment. Provided he adjusts his will to whatever destiny has in store for him, he will be safe, immune to all attacks from the outside world. As the world is ruled by God, or the law of nature, or reason—for nature becomes reason in man—this command is what Troeltsch called the absolute Law of Nature. Now, while the sage remains indifferent to external things and actions, he is nevertheless able to distinguish among them according to their greater or lesser conformity to nature, or reason: some actions are by themselves relatively commendable as against others. The world is relativized as it should be, and yet values, *relative values*, may be attached to it. Here is *in nuce* the relative Law of Nature that will be extensively used by the Church. To those two levels of the Law correspond two pictures of mankind, in its ideal and in its real state. The former is the state of nature—as in Zeno's ideal cosmopolis or in the later utopia of Iambulus (see Bidez 1932: 244ff.)—which the Christians identified with the condition of man before the Fall.

As to the real state of mankind, the close parallelism between Seneca's justification of institutions as results of and remedies to men's viciousness and similar Christian views is well known. What Troeltsch considers essential is the rational aspect: that reason could be applied to actual institutions, either to justify them in view of the present state of men's morality, or to condemn them as contrary to nature, or again to temper or better them in the light of reason.

Thus Origen held against Celsus that positive laws that contravene natural law are not laws in any sense of the term (Caspary 1979: 130), to such effect that Christians were justified in refusing to worship the Emperor or to kill under his orders.

On one point Troeltsch needs an addendum. He has missed or bypassed the importance of sacral kingship in Hellenistic times and

7. See note 2 above.

later on. Natural law, as "unwritten" or "animate" (*empsychos*) law is incarnate in the ruler. It is clear in Philo, who wrote of "incarnate and rational laws," and in the Fathers. According to Philo, "the wise men of ancient history, the patriarchs and fathers of the race present in their lives unwritten laws, which Moses wrote later. . . . In them the law was fulfilled and it became personal" (Troeltsch 1922, note 69, quoting Rudolf Hirzel). And Clement of Alexandria wrote of Moses that he was "inspired by the law and therefore a royal man" (Ehrhardt 1959–69, 2: 189). This is important because we are here in contact with the primitive, sacral type of sovereignty, that of the divine king or priest-cum-ruler, a very widespread representation, present in the Hellenistic world and later on in the Byzantine Empire (see Dvornik 1966). We shall encounter it again later on.

The views and attitudes of the early Fathers on social questions—the State and the ruler, slavery, private property—are mostly considered by the moderns in isolation and from an inworldy viewpoint. We can better understand them by focusing on outworldliness. We should remember that everything was seen in the light of the individual's relation to God and of its concomitant, the brotherhood of the Church. At first sight the ultimate end entertains an ambivalent relation with life in the world, for the world through which the Christian is on pilgrimage in this life is both an impediment to salvation and a condition of it. But we had best think of the whole configuration in hierarchical terms, for life in the world is not simply refused or negated, it is only relativized in relation to man's destiny of union with God and outworldly bliss. The orientation to the transcendent end, as towards a magnet, introduces a hierarchical field, in which we should expect every worldly thing to be situated.

The first tangible consequence of this hierarchical relativization is a remarkable degree of latitude in most worldly matters. As such matters are not important in themselves but only in relation to the end, there may be a great range of variation according to each pastor's and author's temperament and more importantly according to the circumstances of the moment. Rather than searching for hard and fast rules, we should ascertain in each case the limits of permissible variation. They are clear in principle: first the world should not be condemned out of hand, as by the Gnostic heretics; second it should not usurp the dignity that belongs to God alone. We should, moreover, expect the range of permissiveness to be narrower in more important matters than in those of lesser significance and value.

One author has recently stressed the kind of flexibility I am referring to. Studying the exegesis of Origen, Caspary has admirably shown how what seems to me the fundamental opposition plays on a variety of levels and in a variety of forms, and constitutes a network of spiritual meaning, a hierarchy of correspondences.[8] What is true of Biblical hermeneutics is similarly applicable to the interpretation of the rough data of experience. I said a moment ago that things of the world can be taken as hierarchized according to their relative import for salvation. There is no systematic statement to that effect in our sources; yet there is at least one major point on which the difference in valuation should be taken into account. I have shown elsewhere that the modern world has reversed the traditional primacy of relations between men as against relations of men to things. On this point the attitude of the first Christians is unmistakable, for things can only be means or impediments to the attainment of the Kingdom of God, while relations between men involve subjects made in the image of God and predestined to union with Him. This is perhaps the place where the contrast with the moderns is the most marked.

We thus may surmise and we verify that the subordination of man in society, whether in the State or in slavery, poses more vital questions for the early Christians than does the permanent attribution of possessions to persons, i.e., private property in things. The teaching of Jesus concerning wealth as an impediment to, and poverty as an asset for, salvation is addressed to the individual person. As to the social level, the perennial rule of the Church is well known: it is not a rule of property, it is instead a rule of use. It matters little to whom the property belongs provided it is used for the good of all, and in the first place of those most in need, for, as Lactantius put it (in *Divinae institutiones*, 3.21) (against Plato's communism), justice is a matter of the soul and not of external circumstances. Troeltsch happily shows how love within the brotherhood involved detachment from possessions (Troeltsch 1922, n. 57; 1960: 115ff., 133ff.). For all that we know we may suppose that, in the absence of dogmatic stress in the matter, the

8. Actually Caspary distinguishes four dimentions of contrast, or "parameters," of which he gives one only as hierarchical (1979: 113–14), but it is easy to see that hierarchy extends to all of them.

small and largely autonomous early churches may have varied in their actual treatment of property, some perhaps having all in common at some time, while only the basic injunction to help destitute brethren was uniform.

The equality of all men had been declared by the Stoics and others as grounded in their common endowment with reason. Christian equality was perhaps more deeply rooted, set at the core of the person, but it was similarly an outworldly equality. "There can be neither Jew nor Greek, . . . neither bond nor free . . . , no male and female, for ye are all *one man in Christ Jesus*," said Paul, and Lactantius: "No one, *in God's sight*, is a slave or a master . . . we are all . . . his children." Slavery was a matter of this world, and it is indicative of the gulf that separates those men from us that what for us strikes at the root of human dignity and independence was seen by them as a contradiction inherent in worldly life, and which Christ himself had assumed in order to redeem mankind, thus making humility a cardinal virtue for all. All the effort to perfection was turned inside, was internalized, as becomes the outworldly individual. This is readily seen, for instance, in Origen's "tropological" level of exegesis where all Biblical events are interpreted as happening in the inner life of the Christian (see Caspary 1979).

As regards political subordination, Troeltsch's treatment can perhaps be bettered. He follows A. J. Carlyle; the attitude to the laws is governed by Natural Law conceptions, but the power that decrees the laws is seen quite differently and regarded as divine.[9] Actually, Natural Law and sacral kingship are not such perfect strangers. We are again faced with a case where a hierarchical view does better. The cardinal point is found in Paul: all power is from God. But within this overall principle there is room for restriction or contradiction. This is clear in a comment on Paul by the great Origen in *Contra Celsum:*

> He says "There is no power but from God." Then, someone might say: What? That power also, that persecutes the servants of God . . . is from God? Let us answer briefly on that. The gift of God, the laws, are for use, not for abuse. There will indeed be a judgement of God against those who administer the power

9. In his otherwise invaluable book, A. J. Carlyle (1903) had treated in two separate chapters "natural equality and govermment" and "the sacred authority of the ruler."

> they have received according to their impieties and not accord-
> ing to the law divine. . . . He [Paul] does not speak of those
> powers that persecute the faith: for here one must say: "it is
> fitting to obey God rather than men," he speaks only of power
> in general (Troeltsch 1922, n. 73).

We easily see that here a relative institution has overstepped its
limits and come into conflict with the absolute value.

As it was contrary to the ultimate Christian value, political
subordination was attributed to the Fall of man, that is, it was
justified in terms of the relative Law of Nature. Thus Irenaeus:
"men fell from God . . . [and] God imposed on them the restraint of
the fear of other men . . . lest they devour each other like fishes."
The same view was applied by Ambrose to slavery somewhat later,
perhaps because it appeared as an individual matter while the State
confronted the whole Church as a threat. It is noteworthy that a
similar explanation is not given of private property, except by John
Chrysostom, an exceptional character. Once more there is room
here for some variation. On the one hand, the State and its ruler are
willed by God as is everything on earth. On the other, the State is to
the Church as the earth is to heaven, and a bad ruler may be a
punishment sent by God. In general we should not forget that in the
exegetical perspective life on earth since Christ is a mix: he has
ushered in a transitional stage between the unredeemed state of
men under the Old Dispensation and the full accomplishment of the
promise in the Second Coming (see Caspary 1979: 176–77). In the
meantime, men have the Kingdom of God only within themselves.

So far we surveyed the views of the early Fathers on social and
political matters, with the exception of Saint Augustine.[10] He must
be considered apart, for not only does he take us into the fifth
century and the now Christian Empire, but he is such an original
thinker that he renews the conceptual framework that he inherits.[11]

10. The development on Augustine that follows is printed here in English for
the first time. First cut out of the spoken version because of time limits, it was left out
in print because it was felt to be too thin and summary, altogether unworthy of the
subject's greatness. Later a few friends saw the draft, and insisted on seeing it
published; may it make some sense in this context, whatever its shortcomings.

11. We thus diverge somewhat from Troeltsch, although using mainly the
passages he singled out, and still more from Carlyle, whom he relied on. I could not

It is well known that Augustine expressed Christianity with a new intensity of thought and feeling. With him, the Christian message of Paul reveals its whole depth, its paradoxical grandeur. Augustine raised his religion to an unprecedented philosophical level, and in so doing he foreshadowed the future, as if his personal inspiration coincided with the motive force, with the cardinal principle, of the subsequent development. Very pointedly in relation to us, history demands that we should salute him as a genius. Perhaps our sentiment in the matter is the stronger, as we know from his writings about the human limitations, the sufferings, and the efforts through which he soared to such heights.

This makes it all the more difficult to speak of Augustine as he deserves, to form an adequate idea of the sweep and depth of his thought, and yet we ought, even in this brief study, devote a small niche to him or, as it were, a small altar where, by honoring him, we may hope to share in his insight.

Augustine is of his time, and yet he prefigures or rather unfailingly points to what is to come. This is seen from his influence through the Middle Ages and far beyond. Think only of Luther, of the Jansenists—nay, the continuity extends down to existentialism. Perhaps for this very reason he is easily misunderstood, but the perspective outlined here should be of use in locating and grasping him better.

It is not only that Augustine restricts the field of application of Natural Law and extends that of Providence or the Divine Will. The change is more radical. In political matters, the endorsement of sacral kingship is substituted by the absolute submission of the State to the Church, and it is only within this new framework that Natural Law retains a limited value.

Thus a double development on the State in the *City of God* is very clear. Admitting with Cicero that the State is based on justice, Augustine first states forcefully that a State so-called that does not do justice to God and to man's relationship to Him does not know justice and hence is not a State. That is to say, there can be no justice once its transcendent dimension is taken away. This is a

---

consult the book which Troeltsch has especially devoted to Augustine (*Augustin: Die christliche Antike und das Mittelalter*, Munich, 1915). Other references are to Gilson 1969; Brown 1967.

matter of principle, a normative statement. Further on the question is taken up again: having stated that principle, how can one nevertheless recognize that the Roman people has some empirical reality, albeit not being a people in the normative sense? We can acknowledge that the *populus Romanus* is united around something, even if this something is not, as it should be, true justice. Empirically a people is united through its common love for something or, as we should say, through common values, and it is better or worse according to the better or worse values it shares. How then can one say, as Carlyle did, that Augustine's definition of the State does away with justice? (Carlyle's treatment borders on systematic incomprehension, 1903: 164–170.)

Let us look more closely. Until then Christians had considered the State and the world in general as congenitally opposed to and independent from the Church and the realm of man's relationship to God. What Augustine does is to demand that the State should be judged from the world-transcending viewpoint of man's relation to God that is the Church's viewpoint. This is actually a step forward in the imposition of outworldly values to inworldly conditions. It is an inroad of theocracy. Here Augustine augurs the main development to come in following centuries. In the words of Gregory the Great: "Let the terrestrial kingdom serve—or be the slave of—the celestial."

The point is worth pondering, for what is happening here is characteristic of Augustine's general attitude and of his radical and revolutionary claim. When justice is Christianized in this manner, reason is made not only to bow to faith but to recognize in faith something akin to itself, as it were reason itself raised to a superior power. Here is nothing less than a new form of thought corresponding to the immanence-cum-transcendence of God. Such has actually been Augustine's apparently extravagant claim: to philosophize from faith, to set faith, i.e. the experience of God, at the foundation of rational thought. This may have appeared as hubris to an ancient mind, but it can be argued that all philosophers do the same, that any philosophy starts from a personal experience and a personal tendency or design. The fact is that here, under the aegis of the Christian God, the modern era begins, when men will increasingly struggle to embody their personal experience in reason, that is, to reduce the gulf that initially separated reason from experience. (I must confess that this immense phenomenon goes so far beyond my usual concepts as to bring in rhetoric.) Augustine inaugurates a millenary, protean, existential struggle between reason and experience, a struggle unceasingly renewed and propagating from one level to another, which will in the last analysis modify the relation between the ideal and the actual, and of which we are in some manner the products.

The consequences of this tremendous Augustinian mutation are clear in our restricted domain. To begin with, an increased stress on equality: God "has not willed the rational creature made in his own image to have dominion over any but irrational creatures, not man over man, but man over beasts (cattle). Hence the first just men were set up as shepherds of flocks rather than as kings of men." This is almost a Stoic statement, but the wording and the tone brings John Locke to mind. There follows immediately the assertion of sin, equally forceful as was that of the order of nature, for "of course, the condition of slavery is justly imposed on the sinner," the punishment results from the same law of nature that sin contravened (*City of God*, 19.15). Man who made himself a slave of sin is justly made a slave of man. Although this bears on political dominion as well as on slavery, it is noteworthy that the consequence is explicitly, elaborately drawn for slavery only, no doubt because it is in slavery that the subjection of man to man is the most blatant, and God-willed natural equality most directly contradicted. Such antithetical structures are characteristic of Augustine. Here the master is reminded that pride is as harmful to him as humility is salutary for the servant. (It is seen that subordination is not rejected as a general principle.)

Augustine is not much interested in property. He deals with it only incidentally in the struggle against the Donatists, who urged, against the confiscation of their churches by the imperial government, that they had acquired their property by labor—thus anticipating the future argument of Locke, as Carlyle noticed. It is clear that for Augustine private property is exclusively a matter of "human and positive law" (Carlyle 1903: 140–41).

I believe that neither Carlyle nor, when he follows him, Troeltsch does justice to the originality of Augustine's thought in these matters, and I shall add a few remarks on the same well-known passages they refer to. It should first be recalled that, as for most of the ancients, Romans or Greeks, man according to Augustine, is a social creature. Augustine himself was an eminently sociable character. Surely he was no stranger to the idea of hierarchy. There is a hierarchy of soul and body, the more stressed as the body has in Augustine a value and dignity it certainly did not possess with, say, Origen.[12] It is through the soul that we relate to God, and therefore there is a chain of subordination from God to the soul and from the soul to the body. So, when discussing justice in relation to the State, Augustine writes: "When a man does not serve God, what amount of justice are we to suppose to exist in his being? For if a soul does not serve God it cannot with any kind of justice command the body, nor can a man's reason control the vicious elements in the soul" (*City of God*, 19.21; 19.23).

Yet at the same time I believe we can detect in certain details a subtle advance of individualism. The State is a collection of men united through agreement on values and common utility. The definition is Cicero's, but in Cicero it is not as individualistic as it looks in such a translation. In a passage quoted by Augustine in his first reference to the topic, (ibid., 2.21), the concord (*concors*, adj.) of the multitude in the State is that of different orders of people, high, low, and middle, and it is likened to the harmony of different sounds in music; but this reference to the whole is not taken up by Augustine, and one gets the impression that the State for him is made up of individuals while the Church alone is one body.

The definition of what is generally called natural law in *Contra Faustum* (22.7; Troeltsch 1922; n. 69) is close to that of Cicero as celebrated by Lactantius (Troeltsch, ibid.), and yet subtly different: "The eternal law is the divine reason or the will of God, which commands to conserve the natural order and forbids to disturb it." All this is in Cicero except the words "will" and "natural order." If I am not mistaken, their introduction has the effect of separating what was the Law of Nature into two: the order, which is God-given, and the law, which comes also from God but which alone is in the hands of men. It is perhaps not going too far to say that both the transcendence of God and man's own domain receive here a more distinct stress.

Something similar happens with order and justice. Both are defined in terms of distributive justice. Order is (*City of God*, 19.13) "the disposition that attributes their respective place to *similar* and dissimilar things"; and justice "the virtue that distributes to everyone his due" (ibid., 19.21). In another text (*De div. quest.* 31; Troeltsch 1922, n. 73) "Justice is the disposition of mind which,

---

12. Augustine's attitude to the body differs from that of the pagan philosophers as well; see the fine study by Maria Daraki, (1981), esp. pp. 99ff.

once common utility is assured (*conservata*), attributes to everyone his dignity." It is remarkable that justice operates here in relation to individuals within an order or a whole (common utility) but apart from it (and not as if it were said that justice serves the whole through its operation).

It seems to me it is enough to assemble these three passages to feel that they somehow point in a direction that is familiar to us moderns: an increased distance between nature and man, and a tendency to isolate, under the aegis of a God-willed order, a world of men considered essentially as individuals and having only an indirect relation to the order.

Something similar often comes to the mind of the reader of Gilson's *Introduction* to Augustine. Thus, between the theology of Plotinus and that of Augustine, one senses a subtle shift from a hierarchical structure to a somewhat substantialized hierarchy. Gilson notes how the successive entities engendered by the One in Plotinus are each slightly inferior to the preceding one, so that they form a regular downward scale, beginning with Intelligence and then the Soul, while in Augustine the Son and the Holy Spirit are equal to the Father and one with him, and a gap follows, the gap between generation and creation (Gilson 1969: 143–44).

To return to the implications of the State's dependent status: real terrestrial goods like peace cannot be solidly acquired independently of superior goods: peace is not attained, as rulers imagine, by war and victory (*City of God*, 15.4). And this distantiation allows Augustine to take a cold view of the horrors of history: states have their origin mostly in crime and violence: Romulus like Cain killed his brother (ibid., 18.2)—and here we cannot but think of Hume.

At the same time, Augustine is confident in the as yet unrealized possibilities of Christianity, in the unprecedented development that lies in store for it. Against the quietism of the Donatists he urges dynamism and audacity. In the years darkened by the fall of Rome he is full of intellectual enthusiasm, applying Plotinus's vision to the order that history progressively displays; he is inspired by a quite anachronistic, uncanny sense of progress, as when he writes: "I am trying to be among those who write in progressing and who progress in writing" (Brown 1971, 419 *et passim*). One feels that with Augustine the eschatological view under which the early Fathers labored is beginning to change into something like the modern idea of progress (ibid.: 473).

With Augustine the Western Church advances on the path that

leads her into the world and that takes her further and further from her Eastern sister, content with her blessed and deifying shell within the Empire.

Augustine somewhere likens the union of soul and body in man with that of a man and a horse in a horseman (*City of God*, 19.3; Gilson 1969: 58). The soul itself is perceived as living truth, so that Gilson speaks of Augustine's eudemonism (58–59, 66). Here, in the virtual identity of rationality and life, in the divine warrant for their reconciliation, is perhaps the central message of Christianity, which sets it in absolute contrast to Buddhism.

All in all, when faith and feeling thus break into the realm of reason, when history acquires a pattern and the future of mankind is lightened with hope, one feels one is witnessing a rehabilitation of inworldly life, as if it were in the process of being redeemed through an outpouring of outworldly light.

Having thus far reviewed the ideas of the Fathers of the Church that are relevant to our theme, we shall now focus on the evolution of the relation between the Church and the State, that epitome of the world, up to the crowning of Charlemagne in A.D. 800. I shall isolate a remarkable formula of that relation, and show how it was subsequently modified. In the first place, the conversion to Christianity of the Emperor Constantine at the beginning of the fourth century, besides forcing the Church to a new degree of unification, created a redoubtable problem: what was to be a Christian State? The Church was willy-nilly brought face-to-face with the world. She was glad to envision an end to persecutions, and she became an official, richly subsidized institution. The Church could not go on devaluing the State as absolutely as she had done hithero.[13]

The State had after all taken one step out of the world and toward the Church, but by the same token the Church was made

---

13. In an article already referred to (see unnumbered note at opening of this chapter), S. N. Eisenstadt understands me as having attributed the transformation Christianity has undergone, from an outworldly to an inworldly orientation, "to the historical 'accident' of Constantine's conversion" rather than "to some tendencies inherent in Christianity" from the start (p. 1). There is some misunderstanding here, for which my wording of the above paragraph may be partly responsible. Actually it was meant as a description of an historical event rather than a causal explanation of a trend. Globally, my concern has been to show that there has been a transformation, not to explain it, and "all considerations of cause and effect" were explicitly excluded at this fundamental level (above, p. 24).

more worldly than she had ever been. Yet the structural inferiority of the State was maintained, albeit nuanced. The latitude to which I have drawn attention was increased, in the sense that a more or less favorable assessment of the State could be made depending on circumstances and temperaments. Conflicts were not ruled out, but they would henceforth be internal, both to the Church and to the Empire. It was inevitable that the heritage of Hellenistic sacral kingship would collide occasionally with the claim of the Church to remain the superior institution. The frictions that subsequently developed between the Emperor and the Church—and particularly with the first of the bishops, that of Rome—were chiefly around points of doctrine. While the Emperors, mostly for the sake of political unity, insisted on proclaiming compromises, the Church, its ecumenical councils and especially the Pope, were keen on defining the doctrine as the basis for orthodox unity, and resented the rulers' intrusion in the preserve of ecclesiastical authority. A succession of doctrinal divergences obliged the Church to elaborate a unified doctrine. It is noteworthy that most of those debates which issued in the condemnation of heresies (such as Arianism, Monophysitism, Monothelism) centered—predominantly in the East, around the ancient sees of Alexandria and Antioch—on the difficulty of conceiving and properly formulating the union of God and man in Christ. This is precisely what appears to us as the core, the secret of Christianity considered in its full historical development; namely, in abstract terms, the assertion of an effective transition between the outworldly and the inworldly, the *Incarnation of Value*. The same difficulty is reflected in the later iconoclastic movement, where it was perhaps catalysed by the puritanical Muslim influence (the sacred cannot be "imaged"). At the same time, there was clearly a political imperial interest in Arianism and in iconoclasm. Peterson has shown that the adoption of the dogma of the Holy Trinity (Council of Constantinople, A.D. 381) had tolled the bell of political monotheism (Peterson 1951).[14]

Around A.D. 500, after the Church had led an official life in the Empire for some two centuries, Pope Gelasius made a theoretical statement about the relation between the Church and the Emperor which was subsequently enshrined in tradition and abundantly drawn on. Yet modern interpreters do not seem to have done full justice to Gelasius. His clear and lofty pronouncement is widely

14. Leach linked Arianism with millenarism (see note 6 above).

treated as stating the juxtaposition and cooperation of the two powers, or, as I would say, of the two entities or functions. That it contains an element of hierarchy is somehow admitted, but seeing as the moderns are uneasy in that dimension, they misrepresent it or are unable to see its full import. On the contrary, the present comparative perspective should allow us to restore the high stature and logical structure of the Gelasian theory.

The statement is contained in two texts that complement each other. Gelasius says in a letter to the Emperor:

> There are mainly two things, August Emperor, by which this world is governed: the sacred authority of the pontiffs and the royal power. Of these, priests carry a weight all the greater, as they must render an account to the Lord even for kings before the divine judgment . . . [and a little further on] you must bend a submissive head to the ministers of divine things and . . . it is from them that you must receive the means of your salvation.[15]

The reference to salvation clearly indicates that Gelasius deals here with the supreme or ultimate level of consideration. We note the hierarchical distinction between the priest's *auctoritas* and the king's *potestas*. After a brief comment Gelasius goes on:

> In things concerning the public discipline, religious leaders realise that imperial power has been conferred on you from above, and they themselves will obey your laws, for fear that in worldly matters they should seem to thwart your will.

That is, the priest is subordinate to the king in mundane matters that regard the public order. What modern commentators fail to take fully into account is that the level of consideration has shifted from the height of salvation to the lowliness of worldly affairs. Priests are superior, for they are inferior only on an inferior level. We are not dealing either with mere "correlation" (Morrison 1969: 101–5) or with mere submission of kings to priests (Ullmann 1955: 20ff.) but with *hierarchical complementarity*.

Now, I found exactly the same configuration in ancient, Vedic, India. There, the priests looked at themselves as religiously or

---

15. The texts of Gelasius are taken from Carlyle 1903: 190–91 (but see note 17). The translation follows mostly Dvornik's (1966, 2: 804–5).

absolutely superior to the king while materially subject to him.[16] Thus, with some difference in the wording, the configuration is exactly the same as in Gelasius. The fact is astounding, given the vast differences in the respective backgrounds. On the Indian side there was no corporate unity of the faithful, nor any unitary organization of the priesthood, nor, in the first place, was there any stress put on the individual. (The renouncer, of whom I spoke previously, had not yet appeared.) I am thus emboldened to surmise that the configuration in question is simply the logical formula of the relation between the two functions.

The other main text by Gelasius is found in a treatise (*De anathematis vinculo*). Its main interest for us lies in the explanation of the differentiation of the two functions as instituted by Christ. Before him (I must excerpt) "there actually existed—though in a prefigurative sense—men who were concurrently kings and priests," such as Melchisedech. Then "the One came who was truly King and Priest" and "Christ, mindful of human frailty . . . has separated the offices of the two powers[17] by means of distinctive functions and dignities . . . intending that His own [people] should be saved by salutary humility." It is only the Devil that has imitated the pre-Christian blend of the two functions "so that," says Gelasius, "pagan emperors caused themselves to be called sacred pontiffs." There may well be here an allusion to what remained of sacral kingship in Byzantium. For the rest we may find in this text a quite sensible surmise on the evolution of institutions. It is not unreasonable for us to suppose that the original sacral sovereignty (for example, that of ancient Egypt or of China), has in some cultures differentiated into two functions, as it did in India.

It would be enlightening to discuss at length the commentators' difficulties, but I must pick and choose. A recent author, Father Congar, argues that the hierarchical formula of authority versus power is only occasional (Congar 1968). In fact we have heard Gelasius, when dealing with the differentiation, speak only of "the two powers." But is not the distinction the best expression of what Gelasius is saying all along? Congar (ibid.: 256) is right in stating that here the Church does not tend "to a temporal realization of the

16. Cf. my "The Conception of Kinship in Ancient India" (1962; esp. § 3), now in *HH*, App. C.

17. On this point our authors' texts seem (variously) corrupt. We read with Schwartz: *officia potestatis utriusque* (Schwartz 1934: 14).

City of God." As in the Indian case, hierarchy is logically opposed to power: it does not claim, as it will do later on, to transcribe itself in terms of power. But Congar (ibid.: 255–56) also argues that Gelasius does not subordinate imperial to sacerdotal power, but only the Emperor to the bishops with regard to the *res divinae*, and he concludes that, although the Emperor, as one of the faithful, was within the Church, the Church itself was *within the Empire* (his italics). Now, it is not apposite here to introduce a distinction between the function and its bearer which would in fact ruin Gelasius' argument, and of which Carlyle (1903: 169) admits in his own way that it is often disregarded in our sources. Actually the Empire culminates in the Emperor, and we must understand Gelasius as saying that, if the Church is *in* the Empire with respect to worldly matters, the Empire is *in* the Church regarding things divine. On the whole, the interpreters seem to apply to the statement of A.D. 500 a later and quite different mode of thought. They reduce the rich, structural, flexible use of the basic opposition (to which Caspary draws our attention) to a unidimensional, substantial matter of either-or, or black and white distinctions. These will appear only, in Caspary's words, when "with the freezing of political positions as the result of the [investiture] controversy and, more importantly, owing to the slow growth of scholastic and legal modes of thinking, the second half of the twelfth century slowly lost this sort of flexibility . . . and emphasised clarity and distinctions rather than interrelationships" (1979: 190).

We have studied an important ideological formula. It should not be imagined that Gelasius' dicta have either settled all conflicts between the two main protagonists or even received, whether durably or not, the agreement of all concerned. Gelasius himself was led to his pronouncements by an acute crisis following the promulgation by the Emperor of a formula intended to reconcile his Monophysite subjects, the Henotikon. In general, the Patriarchs of Eastern Christendom did not follow blindly the Vicar of St. Peter, and the Emperor first of all had his own viewpoint in the matter. There are signs that something of Hellenistic sacral kingship always remained in Byzantium, at least for the Emperor's own use and in the imperial palace (see Dvornik 1966). Moreover, some Emperors pretended to concentrate in their hands not only temporal but also spiritual supremacy, and sometimes succeeded in doing so. Not only Justinian before the time of Gelasius, but after him in the

West, in different manners, Charlemagne and Otto I assumed the supreme religious functions as part and parcel of their rule.

It would be difficult to imagine a more glaring contradiction to Gelasius' doctrine than the policy the papacy developed from the middle of the eighth century. In A.D. 753–54 Pope Stephen II, in an unprecedented move, left Rome, crossed the Alps, and visited the Frankish king Pippin. He confirmed him in his kingship and gave him the title of "Patrician of the Romans" and the role of protector and ally of the Roman Church. Fifty years later, Leo III crowned Charlemagne as Emperor in St. Peter's at Rome, on Christmas Day A.D. 800.

How the Popes had been led to adopt such a drastic course of action may be understood from their general predicament. We may almost say with Carlyle that it "was forced upon them" by circumstances. On an immediate level, what has happened may be summed up in two points. The Popes have put an end to a situation of humiliation, oppression, and danger, by turning their back on Byzantium and exchanging a remote, civilized but assuming protector for another who is nearer, more efficient, less civilized but therefore hopefully more docile. At the same time, they have taken advantage of the change to press their claim to sovereign political authority in a part of Italy. The Western Emperors may later prove to be less docile than expected, and Charlemagne probably looked at the political rights he guaranteed to the Pope as only a kind of autonomy under his own paramountcy. He did assert his duty not only to protect but to direct the Church.

What is essential for us is the papal assumption of a political function, which is clear from the start. In the words of Professor Southern (1970: 60) commenting on the pact with Pippin: "for the first time in history the Pope had acted as a supreme political authority in authorizing the transfer of power in the Frankish kingdom, and he had emphasized his political role as successor to the Emperors by disposing of imperial lands in Italy." The appropriation of imperial territories in Italy is not quite articulate to begin with: the Pope obtains from Pippin, and later from Charles, the recognition of the "rights" and territories of the "Republic of the Romans" without any clear distinction being made between private and public rights and powers, but this includes the Ravenna exarchate. We cannot yet speak of a papal State, although there is a

Roman political entity. A forged document, of perhaps somewhat later date, the so-called Donation of Constantine, clearly states the papal claim. There, the first Christian Emperor is made to transmit to the Roman See in A.D. 315, along with the Lateran "palace" extensive patrimonial estates and the religious "principate" over all other sees as "universal pope," imperial rule over Roman Italy, and imperial regalia and privileges (see Southern 1970: 60; Partner 1972: 21–23).

What is of primary importance from our viewpoint is the ideological change that is here initiated and will be fully developed later on, independently of what will happen in fact to the papal claim. With the claim to an inherent right to political power, a change is introduced in the relation between the divine and the earthly: the divine now claims to rule the world through the Church, and the Church becomes inworldly in a sense it was not heretofore.

The Popes have, through a historical choice, canceled Gelasius' logical formula of the relation between the religious and the political function and turned to another. For Gelasius' hierarchical dyarchy is substituted a monarchy of unprecedented type, a spiritual monarchy. The two agencies or realms are unified while their distinction is relegated from the fundamental to a secondary level, as if they differed not in their nature but only in degree. The distinction is henceforth between the spiritual and the temporal, as we have known them ever since, and the field is unified, so that we may speak of spiritual and temporal "powers." It is characteristic that the spiritual is conceived as superior to the temporal *on the temporal level itself*, as if it was a superior degree of the temporal, or so to speak, the temporal raised to a superior power, that is a "squared temporal." It is along this line that later on the Pope will be conceived as "delegating" the temporal power to the Emperor as his "deputy."

As compared with Gelasius' theory, the superiority is here stressed at the expense of the difference, and I would venture to call this disposition a perversion of hierarchy. Yet a coherence of a new type is achieved. The new unification represents a transformation of an older unity. For if we remember the archetypal model of sacral kingship we see here substituted for it what we might call kingly priesthood.

This new disposition is pregnant with meaning and with further historical developments. It should be obvious that, in a general sense, the Christian individual becomes here more intensely involved in this world. But to remain on the level of institutions, the movement is, as similar previous movements, double-edged: if the Church becomes more worldly, conversely the political realm is made to participate in absolute, universalist values. It is, so to speak, consecrated, in quite a new manner. And we can thus descry a potentiality that will be realized later on, namely, that a particular political unity may in its turn emerge as a bearer of absolute values, as the modern State. For the modern State is not in continuity with other political forms: it is a transformed Church, as is readily seen in the fact of its not being made up of different functions or orders, but rather of individuals, a point which even Hegel failed to admit.[18]

I cannot even sketch out this further development here. Let me say only that the shift I have just underlined will be followed by other shifts in the same direction, and that this long chain of shifts will issue finally in the full legitimation of this world, together with the full transfer of the individual *into* this world. This chain of transitions can be thought of in the image of the Incarnation of the Lord as the progressive incarnation or embodiment in the world of those values which Christianity had initially reserved to the outworldly individual and his Church.

To conclude, I have proposed that we abstain from projecting our familiar idea of the individual onto the first Christians and their cultural environment; that instead we should recognize a notable difference in the respective conceptions. The individual as value was then conceived as apart from the given social and political organization, outside and beyond it, an outworldly individual as opposed to our own inworldly individual. Helped by the Indian instance, I argued that individualism could not possibly have appeared in another form and developed otherwise from traditional holism, and that the first centuries of the history of the Church showed the first lineaments of the accommodation to the world of that strange creature. I stressed at the start the adoption of the Stoics' Law of Nature as a rational instrument for the adaptation to worldly ethics of outworldly values. Then I turned to a single but highly significant dimension, the political. Initially the State is to the

---

18. Cf. Hegel's *Philosophy of Right* (1942), part 3, section 3, and his impatience in 1831 at seeing the Revolution threatening to burst out anew ("The English Reform Bill" in *Political writings* (1964), *in fine*, and correspondence). Cf. Habermas' "Nachwort" in Hegel 1966: 364–65, and the pointed reference to *Philosophy of Right* (actually § 258: "If the State is confused with civil Society . . .").

Church as the world is to God, and therefore the history of the conception by the Church of its relation to the State is central in the evolution of the relation between the bearer of value, the out-worldly individual, and the world. Subsequently, after the conversion of the Emperor, and then that of the Empire, had forced upon the Church a closer relation to the State, a logical, that is, truly hierarchical, formula was reached by Gelasius, which we may call a hierarchical dyarchy. Yet the truth-value of that formula should not blind us to the fact that, as the Indian parallel shows, it bears no relation whatsoever to individualism. Then, in the eighth century, comes a dramatic change. By a historic decision, the Popes snap their tie with Byzantium and arrogate supreme temporal power in the West. This momentous step was invited by the hopeless situation that had developed, but cannot be explained by it. It expresses a subtle but fundamental ideological shift. The Church now pretends to rule, directly or indirectly, the world, which means that the Christian individual is now committed to the world to an unprecedented degree. Other steps will follow in the same direction, but this one is decisive in general and especially with regard to future political developments. We have thus seen some stages of the transformation of the outworldly individual into the inworldly individual.

The main lesson upon which to meditate is perhaps that the most effective humanization of the world has issued in the long run from a religion that subordinated it most strictly to a transcendent value.

Calvin

It is a weakness of the present study that it stops at the eighth century. I imagine that the thesis would be strengthened if the subsequent developments were followed, as they should, down to the Reformation. I am unable to do so for the present, but in order to remedy the shortcoming in some measure, I propose here a brief consideration of the terminal stage of the process as represented by Calvin.[19] Accepting Troeltsch's account, I shall try to show that it is best reformulated in the language used heretofore.[20]

19. I hope to produce an account of the process as a whole at some later date.
20. This epilogue is thus no more than an exercise on Troeltsch's text. If an excuse is needed for not considering wider literature, I shall say that, judging from a

In what sense can Calvin be taken as standing at the end of a process? In a general sense the process goes on beyond the man. The inworldliness of the individual will progress in the sects, in the Enlightenment, and further on. But from the point of view of what I have tried to highlight—that is, the conceptual interrelation between the individual, the Church, and the world—Calvin marks a conclusion: his Church is the last form that the Church could possibly take without disappearing. Moreover, when I say Calvin, what I mean is the Reformation as culminating—from our viewpoint—in Calvin. Calvin built on Luther; he was conscious only of making Luther's stand explicit, articulate, and drawing its logical consequences. We may thus, for the sake of brevity, avoid considering Lutheranism in itself and retain only those of Luther's views that are presupposed in Calvin, while leaving aside his other views as superseded by Calvin's.

My thesis is simple: with Calvin, the hierarchical dichotomy that charaterized our field of consideration comes to an end; the antagonistic worldly element that individualism had hitherto to accommodate disappears entirely in Calvin's theocracy. The field is absolutely unified. *The individual is now in the world, and the individualist value rules without restriction or limitation.* The inworldly individual is before us.

Actually, this recognition is nothing new, for it is present in every page of Troeltsch's chapter on Calvin, even if it is not expressed in exactly the same words. Early in the book, at the end of the chapter on Paul, Troeltsch pointed forward to this unification. "This principle of the mere juxtaposition of given conditions and ideal claims, that is the mixture of conservatism and radicalism, is first broken only by Calvinism." (1922: 81–82; 1960: 88). The sequence of the passage suggests the possibility of two alternative views: as a consequence of the unification, either, as with Calvin, the spirit animates the whole of life, or, conversely, material life commands spiritual life. Hierarchical dualism is replaced by a flat continuum governed by an either/or choice.

---

few incursions—as into the books by Choisy to which Troeltsch refers, or into Calvin's own *Institutes*—one finds that the questions at issue can easily be answered univocally: there is no twilight, no zone that would call for another angle of vision or another kind of lighting; the contours have been drawn with a firm hand and there is no mistaking them. Indeed there is something slightly uncanny in Calvin's assurance and decisiveness. In this as elsewhere he is quite modern: the rich, complex, and fluctuating world of structure has been banned.

Calvin thinks he is following Luther and yet he produces a different doctrine. Let us therefore start from his particular character or temperament. Troeltsch says that Calvin has a peculiar conception of God. Well, this conception closely corresponds to Calvin's inclinations, and in general he projects everywhere his deep personal inspiration. Calvin is not of a contemplative temper; he is a rigorous thinker whose thought is oriented to action. He ruled Geneva as a skilled statesman, and there is in him a legalistic bent. He likes to promulgate regulations and to discipline himself and others. He is possessed by the will to act in the world and brushes aside through consistent arguments the received ideas that would block his way.

Such a personal disposition throws light on the three fundamental interrelated elements in Calvin's doctrine: the conceptions of God as *will*, of predestination, and of the Christian city as the object on which bears the will of the individual.

For Calvin, God is essentially will and majesty. This implies distance: God is here more remote than hitherto. Luther had removed God from the world by rejecting the mediation institutionalized in the Catholic Church, where God was present by proxy in men singled out as intermediaries (Church dignitaries, priests endowed with sacramental powers, monks devoted to a higher type of life).[21] But with Luther, God was accessible to individual consciousness through faith, love, and, to some extent, reason. With Calvin, love falls into the background and reason applies only to this world. At the same time, Calvin's God is the archetype of the Will, or the affirmation by proxy of man himself as will, or finally, the strongest affirmation of the individual as opposed to, or superior to, reason. Of course, the stress on the will is central in the history of Christian civilization as a whole (from Augustine to modern German philosophy), not to mention freedom in general nor the link with nominalism (Ockham).

The paramountcy of the will is dramatically expressed in the dogma of predestination. The root of it lies in Luther's rejection of salvation through works, which was in the first place meant for the destruction of the Catholic Church, its ritualism, and the domina-

21. This feature seems largely neglected in the history of ideas. Such a type of transcendence will later appear unbearable to German philosophers. Colin Morris happily contrasts Karl Barth's statement that there is no point of contact between God and man with the close presence of God in Saint Bernard and with the Cistercian effort "to discover God in man and through man" (1972: 163).

tion it had established upon the individual soul. Luther had replaced justification by works with justification through faith, and had in the main stopped at that point, leaving to the individual some margin of freedom. Calvin went further, maintaining with iron consistency the complete impotence of man in the face of the omnipotence of God. At first sight, this appears a limitation rather than a development of individualism. Troeltsch therefore sees Calvinism as a particular sort of individualism rather than as an intensification of it (1922, n. 320). I shall try to show that it is an intensification, insofar as the relation of the individual to the world is considered.

God's inscrutable will invests some men with the grace of election, and condemns others to reprobation. The task of the elect is to work for God's glory in the world, and faithfulness to this task will be the mark and the only proof of election. Thus, the elect relentlessly exercises his will in action, and in so doing, while absolutely subjected to God, he will in actual fact participate in Him in contributing to the implementation of His designs. I am trying, no doubt imperfectly, to sum up the nexus of subjection and exaltation of the self found in the configuration of Calvin's ideas and values. On this level, that is, within the consciousness of the elect, we find again the hierarchical dichotomy with which we are familiar. Troeltsch warns us against interpreting Calvin in terms of unfettered atomistic individualism. And it is true that divine grace, the grace of election, is central to the doctrine and that Calvin has nothing to do with man's freedom. He holds that "the honor of God is safe when man bows under His law, whether his submission is free or forced." Yet, if we see here the emergence of inworldly individualism, and if we think of the intrinsic difficulty of this attitude, we might as well look on the individual elect's subjection to God's grace as the *necessary condition* for legitimating the decisive shift.

In effect, until then the individual had to recognize in the world an antagonistic factor, an irreducible *alter* that could not be suppressed but only subjected, encompassed. This limitation disappears with Calvin, and we find it replaced, so to speak, by his peculiar subjection to God's will. If such is the genesis of what Troeltsch and Weber called inworldly asceticism, we had best speak of ascetic, or conditioned, inworldliness.[22]

---

22. Max Weber said very much the same thing in 1910 in a discussion following Troeltsch's lecture on Natural Law: he contrasted "the forms of world-rejecting

We may also contrast Calvin's active participation in God with the traditional contemplative participation that is still Luther's. Instead of taking refuge from this imperfect world in another which allowed us to cope, it would seem we had decided that we should ourselves embody that other world in our determined action upon this one. What is of paramount importance is that we have here the model of modern artificialism at large, the systematic application to the things of this world of an extrinsic, imposed value. Not a value derived from our belonging in this world, such as its harmony or our harmony with it, but a value rooted in our heterogeneity in relation to it: the identification of our will with the will of God (Descartes' man will make himself "master and possessor of nature"). The will applied to the world, the end sought after, the motive and inner spring of the will are extraneous; they are, to say the same thing, essentially outworldly. Outworldliness is now concentrated in the individual's will. This fits in with Toennies' distinction of spontaneous will and arbitrary will (*Naturwille* and *Kürwille*) (Toennies 1971), and it shows where the arbitrariness, (the *Willkür*) has its ground. To my mind it also underlies what Weber called modern rationality.

Our view of Calvin allows for correcting or deepening the paradigm that we used hitherto. Outworldliness is now concentrated in the individual's will. This recognition leads to thinking that modern artificialism as an exceptional phenomenon is understandable only as a distant historical consequence of Christian outworldly individualism, and that what we called the modern inworldly individual has in himself, hidden in his internal constitution, an unperceived but essential element of outworldliness. There is thus more continuity between the two kinds of individualism than we had initially supposed, with the consequence that a hypothetical direct transition from traditional holism to modern individualism appears now not only improbable but impossible.[23]

---

religiosities" to the "Calvinistic religiosity which finds the certitude of being God's child in the to-be-attained 'proving of oneself' (*Bewahrung*) . . . within the given and ordered world"; or again, on the one hand, the "community" of acosmic love characteristic of the Eastern Church and Russia, on the other, the "society" or "the formation of the social structure upon an egocentric base" (Nelson 1973, 148).

Nelson has said elsewhere that innerworldly mysticism needed more explicit acknowledgement than Weber and Troeltsch had given it (Nelson 1975: 236; see note 3 above). This seems to confirm my stress on inworldliness as against asceticism.

23. The two parts of our initial paradigm had been developed more or less

The conversion to inworldliness has in Calvin noteworthy concomitant features. I noticed the recession of mystical and emotional aspects. They are not entirely absent from Calvin's writings, but conspicuously so from his dogma. Even Redemption is seen in a dry, legalistic way, as satisfaction of God's offended honor. Christ is the ruler of the Church (in place of the Pope), the paradigm of Christian life, and the seal authenticating the Old Testament. Christ's own distinctive teaching was not adequate to the regulation of a Christian earthly commonwealth, and therefore the Sermon on the Mount largely disappears behind the Decalogue. The Covenant is between God and the Church, as it had been between God and ancient Israel. Choisy stressed the change from Luther's "Christocracy" to Calvin's nomo- or logocracy.

Similarly, most features corresponding to otherworldliness lose their function and therefore disappear. The Second Coming had already for long lost much of its urgency. The Kingdom of God is essentially, we may say, to be built up piecemeal on earth through the efforts of the elect. To one who is unremittingly struggling with men and institutions as they actually are, the stress on the state of nature or of innocence, the distinction between the absolute and the relative law of nature appear as idle speculations.

But can we really assert that the individualist value now rules without contradiction or limitation? At first sight, this does not seem to be the case. Calvin keeps the medieval idea according to which the Church should dominate the State (or the political government of the city), and in the first place he still thinks in terms of *the* Church identified with the global society. Troeltsch was careful to underline the fact: although many features of Calvinism inclined it toward the sect, and whatever the future developments in the same direction or in that of the "Free Churches," yet Calvin strictly adhered to the idea of the Church as regulating all activities within the social community as a whole. Indeed, he put into effect such a

---

independently and could appear as mutually inconsistent. To put the matter briefly, the holism/individualism distinction supposes an inworldly individualism, while in the inworldly/outworldly distinction the outworldly pole is not opposed to holism (at any rate, in the same manner as the inworldly pole). Actually, outworldly individualism is *hierarchically* opposed to holism: superior to society, it leaves society standing, while inworldly individualism negates, destroys the holistic society and replaces it (or pretends to do so). The continuity we have now described between the two types, especially through the instance of Calvin, reinforces their unity and qualifies their difference. It thus confirms the initial paradigm.

strict regulation in Geneva. This being so, it might be surmised that all trace of holism cannot have disappeared, that with Calvin, as before, some counterweight to individualism would result from the necessities of social life. Troeltsch tells us explicitly that it is not so: "The idea of community has not been evolved out of the conception of the Church and of grace, like the Lutheran ecclesiastical idea; on the contrary it springs from the same principle which appears to give independence to the individual, namely from the ethical duty of the preservation and making effective of election, and from abstract biblicism" . . . (1922: 625–26; 1960: 590–92). Troeltsch quotes Schneckenburger: "The Church does not make the believers what they are, but the believers make the Church what she is," and adds: "The conception of the Church is placed within the setting of predestination" (1922, n. 320). Through predestination the individual takes the upper hand over the Church. This is of course a fundamental change. It becomes more understandable once we realize that Luther, while keeping the idea of the Church, as he thought, unchanged, has already in fact emptied it of its vital core. It remained as an institute of grace or salvation (*Heilsanstalt*), but Calvin's predestination deprived it even of that dignity; actually if not in principle. What remained of the Church was an instrument of discipline acting on individuals (the elect as well as the reprobate, for they are practically indistinguishable) and on the political government. More precisely it was an institute of sanctification (*Heiligungsanstalt*), effective in the christianizing of the life of the city. The whole of life—in Church, family and State, society and economy, in all private and public relationship—had to be molded by the Divine Spirit and the Divine Word as intimated by the Ministers of the Church (and eventually confirmed by the Consistory where laymen were represented in addition to the Ministers). In point of fact, the Church was now the organ through which the elect were to rule over the reprobate and to carry out their task for the glory of God. It kept some features of the old Church, which distinguished it from a sect, but at the same time it had become, for all practical purposes, an association composed of individuals.

To sum up, Calvin did not acknowledge either in the Church or in the society or commonwealth, the Republic or City of Geneva— the two being coterminous in terms of membership—any principle of a holistic kind that would have limited the application of the individualist value. He acknowledged only imperfections, resistances or obstacles to be handled in the appropriate way, and a unified field for the exercise of the elect's activity, that is for the glorification of God.

Notwithstanding the vast chronological gap that remains, let me attempt a provisional conclusion. With Calvin the Church encompassing the State has dissolved as a holistic institution.

Yet Calvin's deed, the unification of the field and the conversion of the individual to this world, was made possible only by the secular action of the Church. It is clear that until then the Church had been the great agent of the transformation we are studying: something of an active mediator between the outworldly individual and the world, which is society at large and in particular the Empire or State.

We are thus enabled, in principle, to replace our initial model with a more precise one. But I must be content with a thumbnail sketch. Between the encompassing value—the outworldly individual—and earthly necessities and allegiances, we have to posit the Church. We see the Church throughout the centuries busy on two fronts—asserting itself against the political institution, and also, so to speak, against the individual. In other words, the Church has been growing on both sides: (a) by subordinating to itself, in principle at least, the Empire, and (b), through the Gregorian reform and the doctrine of the sacraments in particular (Penance), by taking upon herself certain functions and capacities by means of which she smoothed the way to salvation of the common man, but which with the Reformation the individual will later on claim to recover. Luther and Calvin attack in the first place the Catholic Church as an institute of salvation. In the name of the self-sufficiency of the individual-in-relation-to-God they cancel the division of religious labor instituted by the Church. At the same time they accept, or rather Calvin most distinctly accepts, the unification obtained by the Church on the political side.

As a result of this double attitude the field already unified to a large extent by the Church falls by a single stroke under Calvin's inworldly individualism. The Reformation picks the fruit matured in the Church's lap.

In the general continuous process, the Reformation is a crisis marked by reversal on one level: the institution that had been the bridgehead of the outworldly and had conquered the world is itself condemned as having become inworldly in the process.

2 Genesis, II

The Political Category and the State from the Thirteenth Century Onward

1. Introduction

Although this essay bears on the modern conception of the individual and some of its concomitants, it is much more restricted in its scope than the inquiry Max Weber recommended at the beginning of the century.[1] It is comparative in origin and aim. Terms like "individualism," "atomism," "secularism," are often used to oppose modern society to societies of the traditional type. In particular, the contrast between caste society and its modern Western counterpart is a commonplace. Liberty and equality on the one hand, interdependence and hierarchy on the other, are in the foreground. Permanence-versus-mobility, ascription-versus achievement allow for a neat contrariety between the two kinds of social system. We might well ask whether there is as much difference in social practice here and there as between (explicit or implicit) social theories, and I shall point out on occasion that Western society is no stranger to the attitudes and even to the ideas that caste

This text marks the very beginning of the research here presented. The original title was therefore very general: "The Modern Conception of the Individual. Notes on its genesis and that of concomitant institutions." It was first published in *Contributions to Indian Sociology* 8 (October 1965): 13–61. As in the subsequent French version, the introduction is here abridged and the last section rephrased in part. The substance is unchanged.

1. "The expression 'individualism' includes the most heterogeneous things imaginable . . . . A thorough analysis of these concepts in historical terms would at the present time be highly valuable to science" (Weber 1920: 95 n.3, according to Parsons' translation p. 222).

society upholds. Yet on the whole we are here concerned with conceptions only. The effort will be directed at expressing more precisely the Western ideological makeup, as against the traditional Indian case.

A similar contrast is found in political theory between ancient (and some modern) theories, in which the (social or) political whole is primary, and modern theories, in which the rights of the individual man are primary and determine the nature of sound political institutions. To use Weldon's vocabulary (1946),[2] "organic" theories, as represented by Plato's Republic—strongly reminiscent of the *varna* scheme—or Hegel's State, are opposed to "mechanical" theories such as Locke's doctrine of the social compact and the political trust. To distinguish between the two kinds of theories, we shall ask to which concept the stress of value is attached, whether it is the *whole* (social or) political body, or the *individual* human element. We shall speak in this sense of individualism *versus* holism. We may say that the individual, insofar as he is the main bearer of value in modern society, is equivalent to order in traditional society or to *dharma* in classical Hindu terms. This view affords a first means of comparing what at first sight seemed incommensurable and brings to light what is comparatively fundamental in the expression "the individual" as used by moderns. The expression bears in the first place on the individual man, and the notion is characterized by the combination of two elements:

2. Karl Popper (1945) similarly contrasts "open" and "closed" societies. Although in a somewhat different direction, we tread here upon classical sociological ground (Toennies's *Gemeinschaft* and *Gesellschaft*, Durkheim's mechanical and organic division of labor). The use of the same terms by Durkheim and Weldon is not inconsistent in both authors if taken together, but the terms bear on different levels of society, and the discrepancy in their respective reference points to a relation of complementarity: the same modern society that has developed to an unprecedented degree the *organic* division of labor and the factual interdependence between human beings has also asserted the self-sufficiency of the particular human being on the moral and political level by wedding itself predominantly to *mechanical* (individualistic) theories of the State. We might say that while some people behave "mechanically" and think "organically," others will behave "organically" and think "mechanically." Admittedly this is a most approximative formula. The traditional, especially Indian, case betrays its shortcomings, for the caste society is "organic" in its division of labor as well as in its social theory. It is nevertheless true that the ideological affirmation of the individual is accompanied empirically by an unprecedented degree of interdependence. We may suppose that such a chiasmus between different levels always accompanies an ideological differentiation. This is to say, Durkheim's view is to be seen within Toennies's (and Weldon's)—not the reverse.

1. the *empirical* subject of speech, thought and will, indivisible sample of the human species (which I call for analytical clarity the particular man, and which is found in all societies or cultures); and
2. the independent, autonomous and thus (essentially) nonsocial *moral* being, as found primarily in our modern (commonsense) ideology of man and society.

Our problem here is to try to grasp some stages in the constitution and development of the individual in the second sense of the term, and of concomitant representations and institutions. We start from medieval society, which at first sight certainly appears to be closer to the holistic society of the traditional type than to the individualistic society of the modern type.

But one might well ask whether so vast an inquiry is feasible. Does not the present writer risk being judged incompetent and presumptuous? I found that such authorities as Figgis, Gierke, and Halévy had already answered some of our questions for different periods and aspects of the historical development. By summing up and relating to one another their central themes, supplementing them at times, it was possible to present a general, if incomplete, sketch which serves its purpose for the time being.

2. Thomas Aquinas and William of Ockham

In tracing the genesis of man as an individual, i.e. of the dominant modern conception of man, we shall of necessity have to follow the interplay of several levels of thought and kinds of institutions: religion and philosophy, Church and State, political philosophy and law, etc. It is convenient to start from the combination of Christian revelation and Aristotelian philosophy in Thomas Aquinas. The combination is intimate, but we can distinguish its two elements by saying that on the level of religion, faith and grace, each man is a *whole* being, a private individual in direct relation to his Creator and model, and on the level of earthly institutions he is a member of the commonwealth, a part of the social body. We note, on the one hand, that the self-sufficiency of the person is here based on the ultimate values disclosed by revelation, and is rooted in his intimacy with God as opposed to his earthly relationships. On the other hand, the earthly commonwealth is legitimized, with the help of Aristotle, as a secondary value and a rational institution, in contradistinction to the early doctrine of the Church, which disparaged it as a remedy deriving its necessity from original sin.[3]

The conception of the *universitas*, i.e. of the social body as a whole of which living men are merely the parts, obviously belongs to the traditional conceptions of society, and in particular is akin to the Hindu conception of *dharma* and the hierarchical interdependence of the several social statuses. From that stage onward, the evolution will consist in a progressive weakening of this conception in favor of another—that of *societas*, association or partnership. In this process, we shall be content with isolating a few instances or partial stages.

William of Ockham, the great Franciscan scholastic of the first half of the fourteenth century, must be mentioned as being the herald of the modern turn of mind. At first sight, he might seem to put the clock back, as he partly represents a revolt against what I have just called the legitimization of the worldly order, and a return to the founding Fathers and their exclusive stress on revelation. (In the same manner, later, Luther will also revive Saint Augustine and disparage Aristotle.) What is more, Ockham is also, against Aquinas's realism, the systematic expounder of nominalism, the founder of positivism and subjectivism in law, and all this, as will be clear, means a tremendous inroad of individualism.[4]

For Thomas Aquinas, particular beings such as Tom or Harry were "primary substances," i.e. self-subsisting entities of the primary kind; but "universals," like genius or species, that is, categories or classes of beings, were also taken as existing really by themselves and were therefore styled "secondary substances."[5] Ockham, more systematically than Duns Scotus before him, attacks this view. For him, as an expert logician who thinks he is following Aristotle, a sharp distinction must be made between things (*res*) on the one hand, and signs, words, universals on the other; "things

3. In general terms, this is commonplace. Cf. (apart from Villey 1963–see below), Sabine 1963, chap 13, "Universitas hominum." The point is clearly brought out in Cassirer 1946, chap. 9.

4. We shall follow Villey 1963. As this work does not seem to be available in English, copious extracts from it will be given here.

5. Villey, 1963: 204: "The external world is not a mere dust of disorderly atoms, or individuals; it includes an order, classes ("formal causes") and natures ("final causes") in which each of the particular beings belongs, and a whole system of relations between and beyond the particular beings. All this exists objectively, independently of the mind which descries it."

cannot but be 'simple', isolated, separated; *to be* is by definition to be *unique* and *distinct;* in the person of Tom there is nothing other than Tom, nothing that might be distinguished 'really' or 'formally.'" Neither "the animal" nor "man" (not to speak of "humanity" or "mankind") are real beings.[6] In other terms, there are no "secondary substances" as there are for Aquinas, and we must not reify—as we say today—our classes or ideas. Ockham goes so far in his polemics against the Pope as to deny there is really anything like the "Franciscan Order": there are only Franciscan monks scattered through Europe.[7] General terms do have some basis in empirical reality, but they signify nothing in themselves, only an imperfect and incomplete knowledge of real entities, the individual entities (as we may well call them in this view).

What is most important is that we may not infer from the general terms we use any normative conclusion. In particular there is no natural law deduced from an ideal order of things; there is nothing beyond the actual law posited either by God or by man with God's permission, i.e. *positive law*. In the first place it would be contrary to the "absolute power" of God (*plenitudo potestatis*) to be limited by anything but itself. As can be expected, this reference to the power of God will reflect upon human institutions. Law, which in its more fundamental aspect was an expression of the order descried in nature by the human mind, becomes in its entirety the expression of the "power" or "will" of the legislator. Futhermore, while right had been conceived as a just relationship between social

---

6. Ibid.: 206. Ockham would seem here to be very particularly the spiritual father of English minds.

7. Many modern British political scientists come to mind here. Cf. the typical conflict between Gierke and his translator Barker:

Gierke: "The eye resolved upon 'reality' refuses to recognise, in the living and permanent unity of existence of a People, anything more than an unsubstantial shadow; and it dismisses as a 'juristic fiction' the elevation of this living unity to the rank of a person."

Barker (in a footnote): "The reader may possibly sympathise with 'the eye resolved upon reality', and he may thus be led to doubt whether what Gierke calls the *Daseinseinheit eines Volkes* is really a substance, in the sense of a being or person. The unity of existence prevalent in a People may be argued to be the unity of a common content of many minds, or in other words of a common purpose, but not the unity of a Group-Being or a Group-Person."

(Gierke, 1957: 47. Cf. ibid., "The personality of groups," esp. pp. lxxxi ff.; Barker's reservations may well have been sharpened by contemporary events, as his translation was published in 1934).

beings, it becomes the social recognition of the power (*potestas*) of the individual. Ockham is thus the founding father of the "subjective theory" of right, that is to say, the modern theory of law.[8]

Even if Ockham cannot be supposed to have directly influenced the modern development of law—for his writings on the subject are not thought to have been widely known—his whole work is highly meaningful. When we summarily referred to nominalism, and to positivism and subjectivism in the theory of law and right, we witnessed the birth of the individual in philosophy and jurisprudence. When there is no longer anything ontologically real beyond the particular being, when the notion of "right" is attached, not to a natural and social order, but to the particular human being, he becomes an individual in the modern sense of the word. It is noteworthy that the immediate corollary of this transformation is the stress on the notion of "power" (*potestas*), which thus appears from the start as a functional modern equivalent of the traditional idea of order and hierarchy. And it is remarkable that this notion, which plays so great and so obscure a rôle in modern political science, should have appeared at the very beginning of the modern

8. This is of course in keeping with Ockham's nominalism and juridical positivism, but it occurs in a roundabout way which is most curious and instructive. Ockham was no jurist, but a logician. He was led to deal systematically with law in the polemics between the Pope and the Franciscans. Saint Francis of Assisi had wedded his order to poverty, but it became very rich and the Popes finally decided to compel the order to accept the ownership of the estates which they actually enjoyed. It was to attack this policy and to prevent the Franciscans from becoming entangled, contrary to their founder's vow, in worldly affairs that Ockham propounded his new definitions of law and right.

"He transports into the juridical theory of ownership his love of the Christian community life of the Franciscans, and he is thus led to give of the right of ownership a picture purposely impoverished and disparaging, drawn from the viewpint of the monk and with the purpose of justifying the monks' abstention from it" (Villey 1963: 257).

His intention was to restrict the juridical sphere, but he thereby made it independent and, his individualism and positivism playing their part, more absolute and compulsive than it had ever been. As opposed to the mere faculty of using a thing, a right to it is characterized by its sanction, i.e. the possibility of vindicating it before a court of law. "A right is power recognised by positive law": thus says the advocate of poverty heralding the era of private property. It may be objected that the modern idea of property derives from Roman Law. It is more likely that it has been read *into* Roman Law by its modern interpreters, as the same author contends in a development which, if not entirely agreed to by romanists, is highly suggestive to the sociologist (ibid.: 230 ff.).

era. If Ockham does not deal at length with politics he does presage the notion of popular sovereignty and the political contract.[9] In general, and on the social level proper, it is clear that the commonwealth has evaporated, the vacuum having been filled with the freedom of the individual, which Ockham's reaction against Aquinas's laicism extends from the plane of mystic life to that of life in society. Implicitly, we have left the *Gemeinschaft* for a *Gesellschaft*. The religious roots of this first and decisive stage of modern individualism are obvious.

3. From Church Supremacy to Political Sovereignty (Fourteenth to Sixteenth Centuries)

On the question of the birth of the modern State, a set of lectures delivered by F. N. Figgis in 1900 furnishes us with what I believe to be a textbook of unchallenged merit in its main theme. The work is the more precious for us as it allows the comparison with India to proceed smoothly. Figgis sought and found the origin of the theory of the Divine Right of kings in the Divine Right of the Pope. Then, in *Studies in Political Thought from Gerson to Grotius, 1414–1625*, he proceeded to mark the origin of political ideas in late medieval thought and to describe the revolution by which they were emancipated, in short, the birth of the modern theory of the State.[10]

Figgis formally starts from the Council of Constance in 1414. But he gives some attention to writers of the fourteenth century in his Introduction, where he also sketches out the general medieval situation. We may well then situate the starting point at the beginning of the fourteenth century. From his Introduction onward,

9. A reference to the *Lex Regia* is expected in the period. Compare Figgis 1960: 10–11 and notes, with Ockham's "Quod principi placuit legis habet vigorem, cum lege regia quae de imperio ejus lata est, populus ei et in eum omne suum imperium et potestatem concessit" (*Breviloquium* 4.3, from Villey 1963: 223): What pleases the prince has the strength of law, for through the *lex regia* . . . the people have conceded to him all their governance (*imperium*) and power." Similarly the legislative power results from a delegation of power, and finally all rights and law are made up of individual powers (ibid.: 258).

10. Figgis 1960 (first published in 1907). Figgis's eminence, and the immediate comparative value of his work, is due to his having been a religious person who made the effort "to enter into the mind as distinct from learning the outward facts of the medieval world" (see near the end of the first lecture, pp. 35–36, a short excursus on method).

Figgis insists on the triple aspect of his subject: the supremacy of the
Church in the Middle Ages, the revolution which brings about the
supremacy of the State, and the continuity in thought underlying
this transformation. In keeping with our preoccupation, and for the
sake of brevity, we shall concentrate upon the first two aspects,
leaving the third largely implicit.

If we try to set a parallel between the medieval Christian
situation and the traditional Hindu one, our first difficulty will be
found in the fact that, while the Brahmans in India were content
with their spiritual supremacy, the Church in the West also exerted
temporal power, especially in the person of its head, the Pope.
Popularly at any rate, our Middle Ages thus seem to have had a
double kind of temporal authority. Furthermore, as the spiritual
agency did not disdain to clothe itself in temporal power, one might
even wonder whether temporality did not in fact enjoy some
preeminence. As against such surmises, Figgis's central statement
brings us much closer to the Indian picture (1960: 5):

> *In the Middle Ages the Church was not a State, it was the State;*
> *the State or rather the civil authority (for a separate society was*
> *not recognised) was merely the police department of the Church.*
> The latter took over from the Roman Empire its theory of the
> absolute and universal jurisdiction of the supreme authority,
> and developed it into the doctrine of the *plenitudo potestatis* of
> the Pope, who was the supreme dispenser of law, the fountain
> of honour, including regal honour, and the sole legitimate
> earthly source of power, the legal if not the actual founder of
> religious orders, university degrees, the supreme "judge and
> divider" among nations, the guardian of international right, the
> avenger of Christian blood.

We shall take the first sentence, which I have italicized, to mean
two things: first, that the Church, or universal Christendom,
embraced all particular institutions and was the sole society, or
global society in the modern sense; second, that that universal
commonwealth of the Christians had assumed in its spiritual hierarchy the powers which might be called otherwise political, even
though it delegated them, or a part of them, to temporal agencies.
While the first feature, which makes ultimate values to determine
the boundaries of the global society, is found also in the Hindu case,
the second marks off the medieval case, although some similarity is

still found in the hierarchical subordination of temporal to spiritual agencies.

Now, it seems that the statement requires some qualification in the sense that the doctrine of the Supremacy of the Church was neither permanent from the first centuries onwards, nor absolutely unopposed. Figgis, in the passage quoted, says that it had been "developed," and he is more explicit in his *Divine Right of Kings* (Figgis 1914, chap. 3). The *plenitudo potestatis* of the Pope was proclaimed by Innocent III (1198–1216), and the papal doctrine was certainly developed from the time of Gregory VII, in his struggle against the Emperor Henri IV around 1080, to its crowning expression in Boniface VIII's bull, *Unam Sanctam*, of 1302. Some authors would say that the relation between the two principles or powers, the ecclesiastical or papal and the secular or imperial, was not precisely worked out until the last quarter of the eleventh century. (Rivière 1962: 2 ff.). Then, a view which might seduce the modern mind would be to consider the increase in precision and in authoritarianism of the papal claims as the expression of a growing rivalry between Pope and Emperor, or perhaps even as a consequence of the growing impatience of the Emperors in the light of papal pretentions. The papal doctrine was not unopposed in the period: the Emperors had something like their own. Yet, it must be said that this secular doctrine does not look very impressive in the context of the general orientation of minds, of the influence of the theologians—who were all on the ecclesiastic side—and of the coherent articulation of the opposite doctrine. Only a part of the legists espoused the secular cause. All this is very clear from Gierke's classic treatise,[11] especially if we reserve for further consideration the imperial champions of the fourteenth century, Ockham and Marsilius of Padua. The partisans of the State did not deny in essence the superiority of the Church nor its independence and sovereignty in its domain; but they did recall the doctrine of the early Church in its recognition of *sacerdotium* and *imperium* as two independent spheres instituted by God himself, two powers to be coordinated. They rebuked the pretentions of the Church against temporal power and the Emperor: the Church must confine itself to purely spiritual matters. The way in which these jurists tried to unify

11. Otto Gierke, *Political Theories of the Middle Age*, trans. F.W. Maitland (Cambridge, 1900), 7 ff., 20–21, for the general unity; 16–18 and notes for the doctrines of the partisans of the State.

the two powers, to realize the *ordinatio ad unum* which was an all-pervading ideal in the period, shows the relative weakness of their case. Yet they sometimes proposed a relation which recalls the Hindu situation: the State should be subordinated to the Church in matters spiritual, the Church to the State in matters temporal.* We may therefore safely conclude that the papal doctrine summed up by Figgis was, however late its development, really the predominant and also the more coherent doctrine of the Middle Ages. Indeed, it seems to have flowed necessarily from the generally admitted superiority of the Church and from the expression of superiority in terms of positive command. Gierke is on this point in substantial agreement with Figgis for, if Gierke recognizes the presence of two different doctrines, he hastens to add that they were only two variants of the medieval spirit, and that the real opposition was between them both on the one hand, and on the other what he calls the "antique-modern" tendency, i.e. a view based on antiquity but modern in spirit, whose first manifestations, according to Gierke, were the tendency to papal absolutism and the imperial arguments obtained through the study of Roman Law (1900: 4–5).

As to that revolution which was to install the State in the place of the Church as the sovereign institution and the global society of Western Europe, it was a long and manifold process. We must be content to mark some of its successive stages and aspects, after Figgis, but with much simplification.

In the early fourteenth century, while the Emperor has been set at bay, the French king holds in check the papal pretentions and puts the Pope in his pocket. A lawyer from Coutances in Normandy, probably closely linked to the French royal court, Pierre Dubois, in a pamphlet avowedly dealing with the conquest of the Holy Land (*De Recuperatione Terrae Sanctae*), and among startingly modern suggestions, contemplates the confiscation for the benefit of the king of all ecclesiastic properties against pensions to be served to beneficiaries, including the Pope. Later, in the conflict between John XXII and Louis of Bavaria, Marsilius of Padua in his *Defensor Pacis* states: "(1) the complete authority of the civil power, and the purely voluntary nature of religious organization . . .; (2) the consequent iniquity of persecution by the Church;

---

* [Note 1984: What was said above in chap. 1 of Gelasius and the subsequent papal policy should allow for the whole "investiture controversy" to be seen in a new light.]

(3) the original sovereignty of the people, implying the need of a system of representative government."[12] The last point recalls the frequent references of late medieval authors to the *Lex Regia* (Gierke 1900, note 142). Roman law had been assiduously studied under the aegis of Christian theology and philosophy since the eleventh century. Yet the modernism of some conclusions—the first point of Marsilius—is very striking.

The fifteenth century saw the Conciliar movement, and what almost amounted to the application to the Church of a doctrine of popular sovereignty. The Church was going through a grave crisis, the papacy having been in jeopardy for decades, three persons pretending at the time to the function. The Council that met at Constance in 1414, in which scholars of Ockhamist tendency were prominent, aimed in the first place at curing the disease, and succeeded in doing so. The Council viewed the Church as a polity of the kind of a limited or "mixed" monarchy, with the Council, as the body of representatives of the Christian Commonwealth, sharing its government with the Pope. To remedy the situation it was necessary to assert the authority of the Council as superior to that of the Pope. The authority of the Pope was thought to derive from the people and to remain legitimate only as long as it was true to its end, which was edification (*ad aedificationem*). It destroyed itself the moment it was found to work *ad destructionem*.

The Council was permanently to assist and control the Pope, but as soon as the monarchical authority was restored it began to prove more absolute than it had ever been, and the Council was outmaneuvered and lingered on ineffectually for some time. It had paved the way not only for future reaffirmation of popular sovereignty, but for a long period of triumphant absolutism in the Church, and in most European countries.

Thanks to Etienne Gilson[13] we can look at the twin phenomena of the Reformation and the Renaissance as having expressed a *differentiation* between two preoccupations which had on the whole peacefully cohabited within the medieval mind: the religious preoc-

---

12. Figgis 1960: 31–33 (also Dante's *De Monarchia*, etc.); on P. Dubois, cf. Rivière 1962. While Figgis, considering the content, takes Marsilius as more modern than Ockham, his companion in the cause of Louis of Bavaria, on the contrary Villey, stressing the methods, considers Marsilius more scholastic and Ockham more modern (Villey 1963: 217 ff.).

13. Etienne Gilson, *Héloïse et Abélard*, 1938 (esp. pp. 187 ff., 217–24).

cupation, with which Luther becomes impatient of involvement in the world and recognition of the worldly wisdom of the ancients, and the preoccupation with antiquity, which asserts itself in the new humanism as independent of religious tutelage. Such an event could not but have had a revolutionary impact on the relation between spiritual and temporal authority.

On the side of the Humanists, Machiavelli found in Livy the model for his republican city-state, and with the help of the examples of ancient Rome was able to disentangle completely political considerations not only from the Christian religion or from any normative model, but even from (private) morality, to emancipate a practical science of politics from all extraneous fetters towards the recognition of its only goal: the *raison d'État*. According to Figgis, the new absolutism, which was to influence so deeply the practical politicians and statesmen of the following centuries, could have been conceived only because the Church, and certain ecclesiastic orders, had developed a similar one, and because of the factual situation in Italy, where "power" was the real end of action, and which Machiavelli attempted to see coldly, as it really was. It can perhaps be said that the first practical science to emancipate itself from the holistic network of ends was the politics of Machiavelli.[14]

Machiavelli's radical rejection of the dominant contemporary values sets him apart for some time from the main and more effective current of thought, for the rise of temporal power had to be realized through chiefly religious agencies. The Lutheran Reformation dealt a decisive blow to what remained of the medieval order and the Holy Roman Empire. The global society was henceforth to be the individual State, while the core of religion became enshrined in the conscience of each and every individual Christian. The lay power became supreme and was elevated to a kind of sanctity, buttressed by the theory of the Divine Right of kings, on the assumption, which subsequent development was to shatter, of religious homogeneity within the State, the ruler and the ruled sharing the same creed: *cujus regio ejus religio* (cf. in England the Acts of Uniformity). So far, Luther, whatever his intentions may have been, translated into practice a part of the theory of Marsilius of Padua and even some of the tendencies of the Conciliar Party.

14. This brief reference to Machiavelli is insufficient for a comparison with the Indian Kautilya. What the similarity between the two authors immediately suggests is a necessary relation between politics and religion (cf. *HH*, App. C n. 17).

A further change was to result from the juxtaposition in one and the same State (outside Germany) of different confessions, and from the resulting wars of religion. While the *Politiques* were led, in the interest of the State, to advocate the toleration of heresy when expediency recommended it (Machiavelli), the warring confessions were led, contrary to their tendency to uncompromising supremacy, to advocate other views where they were threatened as a minority. Starting with the right of resistance against the persecuting tyran, which made use of the idea of a contract between the ruler and the ruled, this development led to the statement of the individual's right to freedom of conscience, the first of all aspects of political freedom and the root of all others. Jesuit writers on Natural Law developed the modern theory of the State as based on a social and political contract, regarding Church and State as two separate, independent societies, exterior to each other. Finally, "all or nearly all these ideas, making themselves practically effective in the resistance to Philip of Spain, produc[ed] in the Netherlands, its thinkers, its Universities a centre of light whence the political education of the 17th Century largely proceeded" (Figgis 1960: 38).

4. Modern Natural Law

Natural Law and the Theory of Society is the title given by Ernest Barker to his translation of the relevant part of the fourth volume of Otto Gierke's *Genossenschaftsrecht* (Gierke 1957). To sum this book up, even briefly, is the best way of drawing attention to an important aspect of the genesis of the modern idea of man and society. The theory of Natural Law dominates, in the period, the field of political theory and, we may say, that of social thinking. The role of the jurists is as essential as the role of the philosophers in the development of ideas which lead to the French Revolution and its "Declaration of the Rights of Man."

The idea of Natural Law is the warrant, the philosophical justification, of the systematic and deductive theorizing on law, so flourishing and important during the period. It can be traced back to antiquity, and to Thomas Aquinas, but it undergoes a deep change in modern times, so that two theories of Natural Law are sometimes opposed, the ancient or classical, and the modern. Between these two, the difference is of a kind we have learnt to recognize by speaking of respectively traditional and modern views. For the ancients—Stoics excepted—man is a social being, nature is an order, and what can be descried, beyond the actual conventions of each particular City-State, as constituting the ideal or natural basis of law is a social order in conformity with the order of nature (and hence with the inherent qualities of men). For the moderns, under the influence of Christian and Stoic individualism, natural law, as opposed to positive law, does not involve social beings but individuals, i.e. men each of whom is self-sufficient, as made in the image of God and as the repository of reason. This is to say that, in the idea of jurists in the first place, first principles regarding the constitution of the State (and of society) have to be extracted, or deduced, from the inherent properties or qualities of man taken as an autonomous being independently of any social or political attachment. The state of nature is the state, logically prior to social and political life, in which only individual man is considered, and, logical priority blending into historical anteriority, the state of nature is the state in which men are supposed to have lived before the foundation of society or state. To deduce from this logical or hypothetical state of nature the principles of social and political life may appear as an ungrateful and paradoxical task. It is the task which the theorists of modern Natural Law have undertaken, and it is in doing so that they have laid the basis for the modern democratic State. As Gierke said (1957, § 14, I.4, p. 40):

> The State was no longer derived from the divinely ordained harmony of the universal whole; it was no longer explained as a partial whole which was derived from, and preserved by, the existence of a greater: it was simply explained by itself. The starting-point of speculation ceased to be general humanity; it became the individual and self-sufficing sovereign State; and this individual State was regarded as based on a union of individuals, in obedience to the dictates of Natural Law, to form a society armed with supreme power.

In short, the hierarchical Christian Commonwealth was atomized at two levels: it was replaced by a number of individual States, themselves made up of individual men. Two conceptions of the Society-State confront each other in the vocabulary of the period:

> We have here to distinguish the *universitas*, or corporate unity, from the *societas*, or partnership, in which the members remain distinct, in spite of their connection, and the unity is thus

"collective" rather than corporate. (Barker's note on p. 45 in Gierke 1957.)

Societas—and similar terms: association, *consociatio*—has here its strict meaning of partnership, and is evocative of a contract by which the individuals composing it have "associated" themselves in a society. This trend of thought fits the widespread tendency in modern social science, which takes society to consist of individuals prior to the groups or relationships that they constitute or "make" by combination, more or less of their own accord.[15] The word by which the old scholastics designated society, or corporations in general, *universitas*, "whole," would much better fit the alternative view, which is our own, that society with its institutions, values, concepts, language, is sociologically prior to its particular members, the latter becoming human beings only through education into and modelling by a given society. It is unfortunate that, instead of *universitas*, we have to use *societas* or "society" to designate the social whole; but the fact shows the legacy of modern Natural Law and its progeny. Gierke records in great detail the increasing preponderance of the *societas* view as against the *universitas* view of society. At the same time he points out again and again that the opposite view never completely disappeared: "the idea of the State as an *organic whole* which had been bequeathed by classical and medieval thought, was never completely extinguished." Indeed it was difficult to get rid of it once the body social or political was to be considered in its unity:

It is thus a purely 'collective' interpretation of the personality of the People which really predominates in the natural-law theory of the State. The people is made co-extensive with the sum of its constituent units; and yet simultaneously, when the need is felt for a single bearer (*Träger*) of the rights of the People, it is treated as essentially a unit in itself. The whole distinction between the unity and the multiplicity of the community is reduced to a mere difference of point of view, according as *omnes* is interpreted as *omnes ut universi* or as *omnes ut singuli*.

15. As Bentham said of the modern champion of individualism: "Locke . . . forgot that he was not of age when he came into the world. Men according to his scheme come into the world full grown, and armed at all points like the fruit of the serpent's teeth sown by Cadmus at the corners of his cucumber bed"(Halévy 1900–1904, vol. 1, app. iii, p.418).

> The eye resolved . . . [there follows the passage quoted above, note 7]. (Gierke 1957: 46–47.)

Not only ecclesiastical writers like Molina and Suarez but the greatest exponents of the Natural Law theory found a need for the holistic conception. Althusius, building up a federalist order out of a series of *consociationes* of successive levels, called his *consociatio complex et publica* a *universitas* or a *consociatio politica* (ibid: 70). Grotius is praised for his likening the ruler to the eye as a "corporate organ." Hobbes talked of the State as a giant's body but "ended by transforming his supposed organism into a mechanism . . . , an artfully devised and cunningly constructed automaton" (ibid.: 52). After Pufendorf had introduced the term of *persona moralis simplex* and *composita* (somehow the same distinction as between "corporation sole" and "corporation aggregate") in order to bring groups or collective entities on the same juridical level as physical individuals, the same problem was to reappear in the most drastic form in Rousseau, who did more than anyone else to bring the jurists' constructions to the knowledge of the educated public and—however unwittingly—to bridge the gap between specialized speculation and revolutionary action.

All these efforts to express the unity of the social and/or political group answer the main problem of the Natural Law theory: to set up an ideal society or State while starting from the isolation of the individual man of nature. The main device for this purpose was the idea of contract or compact. After 1600, at least two contracts had to be entered into in succession in order to account for the transition. The first, or "social" contract, introduced the relationship characterized by equality or "fellowship" (*Genossenschaft*); the second, or political contract, introduced subjection to a Ruler or a ruling agency (*Herrschaft*). The philosophers reduced this multiplicity of contracts to one: Hobbes by making the contract of subjection the point of departure of social life in general, Locke by replacing the second contract by a Trust, Rousseau by suppressing the Ruler altogether. All this is well known, I recall it only for the sake of a remark on the relation between "social" and "political" and the sense of both in this matter. The "social" contract is the contract of association: it is assumed here that one enters society at large as one enters one or another particular voluntary association. Associations are present here, and perhaps "society" also is, in the sense given it by some behaviorist sociologists. But society at large, *universitas* in the sense of a whole in which a man is born and to which he belongs willy-nilly, which teaches him his language and at the least sows in his mind the material for his ideas, is absent. At best, the "society" implied here is the "civil society" of the economist and the philosopher, not the society of sociology proper. This must be insisted upon to prevent frequent confusion. In the words of a classicist who goes some way towards the sociologist's view:

> Society is not constituted, and never was constituted, on any basis of contract. Society is an all-purposes association—"in all science . . . in all art . . . in every virtue and in all perfection"—which transcends the notion of law, and has grown and exists of itself. In the strict sense of the word "social," there is not, and never has been, a social contract.[16]

In actual fact, the deeper notion of society suffered a partial eclipse in this period and trend of thought, together with the term *universitas*. With the dominance of individualism, as opposed to holism, the social as we understand it was replaced by the juridical, the political and, later, the economic.

5. The Equalitarian and Possessive Implications of Individualism

Before following up some of the earlier manifestations of individualism in its equalitarian aspect, we must bring into focus a well-known distinction. Individualism implies both equality *and* liberty. It is therefore right to distinguish a "liberal" theory of equality, which recommends an *ideal* equality, an equality of rights and chances, compatible with everyone's greatest liberty, and a "socialist" theory, which wants equality to be realized *in fact*, for instance by abolishing private property (Lakoff 1964). Logically, and even historically, it may seem that the transition from rights to facts merely represents an intensification of the claim: equality in principle is not enough, the demand is for "real" equality. Yet, from the point of view adopted here, the transition bridges a discontinuity, a major change in orientation. For example, alleging that all

16. Ernest Barker, p. xv of his Introduction to *Social Contract*, 1947; the words quoted are from Burke in the *Reflections on the Revolution in France* (1968: 194). Burke uses the word "partnership"; he adds that it includes the living, the dead and those to be born.

citizens do not enjoy property equally, one deprives the individual of one of his attributes, private property—which means restricting the range of his liberty—and one assigns corresponding new functions to the social whole.

To see more clearly the relation between liberalism and socialism in this regard, we may resort to our comparative approach. The caste system is a hierarchical system oriented to the needs of all. Liberal society negates both these features: it is equalitarian and it relies on the laws of exchange on the market and on "the natural identity of interests" to ensure order and general satisfaction. The socialist society, in turn, maintains the negation of hierarchy—at least in principle and initially—but it reintroduces a distinct concern for the social whole. It thus combines an element of individualism and an element of holism. It is a new, hybrid form. In socialist and communist movements and doctrines in general, equality has on the whole only a secondary place; it is no longer an attribute of the individual but, one might say, of social justice. As we are concerned here exclusively with the rise of individualism, it will be understood that we are leaving aside the extreme forms of equalitarianism which express the emergence of a contrary tendency (see note 17 below).

The question of equality was touched upon in the preceding section with the distinction between *Genossenschaft*, "fellowship," an association of equal individuals, and *Herrschaft*, an association or group which includes an element of "mastery," superordination or authority. Gierke draws attention to corresponding oppositions, between "collective unity" (corresponding to fellowship) and "representative unity" (as the representative is necessarily set above the group he represents), and between *societas aequalis* and *societas inaequalis*. (Gierke 1957; see Index). When the Natural Law theorists set at the origin of the State two successive contracts, a contract of association and a contract of subjection, they show the inability of the modern mind to conceive synthetically a hierarchical model of the group, and the necessity to analyze it into two elements: an element of equalitarian association, and an element by which this association subordinates itself to one person or entity. In other words, the moment the real being is conceived to be not the group but the individual, hierarchy disappears, and with it the immediate attribution of authority to a ruling agent. We are left with a collection of individuals, and the problem of justifying the construction of a power above them can be solved only by supposing the common consent of the members of the fellowship. There is a gain in consciousness, in interiority, but there is a loss in reality, for human groups do have chiefs independently of formal consent, their structuration being a condition of their existence as wholes. This is where political philosophy and sociology part company.

Comparison between the three great philosophers of the contract in the seventeenth and eighteenth centuries strengthens the case for regarding the contrast between *Genossenschaft* and *Herrschaft* as a crucial issue. We shall see more precisely how Hobbes strains the individualistic and mechanistic view to the breaking point in order to reintroduce the synthetic model of *Herrschaft;* Locke evades the difficulty by taking over from private law the idea of trust; Rousseau refuses to go beyond the *Genossenschaft* and transforms it into some kind of *Herrschaft* by the alchemy of the "general will." What all three authors have in common is the recognition of the difficulty to combine individualism with authority, to conciliate equality and the necessary existence of permanent differences of power, if not of condition, in society or the State.

One of the great psychological motive forces which has been active in the modern development is a sort of indignant protest against ascribed differences in society, including ascribed authority, privileges, inabilities, and, either in extreme movements or later developments, wealth.

Once more, the movement begins in the Church, with Luther. I shall sum up the relevant features of Luther's doctrines as brought together by Lakoff (1964: 25 ff.). There is no difference between "spirituals" and "temporals," all believers have equal authority in matters spiritual; a similar dignity inheres in every man, whether priest or peasant; the hierarchical doctrine of the Catholic Church is but an instrument of papal power; the duality of soul and body is a problem for every Christian, but cannot serve as a model for the organization of the Church and the Commonwealth (an indication of the refusal to think in terms of structure); equality appears—for the first time—as something more than an internal condition, namely an existential imperative; any authority or special function can only issue from delegation or representation: the priests are *"ministers* chosen from among us, who do all that they do in our name," etc. It is clear that all these features hold together: we are confronted with the overthrow of the holistic view, the sudden transition from the hierarchical to the individualistic universe. Very similar psychological dispositions are found at the other end of the development, in Rousseau. As Nietzsche spoke of "resentment" as a Christian feeling, we might speak of, say, envy as a psychological accompaniment of the equalitarian claim. The root of the matter is perhaps to be found in a central sentiment: their quality as Christians makes all men equal and, so to speak, sets the whole of the human essence in each of them. Hence they are dutifully justified to oppose any assertion of humanity which would not be derived from their own interiority. At least this is so for Luther on the level of religion and the Church. Regarding society and the State, he hangs on to medieval holism: "His image of society was organic and functional, not atomistic and acquisitive," says Lakoff.[17]

The equalitarian claim was extended from the religious to the political sphere in the course of the English Revolution (1640–60), especially by the Levellers. Although they were swiftly defeated, the Levellers had had time to draw the full political consequences of the idea of the equality of Christians. The Revolution itself affords one more example of the movement by which supernatural truth comes to be applied to earthly institutions. To quote an historian who cannot be accused of exaggerating the role of religion:

> . . . the essence of Puritanism as a revolutionary creed lay in the belief that God intended the betterment of man's life on earth, that men could understand God's purposes and co-operate with Him to bring them to fruition. So men's innermost wishes, if strongly felt, could be believed to be God's will. By a natural dialectic, those who were most convinced that they were fighting God's battles proved the most effective fighters.[18]

17. The contemporary and enemy of Luther, Thomas Müntzer, the revolutionary leader of the Peasant War, asserted equality in society in the most extreme form. According to Lakoff (1964: 54): "Müntzer at once sums up many of the tendencies of sectarian communism . . . and points forward to the later appearance of militant secular Socialist movements which would seek to transform the world by the violent overthrow of the forces of domination." Certainly Müntzer could be studied as an extreme example of the invasion of religious consciousness into worldly affairs. I have explained above why such communist movements, as the Diggers in seventeenth-century England, or that of Babeuf in the French Revolution, are not taken in consideration here. In a wider consideration, they should take their place beside what survived of the traditional *universitas* notion as parts of the submerged non-individualistic trends. In the case of Müntzer, the fact that the movement was not in essence equalitarian is seen in its dependance on the sanctification of violent action by the *elect*.

18. Christopher Hill 1961: 168; on the definition of Puritanism, cf. Lakoff 1964: 249, n.1.

As to the Levellers in particular, three features are of immediate significance for this study. First, the interplay in their basic ideology of religious tenets and natural law theory, as seen from Lilburne's life and readings, shows how individual religious consciousness serves as a basis for secular developments. Second, the invasion of religious consciousness replaces the English formulation of rights in terms of precedent and privilege by the assertion of the universal rights of man: "From believing that all *Christians* are reborn free and equal, the Levellers proceeded to the assertion first that all *Englishmen* and finally all *Men* are born free and equal" (Haller 1956). Third, the consequence is drawn, contrary to all English tradition, that there should be a written Constitution set beyond the reach of ordinary law. This was proposed in the form of an "Agreement of the People."[19] England was for a short time to have such a Constitution in the "Instrument of Government" of Cromwell's Protectorate.

The Levellers, while proposing to extend widely the electoral franchise by dropping the property qualification, excluded from the vote servants, wage earners, and beggars, on the ground that such people were not in fact free to exercise their right, as they depended on somebody who had to be pleased. At any rate, this limitation appears from the moment the franchise is seriously discussed: in the Army Debates at Putney (1647).[20] Macpherson has insisted on the similarity between the Levellers' theses and the more systematic doctrine of Locke, especially in the Second Treatise (1690). This similarity, perhaps exaggerated by Macpherson but in part unquestioned, between the poor revolutionary craftsmen, traders, and soldiers, and—forty years later—the rich philosopher coming back from a few years' stay in Holland marks the triumph of individual-

19. On the Levellers in general, apart from the books mentioned above and below, cf. Sabine 1963, and Lakoff 1964 (bibl. in the notes pp. 250–51). Lakoff convincingly shows a continuity in spirit between Luther, the Levellers, and Locke on the one hand (notwithstanding Calvinist influences), between Calvin and Hobbes on the other (pp. 47–48, 62 ff.). The Levellers are perhaps relatively marginal in British history, although equality before the law is due to them, but they are central to modern history as a whole (see below, section 8). The very intricate, and apparently still controversial, question of Calvin's indirect influence had of necessity to be left out here. The organization of the Presbyterian Church, with its replacement of bishops by councils more or less representative of the community, is a typical combination of the hierarchical principle with the equalitarian.

20. Detailed discussion in C. B. Macpherson, *The Political Theory of Possessive Individualism, Hobbes to Locke*, 1962.

ism. With his doctrine of trust, Locke characteristically evades the problem of political subjection and maintains the idea of a society of equals governing themselves by consent. Private property appears, not as a social institution, but as a logical entailment of the individual's self-sufficiency. Whatever the precise meaning of the formula may have been to them, the Levellers had already asserted that men were "equal . . . born to like property, liberty and freedom." Locke transports private property into the state of nature, only surrounding it with original limitations which, as Macpherson (1962) shows, he is careful to remove in subsequent steps.[21]

6. Hobbes's Leviathan

That the work of Thomas Hobbes is highly significant in the history of political thought is readily seen from its relation to what precedes and what follows it. On the one hand, the total break with religion and with traditional philosophy (man is not by nature a sociopolitical animal), and through it the elevation of the speculation on the state of nature and on natural law to an unprecedented absoluteness and intensity, together with the enrichment and systematization of the Machiavellian approach; on the other, the profound paradox of a mechanistic view of the human animal issuing in the forceful demonstration of the necessity of sovereignty and subjection; the vindication, that is, of the *Herrschaft* model on a purely empirical, atomistic, equalitarian, basis; and, as a result, the identification of the Individual with the Sovereign, which will be at the very core of Rousseau's and Hegel's theory. In view of this, to characterize Hobbes as a Conservative is insufficient and misleading. It is true that he extolled *Herrschaft* while the main current of political development went toward *Genossenschaft*, and in this sense he was indeed a Conservative. But this assertion has a very limited meaning as compared to the question of who was right. I hope that the following will show in which sense it can be contended that Hobbes

21. I borrowed the epithet "possessive" from Macpherson (1962). On property in Locke, see *MM*, pp. 51–54. It is worth noting that Hegel will give property a place very similar to that which it holds in Locke. Property opens the first part of Hegel's *Philosophy of Right*, which deals with "Abstract Right"—something very similar to Locke's state of nature, since Family, Civil Society, and State appear only in part 3. The reason is not far to seek: "A person must translate his freedom into an external sphere in order to exist as idea" (Hegel 1942 § 41).

was right. The question revolves around the nature of political philosophy. Politics may be studied as a particular level of social life, the more general social background being taken for granted, in which light Hobbes *may* have been wrong in his essential thesis; or modern political philosophy, following the ancient, is actually a mode of looking at society as a whole, in which case Hobbes was more in the right than the Equalitarians.[22]

I do not claim to demonstrate this here. I hope the thesis will become clearer in the section on Rousseau, because Rousseau had a more complete grasp than Hobbes of the social nature of man. Nevertheless, Hobbes's admission of subjection involves such a recognition, all Hobbes's protestations to the contrary notwithstanding: he was actually looking at society, even while speaking only of "man" and "the commonwealth." I must be very brief, and I can only urge the reader to test for himself the following remarks.

To begin with, is there in Leviathan a "state of nature," and if so, what actually is it? It would seem that almost the whole of the first part, "Of Man," is a picture of such a state. Justice is absent, because it is a matter of society, not of nature. And yet, "power," "honour" etc. are there, nay, even "speech" and, based on it, "reason." It thus becomes obvious that this description is that of the social state *minus* something.[23] (Hobbes tells us explicitly that reasoning consists essentially in adding and *subtracting*.) The some-

22. The latter view, incidentally, would have the advantage of explaining the paradox which besets many of the writings on Hobbes, i.e. why those who consider him as wrong and worthy of abhorrence are unable to hide his greatness and influence. He is generally credited with unflagging logic, but is this not an evasion? The reference here is primarily to *Leviathan*.

23. Macpherson (1962) argues similarly, but to him the scene from which Hobbes abstracts his picture of "man" is not the political scene, including civil war, but rather the economic scene. This very unlikely surmise is based mainly on a passage from *Leviathan*, 10: "On Power, Worth, Dignity, Honour, and Worthiness." Power is very generally conceived by Hobbes, it includes Riches among many other things. As all the rest, Worth is defined by Hobbes as something tangible, relative, and dependent on the judgment of others: "The *Value*, or WORTH of a man, is as of all other things, his Price; that is to say, so much as would be given for the use of his Power." It is clear from the context that this is no more than an economic metaphor. When Hobbes deals with economy, he does so from a quite different point of view (chap. 24 "Of the Nutrition and Procreation of the Commonwealth"). The label of "possessive individualism" does not fit Hobbes's philosophy. It is not possessive in any special sense, and, taken as a whole, it is not individualistic either, in our sense of the term, as well as in Gierke's (see note 24 below).

thing which is subtracted from the state of society in the description of "man" as such is simply subjection. The moment the Covenant introduces subjection, we pass from "man" to "the Commonwealth." Another aspect is that the relations between men in this state of nature obviously correspond to the actual relations between States, supposed to be always in the state of nature. Here Hobbes continues Machiavelli on a different level: the war of interests excludes any transcendent norm or value. A third and important aspect of the state of nature is that it contains everything of man which can be described in a mechanistic language: the human animal, the human *individuum* as a system of motions, desires, and passions with all the modifications and complications which speech and thought introduce. These three aspects correspond to the principle under which it has appeared possible and profitable to Hobbes to separate in man, as actually observed in society, two different levels. To us these levels would be much more prepolitical and political than presocial and social. Rousseau will go further in the inquiry regarding the properly social aspects, and as a result, the discontinuity between the two stages, already present in Hobbes, will become still greater in Rousseau.

If we try to apprehend the core of the doctrine, that is to sum up for ourselves the picture of "man" drawn by Hobbes and to see its relation to the constitution of a commonwealth, it is difficult to escape the impression of a dualism between passions and reason, an animal and a rational aspect. Indeed is it not the contradiction between the two that makes it necessary to cross over to the political state, to enter subjection? Indeed, in the Leviathan, what differentiates man from the beast is speech, and reason is grounded in speech, truth and falsehood being attributes of speech. With this proviso, the dualism holds: rationality is given in man in an impure form, mixed with animality, and will blossom into pure rationality only with the construction of an *artificial* commonwealth. To admit with Aristotle that man is naturally social and/or political would be to shut the door to this attainment of pure rationality.

We come now to ask whether Hobbes can be said to be individualist or holist. He is neither. He thus makes our distinction collapse, but the event is interesting, and strictly characterizes Hobbes. There is no doubt that his point of departure is the particular human being, the human *individuum*. But in the prepolitical stage the life of this being is to be judged negatively: "solitary, poor, nasty, brutish, and short." When, following the advice of reason and its own desire for conservation, this being enters the political stage, it lays down a part of its powers. Then man is able to attain security, comfort, and the development of his faculties, but at the price of his subjection. He has not become a self-sufficient individual anymore than he existed satisfactorily as such in the natural state. So it is that, through an approach which seemed to be extremely "individualistic," individualism is brought to heel.[24] The proper life of man is not that of an individual, it is that of a being which is closely dependent upon the State, so closely that it cannot but identify itself for a part with the Sovereign. If Hobbes forbids us to say that man is naturally political, we may nevertheless say that he is artificially but necessarily so: the individual does not enter fully armed into political life. This is the crucial feature which distinguishes Hobbes from so many modern political theorists and brings Rousseau close to him.

At the same time, Hobbes cannot be said to be holist either. In particular the hierarchical ordering of the social body is absent because the State is not oriented toward any end which would transcend it, but is subject only to itself. Ultimately, the *Herrschaft* model is emptied of its inherent hierarchical virtue and is adopted only as an indispensable adjustment of power. The shell, so to speak, but not its inhabitant, value. Nonetheless, there remains the recognition that equality cannot reign supreme and unencumbered, and that man is a social being—and not an individual—insofar as the political level is concerned. In this measure, Hobbes, in contradistinction to Locke, can be taken as a precursor of sociology, albeit dealing only with politics and not with society in its sense of *universitas*. It is precisely this feature that leads those who are interested only and severally in the political aspect to dub him a Conservative. As for the sociologist, Hobbes's teaching taken as a whole is sound, if incomplete. He has some idea of what a society is, while the intransigent theorists of equality have none.

Yet, we have had to acknowledge that for Hobbes the social is

24. Hence the praise of Hobbes in Gierke, who is always anxious to find an assertion of the corporate character of social bodies: "Basing himself upon arbitrarily assumed premises, but wielding a remorseless logic, he wrested a single State-personality from the individualistic philosophy of Natural Law. . . . He had made the individual omnipotent, with the object of forcing him to destroy himself instantly." (Gierke 1957: 61). Polin shows the progress of the idea of the "Person" in Hobbes between 1642 and 1651, as embodied in the sixteenth chapter of *Leviathan* (1953, chap. 10).

restricted to the political. In the end, it is because he looks at the whole society in political terms that he is bound to introduce subjection, i.e. neither hierarchy proper, nor equality pure and simple. We reach here a point which I believe essential to the understanding of the deeper kind of political theory, especially regarding its relation to sociology. In this theory, the social is to a great measure reduced to the political. Why? The reason is very clear in Hobbes: starting from the *individuum*, or the individual, social life will be necessarily considered in terms of consciousness and force (or "power"). In the first place, one can pass from the individual to the group only in terms of "covenant," i.e. in terms of conscious transaction or artificial design. It will then be a matter of "force," because "force" is the only thing the individual can bring into the bargain: the opposite of "force" would be hierarchy, the idea of the social order, the principle of authority; and this is precisely what the contracting individuals will more or less unconsciously have to bring forth synthetically from the common pool of their forces or wills. Hierarchy is the social obverse, force the atomistic reverse, of the same coin. This is how an emphasis on consciousness or consent immediately issues into an emphasis on force or power. Modern political theory, in the best case, is an individualistic manner of dealing with society. It involves an *indirect* acknowledgement of the social nature of man. This must be borne in mind if we are to perceive clearly the further paradoxes of Rousseau and Hegel.

7. Rousseau's "Contrat Social"

In terms of formal characteristics, Rousseau's politics can be taken as an antithesis to Hobbes's. While Hobbes's theory is representative, absolutist, and insists on subjection, Rousseau's is collective, nomocratic, and insists on freedom. But this obvious difference should not hide a less apparent, though deeper similarity, which is found in the very texture of the two theories. Both posit a discontinuity between the man of nature and political man, so that for both the "social contract" marks the actual birth of humanity proper (hence many similarities in the detail). Both start from premises which seem extremely "individualistic"—in accordance with the conceptions of their time or environment—and by straight logic proceed to "anti-individualistic" conclusions. Both are supremely concerned with ensuring the transcendence of the Sovereign—here the Ruler, there the General Will—in relation to the subject, while stressing the identity of Sovereign and subject. In sum: both are intent on welding into a social or political body people who think of themselves as individuals. This explains why their theories appear similarly extreme and paradoxical. As the same may be said—*mutatis mutandis*—of Hegel's theory of the State, we are confronted with an impressive continuity in political thought which deserves investigation.

Rousseau has often been blamed for the French Revolution, and even in our day he is sometimes held responsible for Jacobinism and what has been called "totalitarian democracy" in general.[25] Of course Rousseau and the Revolution belong to the same extreme development of individualism, which in retrospect appears very much as a necessary historical fact, but which some may like to condemn. Yet the revolutionary tide did brush aside several fundamental points of Rousseau's political teaching, however great his general influence may have been. The totalitarian aspects of modern democratic movements are the outcome, not of Rousseau's theory, but of the artificialist project of individualism when confronted with experience. It is true that they are prefigured in Rousseau, but this is so precisely in so far as he was deeply conscious of the insufficiency of individualism pure and simple and labored to save it by transcending it. There is much truth in Vaughan's contention that the gist of the *Contrat social* is "anti-individualistic," even if it is only a part of the truth.[26] Says Rousseau himself in the first version of that work:

25. For a recent indictment of the kind, see Talmon 1952, chap. 3. This author reads Rousseau as a Montagnard of 1793 may have read him, and condemns the revolutionary "presumption that frail man is capable of producing a scheme of things of absolute and final significance" (chap. 1, § c). But whence comes this extreme artificialism? Is it not the inevitable outcome of an individualism which Talmon wisely but unsystematically keeps undeveloped for his own use? As to the thought of Rousseau himself, it is caricatured: Rousseau was a psychotic person whose moral preoccupations landed him into totalitarian politics.

26. It is comforting to find that in this century a number of Anglo-American scholars have retrieved Rousseau's political theory from utter incomprehension. I may therefore be brief and refer the reader to the following works: B. Bosanquet, *The Philosophical Theories of the State* (1910; although more centrally concerned with Hegel, Bosanquet develops an argument very similar to my own, making occasional use of Durkheim to enlighten Rousseau's and Hegel's polities, cf. esp. pp. 88 ff. and xxvii ff., 82, 110, 150); C. E. Vaughan in his standard edition of *The Political Writings of Jean-Jacques Rousseau* (1962), adds to the original works in French an introduction and commentaries in which he insists on the fundamentally

> This perfect independence, this unchartered freedom, even had it never ceased to go hand in hand with primitive innocence, would always have suffered from an inherent flaw, a flaw fatal to the growth of our highest faculties: namely, the lack of that bond between the parts which constitutes the unity of the whole.[27]

It will be seen from this passage that Rousseau goes further than Hobbes in the philosophical "subtraction" which, applied to man as observed in society, leaves us with the man of nature. In the "Discourse on the Origin of Inequality," Rousseau had drawn a picture of natural man, free and equal in a sense, and endowed with a sense of pity, but with his faculties still undeveloped, undifferentiated, a man uncultured and thus neither virtuous nor wicked. He had deplored the fact that above a certain stage of cultural development, the progress of civilization had been accompanied by a growth of inequality and immorality, that "the development of lights and of vices occurred always in the same proportion, not among individuals, but among peoples" (Letter to Ch. de Beaumont, 1763). In the *Contrat social* he attempts to legitimize the social order and rid it of its blemishes. The endeavor is no doubt audacious, and Rousseau strictly hedges it in: his State is small, it is to be a face-to-face democracy. If the task is not quite impossible, it is because, as he says in the Preface to the *Narcisse* (1752): "All these vices belong less to man as such than to man as ill governed."[28]

---

nonindividualist character of the *Contrat Social* (notably 1: 111ff.); I shall quote Sir Ernest Barker, in the introductions to Gierke 1957 and to *Social Contract, Essays by Locke, Hume and Rousseau* (Barker 1947): George H. Sabine, in his *History of Political Theory* (1963), very aptly entitles the chapter on Rousseau "The Rediscovery of the Community." I shall also refer to the recent edition of Rousseau's political writings in *Œuvres Complètes*, vol. 3 (1964) (with comments by several scholars). Cf. also Derathé 1950.

27. Vaughan's translation (1962, 1: 27). The extract is from a chapter in the first version of the *Contrat Social* (I, ii), formerly entitled "Du droit naturel et de la société générale" which is, characteristically, a reply to Diderot (see Vaughan, 1: 423 ff.; Sabine, 1963: 582; Derathé in Rousseau 1964, pp. LXXXVII–VIII): the idea of mankind as a "general society" is an abstraction and, Rousseau adds, "it is only from the social order established among us that we draw ideas about that which we imagine . . . and we properly begin to be men only after we have been citizens." Cf. in the "Gouvernement de Pologne": *ubi patria, ibi bene* (Vaughan 1962, 2: 434).

28. The two quotations are from R. Derathé's introduction to the *Contrat Social* (hereafter abbreviated as *C.S.*) in Rousseau 1964: vol. 3, p. XCIV. On Rous-

The Liberals accuse Rousseau of having grafted a totalitarian sapling on to a democratic trunk. They might have found that the position of the problem was utopian in its absolute affirmation of freedom:

> Some form of association must be found as a result of which the whole strength of the community will be enlisted for the protection of the person and property of each constituent member, in such a way that each, when united to his fellows, renders obedience to his own will [only], and remains as free as he was before (C.S., I, vi).[29]

But they will certainly shudder at the solution which is immediately proposed:

> It must be clearly understood that the clauses in question can be reduced, in the last analysis, to one only, to wit, the complete alienation by each associate member to the community of all his rights.

The People is sovereign, but once its members are assembled, a strange alchemy takes place. From the individual will of all issues a general will, which is something qualitatively different from the will of all, and possesses extraordinary properties. On the one hand, we are not far from Pufendorf's *persona moralis composita*, as different from the sum of the *personae morales simplices* who make it up. But on the other hand the General Will is the Sovereign, and as such, is made to transcend the individual will of the subjects as strictly as Hobbes's Ruler was set above the ruled. What began as a partnership or *societas* actually turns into a corporation or *universitas*. As Weldon says, what began as a "mechanical" system ends in an "organic" system. (Cf. above, note 2). Popper would say that an "open" society has been made into a "closed" one. It is true that Rousseau goes very far to disengage the General Will from its constituent wills. To recall a much quoted passage:

---

seau's experience of inequality and impatience with any dependence, see Jean Starobinski's lofty and perceptive introduction to the 2d Discourse, ibid., pp. xiii ff. "All power comes from God, certainly, but so do all ailments" (*C.S.*, II, iii).

29. The quotations from *C.S.* are from Gerard Hopkins's translation in Barker 1947.

When a law is proposed in the assembly of the people, what
they are asked is not whether they approve or reject the pro-
posal in question, but whether it is or is not in conformity with
the general will, which is *their* will . . . When, therefore, a view
which is at odds with my own wins the day, it proves only that I
was deceived, and that what I took to be the general will was no
such thing. Had my opinion won, I should have done something
quite other than I wished to do, and in that case I should not
have been free. (C.S., IV, ii.).[30]

It is easy to see in this a prefiguration of the Jacobine dictature,
of the Moscow trials, or even of the Nazis' *Volksseele*. But the real
question is what Rousseau actually means by the general will preexisting to its expression in terms of majority vote.[31] My contention is
that we cannot understand it as long as we remain confined to the
purely political plane. A recent critic equates Rousseau's general
will with another mysterious entity, Durkheim's collective consciousness, and commits both to the fire of the democratic hell.
Actually Durkheim himself wrote on the subject:

Since the general will is defined mainly by its object, it does not
consist uniquely or even essentially in the very act of collectve
volition. . . . Rousseau's principle is thus different from that by
which some have tried to justify the despotism of majorities. If
the community must be obeyed, it is not because it commands,
but because it commands the common good. . . . In other terms,
the general will does not consist in the state in which the
collective consciousness finds itself at the moment when the
resolution is passed; this is only the most superficial part of the
phenomenon. To understand it properly, one must penetrate
beneath, into less conscious spheres, and reach the habits,
tendencies and manners [*mœurs*]. Manners are what makes up
"the veritable constitution of States" (II, xii). The general will

30. The general parallelism with Hobbes is obvious. As to Hegel, while he does
away explicitly with the need for basing the law on a vote by the assembled citizens,
he maintains very much the same relation between the private citizen's will and the
law of the State, the law embodying by definition the citizen's truer Will and Liberty,
so that for the latter to go against the law is to go against his own will (Hegel 1942; see
below n. 45).

31. The principle of majority vote is not easy to apply on really important issues
in a closely knit association, and Rousseau was, probably unawares, in line with
preoccupations found in the *Corpus Juris* and in Canon Law; see Gierke 1913, 3: 153
(Ulpien), and 3: 522ff. (Canon Law).

is thus fixed, permanent orientation of the minds and activities in a determinate direction, the direction of general interest.[32]

For Durkheim, then, Rousseau's general will is understandable as the emergence on the political level and in democratic terms of the unity of a given society as preexisting to its members and as present in their thoughts and actions. In other terms, the *universitas* into which Rousseau's *societas* seems to be suddenly transmuted is actually pre-existent to it and underlies it. This is obscured because Rousseau starts from the abstract individual man of nature, and presents the ideal transition to the political stage as a creation of *universitas* as it were *ex nihilo*, as will be seen in the following passage:

> Whoso would undertake to institute a People must work with full consciousness that he has set himself to change, as it were, the very stuff of human nature; to transform *each individual who, in isolation, is a complete and solitary whole, into a part of something greater than himself, from which, in a sense, he derives his life and his being;* to alter the constitution of man in order to reinforce it; to substitute a *partial and moral* existence for the *physical and independent existence* we received from nature. (C.S. II, vii; my italics).

In an artificialist language at once magnificent and misleading, which is typical of the *Contrat Social*, we have here the clearest sociological perception, i.e. the recognition of man as a social being as opposed to the abstract individual man of nature.[33] Indeed, if we imagine ourselves as being exposed to the intellectual climate in

32. Durkheim 1953: 106–7. Although first published posthumously (in the *Revue de Metaphysique et de Morale* 25 [1918]), the study of the *C.S.* is an early work where little advantage is taken of the first version of the *C.S.*, and where the "individualism" of *C.S.* is occasionally exaggerated (e.g. p. 163). The last part of *C.S.* II, xii, very reminiscent of Montesquieu, should be read: "I refer to manners, customs, and, above all, opinions. This is a field unknown to our politicians, yet on these things depends the success of all the rest." Cf. the necessity of "civil religion" (*C.S.* IV, viii) and, in Rousseau's concrete works on Corsica and Poland, his concern with patriotism, religion, games and amusements, etc.

33. Space forbids reproducing passages from other works which show this thought to be one of Rousseau's abiding and central thoughts, as for instance: again I, ii of *C.S.* first version; *Emile*, I (Vaughan 1962, 2: 145, natural man and the citizen); "Lettres sur la vertu et le bonheur," in Rousseau 1861, Letter No. 1, pp. 135–36, etc.; Lettre à d'Alembert, in Rousseau 1856, 1: 257.

which Rousseau lived, we can hardly bring to mind a more categorical statement. The critics who accuse Rousseau of having opened the gate to authoritarian tendencies are really blaming him for having recognized the fundamental truth of sociology, a truth they prefer to ignore. This truth may appear to be a mystery, or a mystification in a society dominated by individualistic representations, as in Hegel or Durkheim; it may appear as dangerous or harmful, nay, it may even be so until it has been properly acknowledged, and the problem thus posed cannot be solved by the ostrich's reaction to danger.

Some would prefer Rousseau to have done away with the abstract individual and the arbitrary idea of contract and to have described his State straight out in "collectivist" terms. But this is to ignore freedom as Rousseau's central concern: he perceived in himself the individual as a moral ideal and an irrepressible political claim, and he maintained this ideal together with its real counterpart, man as a social being. Sir Ernest Barker saw Rousseau as a Janus-like figure looking both backward to (modern) Natural Law, and forward to the German historical school and the romantic idealization of the National State, or, alternatively, beginning with Locke and ending with Plato's Republic.[34] Rousseau labored to reconcile modern and ancient Natural Law, to reintegrate the individual of the French *philosophes* in a real society. Sir Ernest Barker's clear criticism explains Rousseau's failure without detracting from his greatness:

> He would have escaped from a mist of confusion, and avoided the inexplicable miracle of a sudden contractual emergence from a primitive and stupid condition into a civilized blaze of enlightenment, if he had stopped to draw a *distinction between society and the State*. The society of the nation is a given fact of historical evolution, not created by any contract of society, but simply there. The State based on that society may be, or may become at a given moment of time (as France sought to do in 1789), the result of a creative act performed by the members of the society. (Barker 1947: xliii–iv; italics mine.)

Jean-Jacques Rousseau attempted the grandiose and impossible task of dealing in terms of consciousness and freedom not only

34. Barker in Gierke 1957: xl ff.; Sabine 1963.

with politics, but with society as a whole, and of combining the ideal and abstract *societas* with what he could salvage of *universitas* as the nursing mother of all thinking beings. It may be that his abrupt identification of individualism and holism was dangerous when taken as a political recipe, but it was first of all a genial diagnostic of what cannot fail to happen whenever society as a whole is ignored and is submitted to artificialist politics. Rousseau was thus not only the precursor of sociology proper, but as well posed the problem of modern man, who has become a political individual without ceasing to be a social being, a problem which is still with us.

8. The Declaration of the Rights of Man

The French "Declaration of the Rights of Man and the Citizen" as first adopted by the French Constituent Assembly in the summer of 1789, and subsequently modified, marks in a way the apotheosis of the Individual. It had been preceded by similar proclamations in several of the United States of America, but in France it was for the first time made the basis of the Constitution of a great nation, imposed upon a reluctant monarch by popular demonstration, and proposed as an example to Europe and the world. Although cogently criticized in its principle from the start, as notably by Bentham, the example was to work powerfully, indeed irrepressibly, throughout the nineteenth and into the twentieth century.

That the Declaration cannot be fathered on Rousseau is immediately clear. His *Contrat social* contemplated "the complete alienation by each associate member to the community of all his rights" (I, vi) and this is contradicted in Art. 2 of the Declaration, which opens thus:

Art. I. Men are born and remain free and equal in rights. Social distinctions can only be founded upon common utility.

Art. 2. The aim of any political association is the preservation of the natural and imprescriptible rights of man. These rights are: liberty, property, surety and resistance to oppression.

It is not enough to see in the Declaration the outcome of the modern, individualistic, doctrines of Natural Law, for, as Jellinek observed, the main point to be accounted for is the transfer of the precepts and fictions of Natural Law to the level of positive law: the Declaration was conceived as a solemn preamble laying the basis of a written Constitution. The Constitution was felt to be a necessary requirement of artificial rationality. Its purpose was to establish a new State based on consent alone and to set it beyond the reach of political authority itself. The Declaration was to be the quintessence of the Constitution, as the solemn proclamation of the universal principles which it was to enact. Yet the idea of the Declaration was quite consciously taken over from America. An official report to the Assembly on 27th July 1789 approves of "this noble idea, conceived in another hemisphere," and there is ample evidence on this point. As a particular source, Jellinek refers, rather than to the Declaration of Independence of 1766, to the Bills of Rights adopted by certain States, and particularly to that of Virginia of 1776, which was known in France before 1789.[35]

35. Jellinek 1902 (comparison of the texts, pp. 29 ff.; Lafayette's testimony, pp. 14 ff.). A collection of documents entitled *La Déclaration des Droits de l'Homme et du Citoyen* (Paris, 1900) gives American documents in translation (report of 27 July 1789 on p. 34). Cf. Halévy 1900–1904, 2: 50, quoting Etienne Dumont, "it was an American idea." The general point was also made by Cournot and Ch. Borgeaud, who referred to the Levellers' Agreement of the People. This is not to say that Rousseau's influence was entirely absent. Contrary to *Emile*, the *Contrat Social* was admittedly little read until the Revolution, but during the Revolution it was "meditated and learned by rote by all citizens" (Sébastien Mercier, 1791). On 17 August 1789 Mirabeau proposed, in the name of a specially appointed commission, a project of Declaration that was distinctly Rousseauist in its Art. 2. It is true that Mirabeau's secretary, Étienne Dumont, was a disciple of Bentham and that he claimed to have persuaded his co-workers that Natural Rights were a "puerile fiction" (Halévy 1900–1904, 2: 50 and n. 98). On Bentham's criticism of the idea of an "original contract" and of the Bills of Rights of Virginia, etc., cf. Halévy 1900–1904, vol. 1, app. iii, and vol. 2, chap. 1: the French Declarations of Rights are "anarchical fallacies"; the system of absolute equality and independence is physically impossible, "subjection and not independence is the natural state of man." There is no attempt here to enumerate all the influences to be found in the Declaration of 1789 and those following and in the debates which concluded with their adoption. Marcaggi (1904) has shown that on many points (as on private property, above) there was agreement between the physiocratic doctrine and the declarations and intentions of the members of the Assemblée Constituante, but he underrated the American influence and his thesis is unilateral, for the Physiocrats started from the whole and not from the element (cf. *MM*, 41–43). Four different Declarations were adopted in the course of the French Revolution; three of them were in force for some time with the corresponding Constitution: the first for a year, that of 1793 for a few months (and then adjourned), that of Thermidor An III (Declaration of the Rights *and Duties*) for five years.

The Puritans who founded colonies in America had given the example of the actual establishment of a Commonwealth on the basis of a contract. So the famous Congregationalist "Pilgrims" of the *Mayflower* who drew between themselves a Pact of Establishment before founding New Plymouth in 1620,[36] and others after them. We have seen that the Levellers went further in 1647 in stressing, in their Agreement of the People, the native rights of man *qua* man, and first of all his right to religious freedom. This right had been enjoyed by several American colonies since an early date: Rhode Island had it by a charter of Charles II (1663), and North Carolina by its Constitution drawn by Locke (1669). Liberty of conscience was the essential right, the core around which, by integration of other liberties, the rights of man were to take form. Religious freedom, born from the Reformation and the subsequent struggles, was the lever by which the speculations on Natural Law became a political reality. The French could not but endorse the abstract statement of the Individual over and above the State, but that statement was first uttered by the Puritans.

A living embodiment of the transition is found in the person of Thomas Paine, a shopkeeper from England who, as a Quaker, had migrated to the States and risen to eminence there before taking part in the French Revolution as a Deputy in the "Convention Nationale" and a member, with Condorcet, of the Commission appointed to prepare the new Constitution, the Republican Constitution of 1793. Paine wrote two volumes in defense of the Rights

36. "In the name of God, amen. We whose names are underwritten, the loyal subjects of our dread sovereign Lord, King James, by the grace of God, of Great Britain, France and Ireland, King, Defender of the faith, etc. Having undertaken for the glory of God, and advancement of the Christian faith, and the honour of our King and country, a voyage to plant the first colony in the northern parts of Virginia; do by these presents solemnly and mutually, in the presence of God and one another, covenant and combine ourselves together into a civil body politic, for our better ordering and preservation, and furtherance of the ends aforesaid; and by virtue thereof, do enact, constitute, and frame such just and equal laws, ordinances, acts, constitutions, and officers, from time to time, as shall be thought most meet and convenient for the general good of the colony; unto which we promise all due submission and obedience . . ." (*Chronicles of the Pilgrim Fathers*, [New York: Dutton, n.d.], p. 23). It will be observed that the mention of the supreme Being, also present in the preamble of the French Declaration, is more urgent in the Pacts of Puritans. Tocqueville quoted the Pact of 1620 (1961, 1: 34) and insisted on the combination among the Puritans of religion with political theory (ibid., vol. 1, Intro., and vol. 2, chap. 5).

of Man, the difference between which is underlined by E. Halévy. In the first part, Paine defends the rationality and simplicity of the Constituante's politics. His individualism is spiritualist; "through his intermediary, the revolutionary Christianism of the English protestants of America joins hands with the revolutionary atheism of the French 'sans-culottes.' " The second part, which deals with the practical application of the principle, is distinctly utilitarian. Based on the natural identity of interests, it "applies the ideas of Adam Smith to the solution . . . of political problems."[37] This transition is typical of the evolution of ideas which was to enthrone utilitarianism in England all through the first decades of the nineteenth century.

As Paine's second volume appeared in 1792, and as Condorcet worked with the author in 1793, it is perhaps not idle to see a reflection of Paine's ideas in that characteristic of the American Constitution which Condorcet singles out for condemnation. A mathematician and *philosophe* who had played a prominent rôle in the Assemblies, Condorcet was under warrant of arrest during the Terror. In hiding—he was actually to die shortly afterward—he wrote as a testament his short but pregnant "Historical Sketch of the Progress of the Human Spirit," inspired through and through by the idea of the perfectibility of the mind. It ends with a picture of the future (the "Tenth Epoch") and in the last paragraph the Revolutionary threatened in his life proclaims his inalterable faith in progress.[38] History has confirmed many of Condorcet's predictions, but what interests us here is the distinction Condorcet makes between the American and the French Constitutions. He was a tempered equalitarian. He predicted the total disappearance of inequality between nations, including the colonized peoples of other continents, but only a weakening of inequality among one and the same people: the effects of the natural difference in personal endowments would be reduced, but they would not disappear altogether, as this would go against the common interest. Yet

37. Halévy 1900-1904, vol 2, chap. 2, esp. pp. 66, 69.
38. Condorcet, *Esquisse d'un tableau historique des progrès de l'esprit humain,* (1795), 1933. Condorcet says of himself in the concluding paragraph: "It is in the contemplation of this survey that he receives the reward for his efforts . . . it is then that he truly exists with his fellow men, in an Elyseum which his reason was able to create for itself." The artificialist project has become a faith transcending the person's destiny and the horrors of the time. Auguste Comte is not very far.

Condorcet sees the distinctive mark of the French Constitution, and finds the reason for its superiority to the American in the recognition of the equality of rights as its unique and supreme principle. He asserts the Natural Rights of man (while at the same time praising Rousseau). He reproaches the Americans with having continued to search for the balance of powers within the State, and, above all, with having insisted more in principle on the identity of interests than on the equality of rights.[39] Condorcet is obviously thinking of the Constitution he had been working on, and of the *Montagnards'* Constitution of 1793 which supplanted it, more than of that of 1789, which was still royalist. The Declaration of 1789 is as yet close to the American Bills; equality is invoked in its Art. I as against inherited "social distinctions," but it is not listed among the substantive rights in Art. 2 (above). In all subsequent Declaration, equality takes its place by the side of liberty among the rights themselves.[40] It is obvious in his *Esquisse* that Condorcet is not preoccupied only with formal equality, but with factual equality also, insofar as it appears practicable and beneficial. For he writes that the Revolution has done "much for the glory of man, something for his freedom, almost nothing as yet for his happiness"; he deplores the absence of a history of "the mass of families," and advocates a study not only of norms but of facts, of the "effects . . . for the most numerous portion of each society" of changes and enactments, on which to base a policy for the progress of mankind," (1933: 199 ff.) Yet Condorcet is a liberal, a Girondin, who does not set the ideal of equality over and above all others. This was to happen during the Revolution itself, notably in Babeuf's conspiration, a communist movement—

39. Condorcet, 1933: 169. The Virginia Bill has in its Art. III a reference to the "common good" and adds: "the best government is that which is most apt to produce the greatest sum of happiness and surety." Regarding equality, Art. I says only "that all men are by nature equally free and independent..."

40 The draft of a Declaration prepared by its Commission and presented to the Convention on 15 February 1793 has: "Art. I. Les droits naturels civils et politiques des hommes sont la liberté, l'égalité, la sûreté, la propriété, la garantie sociale et la résistance à l'oppression." Apart from the addition of "social guarantee," the general formulation would seem to indicate that the "natural rights" were under fire. This is confirmed by their disappearance from subsequent formulations (perhaps an index of Rousseauist influence). Thus the Declaration adopted on 29 May 1793 (but modified a month later after the adoption of the Montagnards' Constitution) begins thus: "Art. I. Les droits de l'homme en société sont l'égalité, la liberté..." (the rest as on 15 February 1793). Equality has taken precedence.

and thus beyond our confines—as is clear from this appeal: "The time has come to found the Republic of Equals, this great home open to all men. The days of general restitution have arrived. Weeping families, come and seat yourselves at the common table which Nature has set for all her children."

Babeuf was executed, but French democracy remained preoccupied with equality to a degree unprecedented elsewhere. Tocqueville saw this, and he saw also that the French Revolution had been at bottom a religious phenomenon in the sense of a movement which had willed itself absolute and had wanted to recast the whole of human existence, in contradistinction to the American Revolution where democratic political theory remained confined to its proper domain and was complemented and supported by a strict Christian faith. It is all the more interesting to learn that the French sectaries of man as an individual were helped in the formulation of the abstract rights of man by the American Puritans. Once more, Christian religion had pushed the Individual forward.

9. The Aftermath of the Revolution: *Universitas* Reborn

It is often felt that the beginnings of sociology in France are tainted with political "reaction." Auguste Comte, though he professed above all to be a disciple of Condorcet, made no secret either of his debt to the theocrats de Maistre and de Bonald. His positivism is condemned as conservative by a twentieth-century thinker, Herbert Marcuse, in the name of the essentially *critical* philosophy of Hegel and Marx. (Marcuse 1960: 340ff.). I shall try to show that for many reasons this is a superficial view. In the first place the birth of sociology is closely associated with that of socialism in another, and perhaps the closest, of Comte's masters, the genial and desultory Saint-Simon, and in his disciples. This socialist trend receives from the same critic the following explanation:

> The early French socialists found the decisive motives of their doctrines in the class conflicts which conditioned the after-history of the French Revolution. Industry made great strides, the first socialist stirrings were felt, the proletariate began to consolidate (1960: 328, 335ff.).

The handicrafts and light-industry world of the eighteenth century is thus often contrasted with the heavy-industry world of the nineteenth. But whatever truth there may be in it—a question beyond our reach—the explanation is insufficient. It would account for the change of mind of the economists, from the optimism of Adam Smith to the pessimism of Malthus and Ricardo in England, and elsewhere that of Sismondi followed by Marx, but it would not account for the sociological preoccupation, and more generally for the general orientation of the thinkers of the period, which has been truly called one of "anti-individualistic reaction" (Michel 1895).[41]

It is clear from the French literature of the period from 1815 to 1830 and beyond, that the Revolution and the Empire had left behind a void which the best minds were busy trying to fill. If the Revolution had been a triumph of individualism, its liquidation, which appeared retrospectively largely as a failure, brought not only a chronic disappointment but a primary emphasis on values and ideas contrary to those which the Revolution had exalted. The revolutionary ideals were rarely condemned wholesale, as by the theocrats—whose sharpened reassertion of tradition and holism found a wide audience; more often they were either partially rejected, or accepted but considered insufficient, and a search was then made to supplement them. The unprecedented and absolute affirmation of *societas* by the Revolutionaries had run its course, and the need of *universitas* was felt more strongly than it could ever have been by the Romantic individual who was the heir of the Revolution. This is the general explanation for the general reversal of values, from optimism to pessimism, from rationalism to positivism, from abstract democracy to the search for "organization," from the political to the economic and social levels, from atheism or vague theism to the quest for a real religion, from reason to feeling, from independence to communion.[42] For Saint-Simon and the Saint-Simonians, the Revolution, the Rights of Man, and Liberalism had had a purely negative, destructive value; the time had come to organize society, to regenerate it. The State is an industrial association, it should be hierarchized; under competent scientists

41. Henry Michel, *L'Idée de l'Etat* (1895). In Michel's very careful study, the author, writing at the end of the last century, tried to retrieve "individualism" (in a sense slightly different from ours) from the attacks it had suffered in the (mainly French) nineteenth century. He contended that its value had remained entire as regards the ends, but that mistakes had been made in the *a priori* positing of the means. I have also used for this section the survey provided by Leroy 1946-62.

42. Proudhon wrote: "The freest man is he that has the most to do with his fellow men" (Leroy 1946, 2: 50).

come bankers, who are responsbile for the prime means of regulation: credit. Rewards should be unequal, as performances are, but
heritable property is a survival to be suppressed. Moreover, especially for the Saint-Simonians, a new religion, the New Christianism, must bind men together into one body of sentiment. The
critical epoch, which emphasized the individual and reason only,
should give way to a new *organic* epoch. Thus balance and unity will
be restored in the minds of men, for, as Saint-Simon said, "the idea
of God is nothing but the idea of human intelligence generalized."
At the same time, the impious exploitation of man by man will have
come to an end.[43]

The Saint-Simonians thus provided a contrast almost as perfect
as the theocrats, but a more modern one, to the ideals of the French
Revolution. Basically the same preoccupation was shared by men
very different, as Lamennais and Tocqueville. In his *Essay on
Indifference* (1817), Lamennais searched for truth in society itself,
by taking what he calls "common sense," that is, the traditions of all
known societies, as the source and the sign of truth. Elsewhere, he
wrote: "Solitary man is but a fragment of being; the real being is the
collective being, mankind, that does not die."[44]

As to Tocqueville, a Liberal, an aristocrat sincerely rallied to
democracy, he was impressed by the unhappy development of
democracy in France and went to America to study comparatively
and at first hand the conditions which permitted the democratic
United States to live peacefully and happily, and to draw conclusions for his own country.

From this point of view, Hegel himself falls in line with the
French thinkers of the period. Notwithstanding all the obvious
differences, and while recognizing that Hegel's politics have other
aspects, it may be said that, historically, the task which Hegel set
himself to in his *Grundlinien der Philosophie des Rechts* is the same
as that which Comte or Tocqueville were faced with: the task of
redeeming the ideals of the Revolution from the condemnation that
history had pronounced on them in their actual manifestation, or of
building a political or social theory which would enshrine them in a

43. This most insufficient summary is culled from Bouglé and Halévy 1931,
Michel 1895, Leroy 1946.

44. Leroy, 1946, 2: 437 ff. As in Comte, the reference to mankind as a whole,
where Rousseau had already referred to the concrete society, may be taken as a
legacy of the Enlightenment.

viable form. To bracket Hegel together with Marx as a "critical" philosopher of society is to miss the basic meaning of his Philosophy of Right, which is an attempt to *reconcile* all opposites into a vast synthesis and to show simultaneously that this synthesis is present in the modern State, be it Prussian. The modern State, in Hegel's philosophy of it, appears as the consummation of everything that had gone before. There is thus an important positivist aspect in Hegel's political philosophy. His philosophy of law proper is positivistic: law is command, "Will" (and thus "Liberty") in line with what we have found already in Ockham. It is true that he criticizes the positivism of the German historical school of law (Savigny), but he criticizes in a parallel fashion the purely negative, arbitrary, destructive idea of freedom of the French Revolutionaries, and this double criticism leads to the fusion of the two opposites: law is not only *given* in opposition to the individual's freedom, it is also *rational* as the deepest expression of man's freedom. In this synthesis, the truth of positivism and of libertarianism is kept while their limitations are removed. Many other reconciliations take place in Hegel's *Philosophy of Right*, but the latter is not the least important of them all.[45] This is clear from internal evidence. It is also clear from Hegel's immediate posterity branching off into a "right" and a "left," which respectively accepted only the positivistic or the rationalistic ("critical") aspect of his doctrine. The event illustrates Hegel's failure, but the point is that he attempted in his own way something similar and parallel to Comte's or Tocqueville's endeavor. With the Saint-Simonians, too, the parallels are obvious.

What distinguishes Hegel is that, in line with Rousseau and the classical tradition of political philosophy, he persists at looking at *universitas* in exclusively political terms. His "State" embodies actually what we would call society (*universitas*) including the State. As usual, Hegel concentrates on the *conscious* social phenomena. Indeed, in his book, expressions of contempt are not lacking regarding the aspects of the social constitution which have not attained conscious, i.e. practically written expression, such as cus-

45. Hegel, *Philosophy of Right*, (1942). Identification of law, will, and liberty: § 4; the State, pp. 160–61, 279; criticism of the French Revolution: p. 22 (and 227), 27 (and 230), 33 (cf., in the *Phenomenology of the Mind*, the chapter on "Absolute Liberty and Terror"). As it is chiefly in the last section of the book ("Ethical Life") that the individual is transcended, Hegel may appear superficially as more individualist than Hobbes and Rousseau.

tom in general, or the English Constitution. As in Hobbes and in Rousseau, the conscious individual is abruptly called to recognize in the State his higher self, and in the State's command the expression of his own will and freedom. This indirect presentation of society in terms of the State[46] leads to a kind of religion of the State in which Marx saw a mystification.

This rejection of *universitas* by the young Marx is a momentous event. Compared with the French socialists, his position is interesting. While he owes much to them, and goes to the extreme of demanding the abolition of private property, at the same time he does not share in the least their misgivings concerning the Individual and their gropings for a deeper idea of man. The socialist Marx believes in the Individual in a manner unprecedented in Hobbes, Rousseau, and Hegel, and even perhaps in Locke. In Marx, as with the Revolutionaries in 1789, the imaginary creature of Natural Law, which the great philosophers were cautious to transform at some stage of the transition to social life, enters into society fully armed and with a strong sense of self-sufficiency. Such a reassertion might not have been possible before the 1840s. At first sight the theory is contradictory, and compared with the Saint-Simonians' ramblings it is sociologically much impoverished. But it may be that precisely its simple and rigid individualism and artificialism has made for its success.[47]

As opposed to all this, Montesquieu and, later, Rousseau had seen the constitution of States against the background of the customs and *mores* of peoples. Tocqueville in his turn studied politics in the context of social life in general, and in particular relation to the body of socially shared ideas and values. Regarding the relation between religion and politics, it may be said that in comparison with Hegel's definitive and abrupt, if somewhat obscure, identification, and with Comte's overvaluation of Humanity as opposed to the concrete global society, the conclusions of Tocqueville's relatively modest American inquiry look today more profound and nearer the truth, possibly because his comparison was inspired by a true sociological spirit. Tocqueville concluded that a democratic polity is viable only if certain social conditions are fulfilled. The sphere of politics cannot absorb that of religion, or ultimate values in general.

46. This point was fully recognized by Bosanquet (1910).

47. On the relation in Marx between individualism, economism, and the artificialist project, cf. *MM*, part 2.

On the contrary, it should be complemented, and supported by it. (*HH*, 14)

In general the French thinkers of the revolutionary aftermath were led to consider man as a social being, to stress all the social factors, which constitute the raw material of personality and explain ultimately that society is not reducible to an artificial construct for the combination of individuals. Language, the more obvious of such factors, was emphasized by Bonald, who attributed its origin to God. Religion was highly appreciated by the Saint-Simonians as a source of social cohesion: they insisted on religion and sentiment for rebuilding the social body. And the ridicule into which they sank should not, any more than Comte's mysticism, which was perhaps only premature, hide the importance of their insight. The emphasis was, at least in part, on aspects of social life that are less conscious than the political aspect. The efforts of all those men tended to unearth, below the obvious discreteness of human consciousness, the social roots of man's being. At the same time this marked a rebirth of *universitas* and the beginnings of sociology proper, at least in the French tradition. In this perspective, the modern State corresponds to only a part of social life, and there is no absolute discontinuity between the self-conscious polity of modern society and other types of society which are considered by the political philosopher as standing somewhat below the threshold of fully-grown humanity.

There is obviously here, in the twin emergence of sociology and socialism in France, an important ideological phenomenon which cannot be understood as a mere consequence of the industrial revolution. Besides, in France the latter was still to come, and cannot be talked about before 1830.

Actually, it all looks as if the revolutionary tidal wave had been followed by a deep hollow, in which something of the holistic bedrock representations that we have detected, submerged but not absent, all along the rise of individualism, came to the surface.[48] Comparatively, the fact shows that modern society is not as far removed from the traditional type of society as its peculiar values tend to make us believe. The fact also points to a proper understanding both of sociology and of socialism. Sociology represents in

---

48. A parallel can be drawn between the global fact—the French Revolution and its consequences—and the paradoxical doctrines of Hobbes and Rousseau: in a sense history shows them to have been right.

the guise of a specialized discipline that awareness of the social whole which was embedded in common sense in nonindividualistic societies. As to socialism, it is a new and original form retrieving the preoccupation of the social whole while retaining a legacy of the Revolution—combining, that is, holistic and individualistic aspects. One cannot speak of a return to holism, for the hierarchical principle is rejected, and it is clear that individualism also is here split in two, part of it accepted and part rejected.[49]

This is of course only a brief characterization from the viewpoint of the history and comparison of ideologies. Yet it throws some light on the position of the "critic" cited earlier. It would also be of some use for the study of ideological developments in the nineteenth and twentieth centuries, but this goes beyond our present concern. This last section aimed merely to complete the sketch of the rise of individualism in political and social matters by taking note of the ideological consequences of the French Revolution, by registering, as it were, what history tells us directly of the relation between the ideology of 1789 and social reality as a whole.

49. Cf. above, sec. 5. The great variation in the place given to equality among the French socialists—very important with Proudhon as against Saint-Simon and Fourier—seems to be an index of their mixed attitude to the 1789 Revolution.

3 Genesis, III

The Emergence of the Economic Category
(A Reminder)

In the genealogy of modern concepts, politics is followed by economics. Just as religion gave birth to politics, politics was to give
birth to economics. This further phase in the modern process of the
differentiation of categories is described elsewhere at book length,
but it was felt that it ought to be represented here in a condensed
form in order to offer the reader a wider conspectus of the research
and a more complete idea of the general historical perspective.

To define economics is not easy. In his monumental *History of
Economic Analysis*, Schumpeter does not give any definition; he
defines such terms as "economic analysis," etc., but from the start
he takes "economic phenomena" for granted (1954, intro.). It is
difficult to propose a definition that would be universally accepted,
particularly if it was to be a definition which the economists of
the past as well as those of the present could approve. This difficulty might be one reason for Schumpeter's silence, for certainly
Ricardo did not deal with "scarce resources." This difficulty to
achieve a definition is probably a general modern phenomenon: not
only is it true of the sciences in general, but it can also be said of
modern man that he knows what he is doing ("analysis") but not
what it is "really about" ("economic"). Schumpeter writes of
Adam Smith and others: "They failed to see that their ethical
philosophies and political doctrines were logically irrelevant for the

Reproduced here, preceded by two brief extracts, is the section of *From Mandeville
to Marx* (Dumont 1977) dealing with the conditions of differentiation of the category, pp. 23–25, 5–6, 33–38. Notes and detailed references are omitted.

explanation of economic reality as it is . . . . They had not yet a clear conception of the distinctive purposes of analysis—have we?" (1954: 558–59).

The difficulty of definition is still greater from a comparative point of view, namely in anthropology. Anthropologists are strongly motivated to identify an economic aspect in any society, but where does it begin and where does it end? In recent years, two antithetic viewpoints have been expressed. The proponents of the formal one insist with good reason that economics is identical with its concept, and they propose as a consequence *their* conceptions of the alternate uses of scarce means, of methods to maximize gain, etc. The supporters of the substantive view argue that this attitude would be destructive of what is really the economy "out there" as an objective and universal datum—briefly, the ways and means of the subsistence of men. If a point of view that issues in such a divorce between the concept and the thing clearly shows itself to be inapplicable, then we have here a significant situation: what is meaningful in one world is simply not meaningful in another. Thus Karl Polanyi, taking the latter position, threw overboard "economics" in their contemporary version ("economizing"), to retain "the economy." This is not only an inconvenient language, but it represents also a regrettable step backward on the part of a scholar to whom we owe so much. True, Polanyi hastens to add, in conformity with the fundamental thesis of his previous book, *The Great Transformation*, that, in contradistinction to us, other societies have not segregated economic aspects—that they are found everywhere "embedded" in the social fabric (Polanyi 1957b: 243ff.). If there is any consensus in the matter, it is this: that to isolate economic phenomena the anthropologist has to disembed them—on the face of it a hazardous and probably destructive procedure, a Procrustean operation. It is particularly difficult—and, I would add, unrewarding—to separate political and economic aspects. This is no wonder, as we shall witness in our own culture the birth of the economic viewpoint from within the political; but when it is proposed to distinguish more and more sharply a "political anthropology," an "economic anthropology," it does not make sense with respect to the progress of knowledge. Quite the reverse; it is indicative of a renunciation of the anthropological inspiration ("only connect!") in favor of our modern tendency to increase compartmentalization and specialization.

It should be obvious that there is nothing like an economy out there, unless and until men construct such an object. Once it has been built, we are able to descry everywhere in some measure more or less corresponding aspects that we should in all rigor call "quasi-economic" or "would-be economic." Of course they should be studied, but the proviso ("quasi-") is operative. In other terms, the place of such aspects in the whole is not the same here and there, and this is essential to their nature.

Now, if the object—"the economy"—is a construct, and if the particular discipline that constructs it cannot tell us how it does it—if it cannot, that is, give us the essence of economics, the basic *presupposition(s)* on which it was built up—then we should find it in the *relation between economic thought and global ideology*, that is, in its place in the general ideological configuration. This supposes of course that we are equipped to identify this relation; and, as our comparative equipment is, as I said before, incomplete and tentative, it may be that we shall find this relation only incompletely. In that sense, the question will have to remain open. But such is our initial hypothesis.

Individualism, in its present definition as an overall valuation, goes together with one or two features of great import that will come forth in the following study but that it is perhaps as well to introduce immediately. In most societies, and primarily in the higher civilizations, which I shall designate henceforth as the "traditional societies," the relations between men are more important, more highly valued, than the relations between men and things. This primacy is reversed in the modern type of society, in which relations between men are subordinated to relations between men and things. This is a point Marx has stressed in his own manner, as will be recalled later on. Closely combined with this reversal of primacy, we find in modern society a new conception of wealth. In the traditional type of society, immovable wealth (estates) is sharply distinguished from movable wealth (money, chattels) by the fact that rights in land are enmeshed in the social organization in such a manner that superior rights accompany power over men. Such rights or "wealth," appearing essentially as a matter of relations between men, are intrinsically superior to movable wealth, which is disparaged, as is natural in such a system for a mere relation between men and things. Again, I find that Marx perceived clearly the exceptional character of those small commercial societies in which movable wealth had attained an autonomous status: "Wealth appears as an end in itself only among the few merchant peoples . . . who live in the pores of the ancient world like the Jews in medieval society" (1953: 387, on precapitalist formations).

With the moderns, a revolution occurred in this respect: the link between immovable wealth and power over men was broken, and movable wealth became fully autonomous in itself, as the superior aspect of wealth in general, while immovable wealth became an inferior, less perfect, aspect; in short, there emerged an autonomous and relatively unified category of wealth. It should be noted that it is only at this point that a clear distinction can be drawn between what we call "political" and what we call "economic." This is a distinction that traditional societies do not admit. As an economic historian recently recalled, in the modern West "the ruler abandoned, voluntarily or involuntarily, the right or practice of arbitrary or indefinite disposition of the wealth of his subjects" (Landes 1969: 16). This is a factual precondition for our familiar distinction.

The Conditions of Emergence of the Economic Category

The modern era has witnessed the emergence of a new mode of consideration of human phenomena and the carving out of a separate domain, which are currently evoked for us by the words *economics, the economy.* How has this new category appeared, a category that constitutes at one and the same time a separate compartment in the modern mind and a continent delivered to a scientific discipline and that, moreover, embodies a more or less paramount value of the modern world? It is convenient, and not too arbitrary, to take the publication by Adam Smith in 1776 of the book entitled *An Inquiry into the Nature and Causes of the Wealth of Nations* as the birth registration of the new category. What is it, then, that has happened in the *Wealth of Nations,* and in what relation does the book stand to what was there before?

Stressing the continuity between the Scholastics and subsequent writers down to the eighteenth century and the contributions of theologians and canonists from the fourteenth to the seventeenth century, Schumpeter wrote that, in the latter's works, "economics gained definite if not separate existence" (1954: 97). Our problem focuses precisely on the "separate existence," on the separation from existing viewpoints and disciplines through which economics began to exist as such, whether it was designated as "political economy" or otherwise.

For such a separation to occur, the subject matter had to be seen or felt as a system, as constituting in some manner a whole apart from other matters. This condition can be analyzed into two aspects: the recognition of some raw material, and a specific way of looking at it. The first aspect was present early, the second only later. This is what Schumpeter tells us when he speaks for the intermediate stage of a "definite but not separate" existence of economics. The canonists dealt with an array of questions relating to the public good that bore on what we call economic matters; however, those questions appeared in their works unconnected or only loosely connected among themselves, and they were treated, not from a specific, but from a more general point of view. Similarly, the writers called "mercantilists," of the seventeenth and eighteenth centuries, mingled the phenomena we classify into *economic* and *political*. They considered economic phenomena from the point of view of the polity. With them, more often than not, the end is the prosperity and power of the State. "Political economy" appears in that period as an expression designating the study of particular means—"economical" means—to that end, that is to say, a particular branch of policy (Heckscher 1955). Actually, the general subservience of wealth to power in that period has been challenged (Viner 1958), yet I think it is safe to assume that, while the two were thought of as closely interdependent, wealth remained on the whole subordinated to or encompassed in power.

To make a brief comparative remark, I note that in the Indian civilization, while the political had been distinguished from and subordinated to the religious, the economic was never conceptually detached from the political. "Interest" remained an attribute of the king (H.H., 303ff.). Moreover, it is clear that this feature is linked with the fact that immovable wealth remained, as associated to power over men, the only recognized form of wealth, as in the configuration I noticed above. Therefore, the preoccupation of our mercantilists with trade and money appears comparatively pertinent.

True, there never was a "commercial or mercantile system" as Adam Smith later presented it. In particular, we have it on Schumpeter's authority that no serious writer ever believed that the wealth of a state or nation consisted in the accumulation of treasure

(1954: 361–62). What seems to be the case is that, once it had attained its independence, economics began to look down upon its humble beginnings and disparaged everything that had gone before, to the point of disregarding many valuable insights. Schumpeter regrets this discontinuity (ibid.: 376), but there are reasons for it. In particular, it is natural that the champions of what was popularly known as Free Trade became impatient with those who had adopted or had, at any rate, started from the point of view of State intervention. But then another question comes up: if the writings of those whom we shall go on calling, for convenience, the mercantilists are not entirely devoid of merit, how far is it true that they presented only disconnected statements and no system? All considered, we may at the most speak of partial systems in the making (Schumpter 1954; see also the plan of Heckscher 1955 and his remark in Coleman 1969: 34). To be brief, we shall concentrate on one aspect that is crucial regarding the lack of unification of the field: the close relation to the State has this consequence, that *international transactions are considered in one manner, and transactions within the State or country in another.*

Thus, what Schumpeter singles out as perhaps the foremost achievement of the period, Malynes's "automatic mechanism," is a partial theory of equilibrium in international trade which was to receive its definitive formulation from Cantillon and Hume (Schumpeter 1954: 365). To see the point more clearly, we may refer to a basic ideological change that occurred in the period. The primitive idea is that, in trade, the gain of one party is the loss of the other. This idea was popular, and it came spontaneously even to acute minds like Montaigne. I am tempted to call it a basic ideological element, an "ideologeme," and to see it in relation to the general disparagement of trade and money that is characteristic of traditional societies in general. To think of exchange as advantageous to both parties represented a basic change and signaled the advent of economics. Now this change occurs precisely in the mercantilist period, not suddenly, but progressively. The ideologeme lingers on; while it recedes from the domain of internal trade—be it only because, considered globally, the gains and losses of particular agents cancel each other out—it is found in full force in the domain of international trade. It lies at the root of what Heckscher calls the "statism" of the economy as opposed to the dynamism of the State: the sum of wealth present in the world is taken as constant, and the aim of the policy is for one particular State to get the greatest possible share of that total and constant sum of wealth. Thus says Colbert (Heckscher 1955, 2: 24 ff.).

On a different level, it is striking to find in a thinker of Locke's caliber a clear trace of the heterogeneous conception of internal and external transactions and of the inability to unify the field across national boundaries. Reasoning about the optimum amount of money a country ought to possess, Locke sees the price of the goods in international trade as determined solely by internal conditions, namely, by the internal price in the exporting country. External trade, that is, is not conceived as a sort of trade existing in its own right but only as an adjunct to internal trade, not as an economic phenomenon per se but as a set of transactions in which the price is determined by economic (internal) phenomena (ibid., 2: 239–42).

Thus, mercantilist literature clearly shows that, if a separate domain were to be recognized as economic, it must be carved out of the political domain: the economic point of view demanded to be emancipated from the political. Subsequent history tells us that there was another side to this "emancipation": economics had to emancipate itself from morality. (This is an inexact formula, but let it serve for the time being.)

This point may seem strange at first glance, but the necessity can be understood—or, at any rate, we can familiarize ourselves with the climate in which it appears—by a brief reflection. One may well ask, in a quite general manner, whether there can be a social or human science that would not be normative. We social scientists mostly contend or suppose not only that such can be, but also that such should be the case; in imitation of the natural sciences, we hold that science is value-free. But the philosopher can argue a priori that a science *of man* is by definition normative, and he will support this statement by denying either that our social science is really a science, or that it is devoid of value judgments. We may perhaps leave the question open regarding a hypothetically global science of man in society, but the philosopher's doubt is strongly reinforced if we consider the case of a *particular* social science—of a social science, that is, that studies only some aspects and not others of social life, as is the case with economics.

Here the philosopher will ask whether the initial postulate by which such a science ideally separates, that is, constitutes itself, can possibly be free of value judgment. Rather than discussing the question in the abstract, I observe that the history of the genesis of economics and of its first or "classical" phase fully confirms the philosopher's surmise. Gunnar Myrdal has shown that a normative aspect clings all along to economics. As to the genesis itself, we shall see in some detail that the distinctness of the economic domain rests on the postulate of an inner consistency *oriented to the good* of man. This is easy to grasp, in the circumstances: the emancipation from politics required the surmise of inner consistency, for otherwise order should be introduced from the outside. But that was not quite enough, for supposing it was shown that the inner consistency worked for evil, then again it would have required the politician and statesman to intervene. We may observe, en passant, that the assumption of consistency itself may be viewed as the residue, within an avowedly purely descriptive social science, of its normative or teleological foundation. In the eagerness with which the founders of economics took hold, in the most uncritical manner, of any correlations that presented themselves immediately to their minds, we see a reflection of this sine qua non condition. When Schumpeter wonders at such arbitrary assumptions as, for instance, the ubiquitous notion that foodstuffs, by their very existence, create the population that will consume them, he simply forgets the paramount need that engendered such beliefs, the need for immanent laws to guarantee the independence of the domain and of the consideration applied to it. Thus James Mill:

> The production of commodities . . . is the one and universal cause which creates a market for the commodities produced . . . [and further,] the quantity of any one commodity [produced] may easily be carried beyond its due proportion; but by this very circumstance is implied that some other commodity is not provided in sufficient proportion. (Mill 1808: 65–68)

That the independence of economics from politics was not given immediately and without struggle or contradiction is seen indirectly as well, when one finds that it is not only in our times or in political circles that pleas for reintegration or subordination were made, but that all along, in economic circles, the question was present in some minds.

As to the second aspect: that the internal consistency of the economic domain is such that it is beneficent if left to itself is transparently expressed in the axiom of "the natural harmony of interests," as Elie Halévy called it. Not only are the interests of two parties in a transaction not opposed, as it was originally believed, but individual interest is also congruent with the general interest. We shall have to inquire into the genesis of this remarkable notion and its place on the global ideological map. That it was most of the time accompanied by the notably different notion of "the artificial harmony of interests" illustrates my preceding point.

The immediate impression is that it was not a simple matter to fulfill these conditions. We shall admit that they are all assembled for the first time in the *Wealth of Nations*. This fact accounts for the success of Adam Smith's book in subsequent times, its unique historical importance, even for those who would admit with Schumpeter that there is little in it that is orginal and that in some respects the compilation could have been more complete or better (1954: 184–86 etc.). Regarding internal consistency, it is generally recognized that the decisive step was made by Docteur Quesnay and the Physiocrats, and there are good reasons to believe that without them the *Wealth* would not have seen the light of day or would have been a very different book. At the same time, Smith's divergence from Quesnay is at least as marked as his dependence on him.

The point can be related to our external conditions: with Quesnay, economics is not made radically independent from politics, nor is it severed from morality. Characteristically, with him it cannot be said that all economic interests harmonize by themselves, while in Adam Smith they do so, in principle if not always in fact. To account for this aspect of the *Wealth*, we must turn to works that are not generally recognized as landmarks in the history of economic thought. It is indeed only natural that we do so, for we then deal with the relations between the economic and the noneconomic. I found Locke's *Two Treatises of Government* enlightening as regards the relation with politics and, similarly, Mandeville's famous/ infamous *Fable of the Bees*, as regards morality. The link with Adam Smith, admitted in the case of Mandeville, is to my mind no less clear, *pace* Schumpeter, in the case of Locke, whether it is direct or indirect.

4   A National Variant, I

German Identity: Herder's *Volk* and Fichte's *Nation*

All through the research presented in this book, it is supposed that there is a system of ideas and values that characterizes modern societies—especially those societies in which modernity appeared and developed—which we call modern ideology. It may be objected that such an ideology does not really exist, for what might be so called varies from one country or one major language area to another. There are, for example, English, French, German subcultures within European culture. But the fact entails simply that we ought to take those subcultures, or the corresponding ideologies, as so many variants—of equal status—of modern ideology. Ideally, a concrete knowledge of modern ideology would be attained if we could pass from one variant to another in a systematic fashion, as if by applying a set of transformations.[1] In fact, the first point that requires notice is that our more or less national subcultures, although they do participate in the same modern culture, do not by any means communicate between themselves as immediately

Communication given in French in a Honda Foundation symposium in Paris, October 1978, and in English before the International Society for the Comparative Study of Civilizations (U.S.) in Northbridge, California, March 1979. Published in parts in two memorial volumes: *Ethnicity, Identity and History: Essays in Memory of Werner J. Cahnman*, edited by Joseph B. Maier and Chaim I. Waxman (New Brunswick: Transaction Books, 1983), and *Civilizations East and West: A Memorial Volume for Benjamin Nelson*, edited by E.V. Walter (Atlantic Highlands, N.J.: Humanities Press, 1985).

   1. For two examples of the practical problem set to the anthropologist addressing readers of different European nationality (initiation to sociology, and kinship theory), see *HH.*, p. xxiii and n. 18.

and easily as one might suppose, and as common sense does suppose—especially French common sense; as we shall see, French common sense hardly recognizes at all the existence of different subcultures.

Modern culture has a powerful universalist slant which leads to rejecting the differences, when actually encountered, from the cognitive domain. We speak of differences in "national character," and each European country entertains stereotypes about its neighbors, the implication being that the cognitive map is the same everywhere, and differences merely a matter of psychological or behavioral idiosyncrasies.

National subcultures are to some extent opaque to each other—those of France and Germany for example. That the conflicts and estrangement of the nineteenth and twentieth centuries do not result only from the confrontation of two national states, one older, the other younger, is shown by the dispute among historians about Alsace-Lorraine after 1870 and by the qualms of conscience and tortured reexaminations of several notable French Germanists-cum-philosophers around 1914. It is testified to again by two outstanding witnesses, Heinrich Heine and Ernst Troeltsch, who perceived, the former as the heir to Romanticism, the latter as a historian and sociologist who had lived through the First World War, the distance between the two nationally predominant modes of thought and the difficulty of making them communicate.

Although there have been notable contributions, the problem is still before us. Looking at it from the French side, we see that this is so because no one can get out of his own national variant, no one can stop identifying it implicitly or unconsciously with the only "true" one or with modern ideology at large, in order to place it on a par with the alien variant. In other words, there has been a lack of distantiation, of a fulcrum located outside the double system, and setting in perspective modern ideology itself.

Now this is precisely what social anthropology can offer; in the present case, the fulcrum is provided by the results of an earlier comparison between India and the modern West. They consist essentially of two tools that will appear further on, the holism/individualism distinction, and the hierarchical relation. The approach has been applied to a general study of German ideology and, in particular, German thought between 1770 and 1830. The research is well advanced, but has not yet been written up as a whole. What follows represents a chapter detached from it, dealing with the contribution of Herder and Fichte to the German conception of collective identity and, through it, to German identity itself.

For clarity and conciseness, I shall present the particular theme in the light of my general conclusion, but this means short-circuiting in the exposition the order of the inquiry. I must draw attention to this point in order to prevent any misunderstanding. As implied above, the basic procedure consisted in a comparison of configurations of ideas; the study was therefore essentially static and morphological, neither dynamic nor directly concerned with interaction. As the study developed, however, it appeared with increasing force that German culture should be looked at not in isolation but as involved in a vital relationship with its environment. This connection will be documented here in the instances of Herder and of Fichte. Actually it extends to the whole field of study; that is why I take the liberty in what follows of anticipating the general—as yet unproven—conclusion of my work, and of speaking of "interaction," "acculturation," and the like.

Beginning in the eighteenth century, especially with the *Sturm und Drang* movement, and throughout the age of the French Revolution and Napoleon's Empire, German culture exhibits, at the level of learned humanism, an unprecedented development. This development brings about on the one hand complete emancipation in relation to French culture, which previously dominated the scene to the extent of appearing coterminous with culture in general, or universally valid. On the other hand, the same development not only lays the basis of modern German ideology but builds it up in its essential framework. I should add, but it is hardly necessary, that this same movement of thought has been of the first importance not only for Germany but for modern ideology—or culture—in general.

For this very reason, to present it as I just did is likely to arouse protests: it will be argued that the great philosophical systems are part of our universal patrimony and have nothing to do with national ideologies. Even if one admits that German thought was goaded on, so to speak, by the French and English Enlightenment and the French Revolution, one will hesitate to see in that thought itself the result of an interaction between national cultures. After all, the French Revolution itself is more than a French phenomenon. It is part and parcel of modern culture at large. And perhaps I should make it clear that I do not propose to reduce German thought to the conditions of its genesis any more than the truth or value of a statement is reducible to the circumstances in which it was arrived at. Especially for the anthropologist, a feature is no less universal for its being rooted in a particular tradition. In the main, however, the question is whether the proposed approach throws light on the matter; the objections must give way if the new perspective gives a better account of the data than the more habitual views.

In 1774, at the time of the short-lived *Sturm und Drang* movement, or German preromanticism, Herder, who is thirty years old, publishes "Another Philosophy of History" (*Auch eine Philosophie der Geschichte*).[2] The title indicate a reply to Voltaire, and, while the philosophy of history it propounds is complex, the short book (110 pages in the edition of the complete works) is in essence an impassioned polemic against the Enlightenment with it platitudinous rationalism and its narrow conception of progress[3] and, above all, against the hegemony of that universalist rationalism which despises all that is foreign to it and presumes to impose its senile refinement everywhere. Herder rehabilitates everything that the French and English eighteenth century rejected or ignored: the barbarous Middle Ages, Ancient Egypt sacrificed to the glory of Greece, and perhaps most important, religion. Instead of history consisting in the accession of reason, a reason disembodied and everywhere identical to itself, Herder sees in history the contrasted interplay of individual cultures or cultural individuals, each constituting a specific human community, or *Volk*, in which an aspect of general humanity is embodied in a unique and irreplaceable manner. The German *Volk*, bearer of western Christian culture, is the modern example of the category. In the flow of history there is not only simply progress (*Fortschritt*) but, within each of the two civilizational complexes, the ancient and the modern, what one may call a succession of "forward strivings" or blossomings (*Fortgang, Fortstreben*), all "of equal necessity, equal originality, equal merit, equal happiness."[4]

In sum, in the face of the dominant universalism, Herder in

---

2. Rather than the edition in the Complete Works (Herder 1968) I have used the French (bilingual) edition by Max Rouché (Herder 1964).
3. Notably in Iselin 1764.
4. On the complexity of the historical movement according to Herder, cf. Rouché's introduction in Herder 1964: 48–76.

1774 asserts with ardor the diversity of cultures, each of which he extols in turn. He does not ignore the borrowings by one culture from another, always accompanied by a thorough modification of the borrowed element. He even notes fleetingly that each excellence is paid for by some shortcoming, so that all those perfections are unilateral or incomplete.

We may say that, by anticipation, the basis is laid here for a right of cultures or "peoples" in contrast to the future Rights of Man. This implies a deep transformation in the definition of man: as opposed to the abstract individual, a representative of the human species, endowed with reason but stripped of all particularity, man for Herder is what he is, in all his modes of thinking, feeling, and acting, by virtue of his belonging to a given cultural community. This view, as much else in Herder, is not absolutely new. One thinks in the first place of Rousseau, who parted with the *Encyclopédistes* precisely on this point, as a "citizen of Geneva" fully acknowledging the social nature of man, that is, his belonging to a concrete society as a necessary condition of his education into a man.

We have here a fundamental difference in the conception of man. In the last analysis, either the fundamental value is attached to the Individual, and we may speak in this sense of the "individualism" of Voltaire and the authors of the *Encyclopédie*, or the fundamental value is attached to the society or culture, to the collective being, and in that sense I shall speak of "holism" as emerging in Rousseau and Herder.[5] If, as I believe, the accession of individualism to predominance distinguishes modern culture from all others, certainly from the great civilizations, we face here, in the resurgence of a holistic aspect in modern culture, an important fact of history. Yet we must note an unprecedented novelty. In traditional holism, the society is exclusive, humankind coincides with the society formed by *us*, and strangers are devalued as being, at best, imperfect men. By the way, even modern patriotism is tinged with that feeling. With Herder, on the contrary, all cultures are recognized as equal in principle. It should be clear that such an assertion

5. The holism/individualism distinction does not represent the introduction of an alien viewpoint in relation to German culture. It differs from that of Toennies, *Gemeinschaft/Gesellschaft*, only by its articulating the hierarchy of values, and Toennies's distinction itself owes its interest to its being an analytic reflection of the tendencies in German thought in the nineteenth century (cf. below, the first part of chap. 8).

is possible only because cultures are viewed as so many individuals, equal among themselves notwithstanding their difference; *cultures are individuals of a collective nature*. In other words, Herder on the one hand discards individualism in favor of holism on the level of the elements, that is, when he considers individual human beings; but on the other hand he uses the individualist principle by transferring it to the level of compounds, so to speak, that is, when he considers collective entities that before him were unacknowledged or subordinated. It would therefore be wrong to see Herder as rejecting wholesale the individualist—mainly French—culture, for at the same time he accepts a major feature of it in order to assert against that very culture the existence and value of German culture and, with it, of all others that have flourished in history. Therefore, taken globally, Herder's reaction must be located *within* the modern value system. His holism must be seen as contained within the individualism that he fiercely attacks—and the circumstance may well account for the style of the book, which is tense, screaming, almost panting.

Later, in the more serene climate of Weimar, Herder will attempt to reconcile universality and concreteness in his *Ideen* through the notion of *Humanität*, which embodies the tension between the two poles and which, perhaps for this reason, he despairs of defining.[6] The strident protest of the 1774 booklet is much clearer. It presents a momentous case of what anthropologists of our day have called acculturation.

It may be said in all rigor that Herder posits a German subculture by the side of the French one *within modern culture*. Moreover, in doing so he lays the basis for what will be later the "ethnic theory" of nationalities as against the "elective theory," in which the nation rests essentially on consensus, on Renan's "everyday plebiscite." We have just seen that the ethnic theory rests at bottom on the same equalitarian—i.e. individualistic—basis as the elective theory does. The two theories are therefore not completely independent of each other as is often assumed nowadays. They both apply, albeit on different levels, the same modern principle of equalitarian individualism.

Let me emphasize the articulation of holism with individualism

6. Isaiah Berlin noticed the incompatibilities introduced by Herder, and the fact that his views could develop explosive possibilities until our days "and perhaps beyond" (Berlin 1976: 209–13).

in the Herder of *Auch eine Philosophie* and formalize it in hierarchical terms. Herder asserts each concrete culture as a concrete entity in which individuals are merged, and thus presents a holistic protest against the individualism of the Enlightenment, but this protest actually takes place at a subordinate level. The superior level, for Herder himself, is the global level of consideration, on which all cultures are present as individuals with equal right. As against the ethnocentricism of naive holism, this shows adherence to modern individualism—transferred from the elementary to the collective level. Holism is here encompassed in individualism; it is a case of the *encompassing of the contrary* by which I defined hierarchy elsewhere.[7] To explain this briefly, there is no better example than the creation of Eve from one of Adam's ribs in the first book of Genesis. God creates Adam first, the undifferentiated man, the prototype of "mankind." Then he somehow extracts from that undifferentiated being a being of different sex. Adam and Eve stand face to face, prototypes of the two sexes. In this strange operation Adam has changed identity: from being undifferentiated, he has become a male. On the other hand a being has appeared who is both a member of the human species and different from the main representative of this species. Adam—or "man" in our language—is two things in one: the representative of the species, and the prototype of the male individuals of that species. On one level, man and woman are identical; on a second level woman is the opposite or contrary of man. These two relations together characterize the hierarchical relation, which cannot be better symbolized than by the material encompassing of the future Eve in the body of the first Adam. This hierarchical relation is, very generally, that between a whole (or a set) and an element of that whole (or set): the element belongs to the whole, or set, and is in this sense consubstantial or identical with it; at the same time the element is distinct from the whole, or set, and stands in opposition to it. There is no way to express the hierarchical relation in logical terms other than by juxtaposing at two different levels these two statements, which contradict each other if taken together. That is what I designate as "encompassing the contrary." I recalled the Biblical example be-

---

7. Cf. *HH.*, Postface, pp. 239 ff. (from which the Adam and Eve example is borrowed), and also the application to the right hand/left hand opposition, below chap. 8, second part.

cause its vivid image will make more understandable the aspects of German thought with which we are concerned here.

I am aware that the reader might prefer to look at the combination of holism and individualism in Herder in a different way; yet I am convinced that my formulation of it is right or, rather, that it is the most pregnant one from a comparative point of view of cultures and their interaction. It is confirmed by other Herderian traits, which I cannot go into here (one need only think of the later *Humanität*). The combination must be such as I describe it for Herder's thought to fall *within* modern culture and not outside it, and for its subsequent impact to have been such as we know it. Moreover, if we admit that ethnocentricism is strong everywhere, and if by anticipation we assume that German culture will show throughout a powerful tendency toward holism, we may ask ourselves how well the Herderian equality between cultures will stand the test of subsequent generations of German thinkers. It is a fact that Herder's successors have more often hierarchized contemporary cultures or nations, with their own at the top of the value scale, than they have valued them equally.

We may single out one hierarchical trait in Herder's first philosophy of history. In each historical period, one particular culture or people comes to the fore and expresses for a time humanity at large, while the other contemporary cultures remain in the background, more or less subordinate. Thus in antiquity there is a succession in which the Oriental, the Egyptian *cum* Phoenician, the Greek, and then the Roman cultures each have universal value as embodying an age of ancient humanity, from infancy to old age. This identification of a given culture with humanity as a whole for a particular epoch is common among German thinkers after Herder, and we shall find it again, applied to modern times, in Fichte.

Before leaving Herder, I should stress that I have singled out only one aspect in his writings, an aspect fundamental for Herder's posterity both within and outside Germany. In German thought, Herder is at the origin of one of the two currents or lineages of thought, the more distinctly romantic one; but his thought also spills into and influences the other, more universalistic current. Outside Germany he has deeply influenced the acculturation and nationalism of peoples later exposed to the full impact of modern values, especially the Slavic-speaking peoples of central and eastern Europe. The fact is well known and should cause no surprise given the formula we have isolated, which looks like a formal blueprint for (positive) acculturation to modern conditions independently of time and place.

The social and political philosophy of Fichte still poses a problem today. Fichte explicitly set out to be the philosopher of the French Revolution. Yet he has often been considered in Germany, notably by the historian Meinecke writing before the First World War, as a precursor of pan-Germanism or of the theory that binds the State to the collective will-to-power of a people. On the other hand, Martial Guéroult, the French philosopher who has given a painstaking exegesis of Fichte's system, has been deeply concerned with showing that Fichte throughout his life and writings remained perfectly faithful to the Revolution, and that whatever else is found in Fichte on that level is quite secondary, whether it be his deeply German manner of thinking and feeling, or his "German messianism," not to speak of the misunderstandings and falsifications he has been submitted to.[8] In the face of such conflicting opinions, I should like to show that we can better account for the social philosophy of Fichte and for its subsequent destinies by starting from the difference between the two subcultures, German and French. I shall mainly endeavor to show the presence in Fichte, decidedly equalitarian though he is, of a hierarchical form of thought the equivalent of which it would be difficult to detect among the French revolutionaries.

Let us go straight to the heart of the difficulty, the *Addresses to the German Nation*—those lectures delivered by Fichte in Berlin—then occupied by Napoleon's troops—after the Prussian defeat at Jena. From the divergent interpretations and contradictory valuations of our two witnesses we can extract a minimum of agreement. For Guéroult, Fichte remains true to the revolutionary ideal, while according to Meinecke he goes one step forward—but only one step—toward the truly German, more or less pan-Germanist, conception of the State. We observe that both authors are actually agreed on one point: that there is a universalist component in Fichte's thought (which Guéroult praises while Meinecke deplores it). Let us take this common admission as our point of departure. We shall even admit with Guéroult that this universalism is the essential or encompassing component in the *Addresses* and in Fichte's social thought in general. Yet it does not itself account for

8. Meinecke 1915: 96–125; Guéroult 1974: 142–246.

the exaltation of the German nation, which is the more striking as that nation was in fact—unlike Prussia—nonexistent in those days. We are thus bound to search for another element that combines with Fichte's universalism to produce his nationalism.

There are two lineages in German thought. As against the Herderian or, one might say, historicist or monadic lineage, which has as its basic tenet the specificity and irreplaceability of each culture or people, Fichte belongs with Kant and even with Hegel to the universalist lineage. Meinecke can reproach him for extolling in the last analysis not the concrete nation as a particular corporate will-to-live, but the *nation de raison*, the nation as a rational, universal entity. Of course it is true that the universalist or cosmopolitic ideology does not bar patriotism. The French *levée en masse* of 1793 seems to bear witness to the fact, and it is easily understood: if I conceive of myself as an Individual, a representative of the human species, I nevertheless live in fact in a given society or nation, and I spontaneously look at this more restricted circle as the empirical form that the human species takes for me, so that I may feel an attachment for it without justifying my feeling explicitly through what differentiates my nation from others. Yet this is not enough in Fichte's case. His stance is essentially that the German spirit is characterized by universality—on the face of it a quite ambiguous statement.

The devoted French biographer of Fichte, Xavier Léon, has shown that, in the *Addresses* and other texts of the same period, Fichte put forth theses bearing a certain likeness to those of romantics like August Wilhelm Schlegel and Schelling. On the present issue, Fichte admits with Schlegel that the German people is destined to dominate the world, but he thoroughly modifies the meaning of the assertion by basing it on the identity of universality and Germanness, a trait which was, incidentally, already present in his slightly earlier *Patriotic Dialogues*.[9] It is all essentially a matter of humanity and its development. The ambiguity lies in the fact that, when Fichte insists on the regenerative function of the German people and on the resulting attribution of precedence to Germany, we do not know whether he is unilaterally applying universalism to a particular population, as by a sort of hypertrophied patriotism, or asserting the hegemony of a will-to-live that uses universalism merely as a prop. If we want to remain close to Fichte's thought, I

9. Léon 1954–59, 2.1: 433–63; 2.2: 34–93.

think that we must maintain that for him the two aspects do not exclude each other as they do for his interpreters, but coincide. Strange as it looks, this coincidence is something we must try to understand.

As already stated, Fichte is on the whole a stranger to the Herderian and romantic notion of the blessed diversity of cultures or peoples as so many facets of the richness of the universal Whole. When he does use this notion in the thirteenth address, it is part of a clever argument directed precisely against the romantic dream of a new Christian-Germanic Empire. More generally, although in this period Fichte adopts the current stereotypes of the excellence of the German character, the German language, etc., he does so essentially in order to state a *hierarchy* among peoples *in the name of the very value of universalism*. Now I contend that, apart from any borrowing from the romantics, it is possible to show the presence in Fichte's thought in general, along with a strong individualistic-cum-universalistic stress, of a holistic aspect and, more especially, a hierarchical component. I shall leave out here the holistic tendency, which is strong in the authoritarian socialism of the *Closed Commercial State* and is also encountered in other texts, uneasily cohabiting with individualistic features—but such is after all often the case in modern thinking, including that of sociologists.[10] What is more noteworthy is the emergence, throughout Fichte's work and in clear contrast with the thinking of the Enlightenment and the French Revolution, of a hierarchical form of thought.

Fichte is fiercely equalitarian on the political level, in contrast with Kant and with most other Germans—though in agreement with Herder (and Rousseau)—and in perfect consonance with the French Revolution in its Jacobin development. Is it not therefore surprising to find an example of formalized hierarchy in the very book the young Fichte devotes in 1793 to the defense of the Revolution, the *Contributions to the Rectification of the Judgment of the Public*? A single diagram is found in the book. It is intended to show the State as subordinate to the individual. It shows four concentric circles of which the largest includes—or in my language encom-

10. Cf. for the Durkheimians *HH.*, n.3*a*; also below, chap. 8; closer to our topic, Karl Pribram, in a seminal essay written in 1922, has given the name "pseudo-universalism" (= pseudo-holism) to the ideological formula that he showed to be common to Prussian nationalism and to Marxian socialism (Pribram 1922—quoted at length below, chap. 6, from a slightly different angle).

passes—the second, and so on: the "domain of consciousness," i.e. individualism in its moral form, embraces the domain of natural law; the latter in turn that of contracts in general; and the domain of contracts that of civil contract or the State. Here, repeated thrice, is precisely the encompassing disposition through which I have defined hierarchy.[11] It is remarkable that this argument is found in a vindication of the French Revolution against the attacks of Burke and Rehberg. Of course there is no conflict at all between this schema and Fichte's purpose, for it deals with pure hierarchy, which has nothing to do with (political) power. Yet it is paradoxical that a staunch equalitarian should resort to a form of pure hierarchical thought. I bet that one would be hard put to it to find anything similar in revolutionary France at that time. At this early date, Fichte presents, along with the equalitarian conviction which brings him into communion with the Revolution, a quite different form of thought.

An element of social hierarchy occurs in a passage of the *Closed Commercial State* in which the needs of the several social categories are carefully distinguished. The scholar or scientist, in the interest of what we could call the output of his work, needs rich foods and a refined environment, while at the other end of the social scale the peasant is able to assimilate coarse meals, which are sufficient for him. The trait is interesting in contrast to the stress on the equalitarian principle in the book at large, and still more so in contrast to the French developments in the direction of a state-regulated economy, to which Fichte's model runs parallel.[12]

The examples of hierarchy I have just referred to are still details, local, almost anecdotal occurrences. Far more weighty— indeed, decisive in my view—is the hierarchical opposition at the very heart of Fichte's system of philosophy, in that dialectic of the "I" (or self) and the "Non-I" (non-self) which constitutes the foundation of his *Wissenschaftslehre* (1794), the "transcendental dialectic," as Philonenko calls it (in Belaval 1978: 173), that establishes the conditions of all knowledge. The demonstration lies at hand, for it is the "I" that posits the "Non-I." As in the case of Adam and Eve, there are two levels in the relationship: on the first

11. J. G. Fichte 1845, 6: 39–288; the figure is on page 133. The reader might think that Fichte's circles, or some of them, indicate only subdivisions and do not imply contrariety. He is referred to Fichte's own commentary. Cf. Philonenko 1968: 162.

12. X. Léon 1954–59, 1: 101–4, makes a parallel with Babeuf.

level, the I or self is undifferentiated, it is the absolute I or self; on the second level, the self posits within itself the non-self, and ipso facto posits itself as against the non-self, so that we have, facing each other, the self and the non-self. The non-self is, on the one hand, contained within the self, on the other hand it is the opposite of self. This strictly hierarchical disposition of the Fichtean dialectic is noteworthy from many angles, especially perhaps with regard to Kant and to Hegel. On the one hand it is this hierarchical disposition that allows Fichte to integrate into a whole Kant's two Reasons, pure Reason and practical Reason. On the other hand, Hegel's dialectic will be no more hierarchical.

The fact takes some wonder, and is worth pondering, for the young Hegel was intent on totality and had finally reached a hierarchical definition of it when he wrote, in his last fragment at Frankfurt that Life was "the union of union and non-union" (*Verbindung und Nichtverbindung*).[13] Here, if anywhere, is that "encompassing of the contrary" by which I proposed to define hierarchy.

This formula of the young Hegel is no *obiter dictum*. It is central to what has been called by the editor the "Fragment of a System," a text that, even grievously incomplete as we have it, marks the conclusion of the whole period of the "early theological writings" and is roughly contemporary with Hegel's resolve to join Schelling in Jena and enter the career of philosophy proper. The importance of the formula is confirmed from the fact that we can follow it up in subsequent writings. In Jena it is identity that must be conceived as "the identity of identity and non-identity," and in the *Logic* we find the infinite as the union of the infinite and the finite.[14]

Yet there is no gainsaying the fact that this unmistakable hierarchical aspect is eliminated from Hegel's definitive thought. What has happened? It is certainly not the case that Hegel turned his back on the formula in which he had condensed the yearnings of his youth. Rather, a gradual transformation took place, which was

---

13. Hegel 1907: 348; trans. 1948: 312.

14. The first two formulas are brought together in Taminiaux 1967: 234. Among recent interpreters, only Michael Theunissen and to a lesser extent Charles Taylor (1975) have, to my knowledge, recognized clearly the hierarchical aspect of those formulas. Theunissen mentions them repeatedly; indeed their common matrix is central to his general argument (Theunissen 1970: 8, 15–16, 35, 47–49, 50, 55–56, 68, 72, 126–27, 161–63, etc.).

signaled, in Jena and later, by changes in vocabulary indicative of conceptual modifications and shifts. The totality that in the Fragment was called Life became the Absolute, and then the absolute Spirit, that is to say the Absolute as subject. All this is known, but the hierarchical perception itself has remained almost unnoticed, and so has its subsequent fate, enlightening though it is.[15]

What became of it can, I think, be seen most graphically and economically from the section of the *Logic* that deals with the dialectic of the infinite and the finite, to which a recent exegete attributes a central place and exemplary value.[16] In this long and toilsome discussion, a real *Auseinandersetzung*, Hegel asserts not only, as hinted above, that the infinite contains the finite, but also conversely that the finite contains the infinite. The reader who allows that the latter statement is obviously not true *in the same sense* as the former, who bears my remarks in mind and immerses himself in the intricacies of the development, is likely to conclude as I do that Hegel here labors very hard to eliminate the dissymmetry inherent in the relationship and give equal status to its two poles. Infinity, which attached, to begin with, to the encompassing of the contrary, will in the end have been transferred to the *process* of transition from one pole to the other, and to *negativity* as the motive force or principle of this process.[17] All in all, infinity has transited—whether wholly or only partly—from the domain of wholeness or transcendence to that of immanence and dialectics. From this particular discussion, it seems that Hegel's effort, or a considerable part of it, was precisely directed at the elimination of the hierarchical aspect, and that his dialectics owes to that intention a good deal of its complexity.

Of course this is not to say that hierarchical aspects cannot be detected in Hegel's system as a whole, especially in its architectonics. It reappears explicitly, or almost so, at the supreme level,

15. Even with Theunissen the encompassing of the contrary, if it surfaces here and there, is not systematically isolated, and perhaps for this reason early formulas are brought to bear indiscriminately on later texts where they may not always be relevant (as when Hegel is corrected, pp. 126–27, or about the infinite pp. 8, 49).

16. Taylor 1975: 240–44, esp. p. 242 *init.*

17. This movement seems to me somehow implied in Taylor 1975. First (p. 240), "the Hegelian notion of infinity is of a whole which is not conditioned or bounded by something else"; then (p. 242), "of a whole whose inner articulations and process unfolds of necessity"; and finally (p. 244), of "the life inherent in the coming to be and passing away of the finite."

that of Absolute Spirit (Theunissen 1970), and implicitly, almost
shamefacedly, at less exalted levels, at any rate in the social philosophy (Objective Spirit), for it is clear that Hegel's State, as holistic,
encompasses in our sense of the term civil society and its individualism. We cannot here enlarge on those aspects and must be content
with stating that hierarchy, although implicitly present at first, has
been somewhat forcibly expelled from the core of Hegel's philosophy—an event of tremendous impact if one thinks of his posterity.
Everything looks as if Hegel had sensed the incongruity that we
detected in Fichte's *Contributions* and had eliminated it. With
Hegel, the equalitarian value has grown more ambitious and exclusive. The acculturation to the French Revolution has gone one wide
step deeper, so to speak. To highlight this point was the intention of
this brief Hegelian excursus.

Let us return to Fichte. We saw that, from the *Contributions* of 1793
to the *Addresses* of 1807–8, including the transcendental fulcrum of
the *Wissenschaftslehre*, a hierarchical component is found in Fichte.
We are now in a position to answer the question we asked earlier
about the *Addresses*. What Fichte has added to the universalistic
individualism of the French Revolution, aside from occasional borrowings from the romantics, is precisely this deep hierarchical
perception. It is no wonder that for Fichte, one particular people,
opposed to other peoples as the self is opposed to the non-self,
embodies humanity at a particular time. It embodies, that is, the
human self as a whole. Thus Fichte may at this point join the
predominant current of German thought, and the romantics in
particular.

At this juncture, it is apposite that we should try to see more
precisely the relation between Fichte's thought and the German
ideological pattern in general. There is a powerful holistic trend in
German ideology at large, and in conjunction with it we may, I
think, admit that—as is commonly held by foreigners, and not by
them alone—the German people as a whole were, in our period and
beyond it, strongly inclined to obey the powers that be. Admittedly,
this is a stereotype, but for the present purpose we shall take the
statement as true in comparison with other western European
peoples and the French in particular. In agreement with this general
background, the great majority of German intellectuals admitted
the necessity of subordination in society. Thus, according to Kant,
man is an animal that, in society, needs a master. Now what is true

within society is true, *mutatis mutandis*, outside it, and given a plurality of nations it was only natural, from such a point of view, to believe that some should dominate others. Combined with the ethnocentricism that is found universally—the valuation of "us" as against "others," strangers—we have here the social basis of what has been called "pan-Germanism."

In this environment there were few champions of equalitarianism among thinkers of influence, but the few that existed were determined. Herder and Fichte, both of lowly origin and in their youth dependent on the affluent, hated the domination of man over man. It is remarkable that they were nevertheless able to think in hierarchical terms, for it means that they spontaneously disentangled hierarchy—essentially a matter of values—from political (and economic) power. The two are widely confused, as we know only too well. On this point the contrast with Rousseau, whose insertion in society was very similar but whose social milieu was different, seems decisive. That the thought of the staunchly equalitarian Fichte was as essentially hierarchical as we have shown is thus an index of the strength of the holistic component in German culture.

We can now see clearly how insufficient it is to consider Fichte either as a faithful follower of the French Revolution, only secondarily endowed with German characteristics, or as a precursor of pan-Germanism unable to rid himself completely of the abstract universalism of the French. Extending the use of the word *translation* from the linguistic to the cultural domain, one may say that Fichte translated the French Revolution into German. A convinced equalitarian, he did not admit of subordination in society as grounded in the nature of man; but at the same time he maintained a strong sense of hierarchy—indeed, he was able to give hierarchy a philosophical form, albeit indirectly. Moreover, as Herder did before him, he applied modern individualism on a collective level, making a people or a nation into an individual of a superior order, and again as Herder he saw humanity as embodying itself in modern times in the Germanic culture-people, or the German nation.

Perhaps a little more can be said here about hierarchy and German ideology. If there is any truth in the stereotype that represents the German people—in contrast, for instance, to the French in the same period—as having a propensity to obey, if it is true that in German thought, again in contrast to others, the necessity of subordination in society is more often admitted than denied, then we would expect some of the great German philosophers who have dealt at least occasionally with the problems of society to have searched for the values that might justify subordination, and, just as I have been led to do by the exemplary Indian case, to have explicitly isolated hierarchy as distinct from, if combined with, power. This is not the case. At any rate, the whole of German idealist social philosophy can be, and has often been, surveyed without any mention of hierarchy proper. How can this fact be understood? A first answer is obvious: as we have seen with Hegel, those philosophers worked under the spell of the French Revolution,[18] and they were more oriented toward the powerful contemporary individualist and equalitarian trend than toward the plain elucidation of their own social makeup. But our question is wrongly put; witness the hitherto unsuspected but glaring presence of the hierarchical form of thought at the core of Fichte's philosophizing. True, Fichte does not directly name what I called the hierarchical opposition, but he does spontaneously set it to work and, thus, virtually operates the distinction between hierarchy and power. Yet the point is not acknowledged, not "thematized." And we can well fancy why not. Fichte's equalitarianism was limited to the refusal of subordination in society; it did not prevent him— perhaps it did not *yet* prevent him—from hierarchizing ideas, but for this to be possible the two domains had to remain separate. In other words, Fichte could not possibly recognize the encompassing form of thought as hierarchy, that is, as something that, although distinct in principle, is nevertheless present in combination—lawfully even if not factually—in social subordination. Fichte's achievement in this regard is remarkable when compared with the young Hegel's confusing under the category of "domination" (*Herrschen*) despotic power, the transcendence of God among the ancient Jews, and the transcendence of the Kantian imperative.[19] Fichte may have reached the limit which no human mind could transcend under the circumstances, that is, at a time when an all-powerful equalitarian ideal inspired minds like his.

Here is perhaps a fateful turn of history. Let us allow ourselves a wishful reconstruction: let us suppose that Fichte or some other thinker had crossed the limit and clearly distinguished hierarchy

18. For the role played here by the Lutheran background, see the next chapter.

19. Hegel 1907, *passim*. Most characteristic is the passage on pp. 265–66 (trans. p. 211).

from power, and that this acquisition had, in time, slowly permeated the common German consciousness. The German people, predisposed as it was to accept subordination, would then have learned to distinguish between factual power and its legitimacy with reference to values, and the Germans could have avoided plunging into the outrageous and apocalyptic masquerade that we have lived through and that has left its scar on them as well as on us.

One significant point has still to be elucidated. We encountered in embryo what was later to become pan-Germanism. The fact must be understood comparatively, in order to dissipate what looks strange or aberrant about it. Let us come back to the ideology of the nation. In a comparative perspective centered on the ideological aspect, the nation—as found, say, in western Europe in the nineteenth century—is the sociopolitical group corresponding to the ideology of the Individual.[20] It is thus two things in one: a collection of individuals and, at the same time, a collective individual, an individual on the level of groups, facing other nations-individuals. On the face of it, the two aspects should be hard to combine, and the point is confirmed by a comparison of the French and German subcultures.

If we consider the two *predominating* ideologies in each country, we may characterize them as follows. On the French side, I am a man by nature and a Frenchman by accident. As in the philosophy of the Enlightenment in general, the nation as such has no ontological status: on that level, there is nothing but a void between the individual and the species, and the nation is simply the largest empirical approximation to mankind to which I have access in actual life. If you tell me this is not true but merely an abstraction of the mind, I'll ask you to seriously consider the lines of forces of political life in France, or the evolution of French public opinion around the two world wars. This being so, the nation as a collective individual—in particular, acknowledging other nations as different from the French—is very weak at the level of global ideology. The same is true of the antagonism between nations: the French liberals, as the Revolutionaries before them, seem to have thought that constituting European and other peoples into nations would be

20. See "Nationalism and communalism," *HH*. App. D. What follows is taken from Dumont 1971a: 33–35.

enough to solve all problems and ensure peace. In the last analysis, they conceived the nation only as the framework for the emancipation of the Individual, the latter being the alpha and the omega of all political problems.

On the German side, we shall take the ideology at the level of the great authors, but I see no reason to suppose disagreement on this point between them and the common people. Here I am essentially a German, and I am a man through my being a German: man is immediately acknowledged as a social being. Subordination is generally recognized as normal, necessary, in society. the need for the emancipation of the individual is less strongly felt than the need for a supporting environment and for communion. Thus the first aspect of the nation—a collection of individuals—is weak. On the other hand, the second aspect—the nation as a collective individual—is very strong. Therefore, while the French were content with juxtaposing nations as so many fragments of mankind, the Germans, acknowledging the individuality of each nation, were preoccupied with *ordering* the nations within mankind in relation to their value—or to their might. We observe that the old ethnocentricism or sociocentricism which exalts *us* and disparages *others* did survive in the modern era, but in two different ways: the Germans saw themselves, and tried to impose themselves, as superior *qua* Germans, while the French consciously postulated only the superiority of the universalist culture, but identified with it so naively that they looked on themselves as the educators of mankind.[21]

In the final count, and beyond their apparent contrast, the universalism of one group and the pan-Germanism of the other served a similar function. Both expressed an antinomy internal to the nation as being both a collection of individuals and a collective individual, that is to say both translated into tangible fact the difficulty of getting a tolerable image of social life (intra- and intersocial life) in terms of modern ideology. The difference is found again in the respective shortcomings. The issue lies beyond our purview, but a general impression may perhaps be given. On the one hand, everything looks as if French ideology had managed

---

21. As the Publisher Bernard Grasset did in 1930 in a letter he postfaced to a translation of a book by Friedrich Sieburg, *Dieu est-il français?* (Sieburg 1930: 330, 335, 340, 342, 346).

to remain pure and poor, unsullied by any contact or compromise with the actual, through two centuries of trials and ordeals. On the other hand, German ideology, born of acculturation, having amalgamated traditional and modern features, was relatively rich and open, but it was liable to lead to grievous error, as the amalgam was too easily taken for a genuine synthesis.

5   A National Variant, II

The German Idea of Liberty According to Troeltsch

In a 1916 text reprinted in 1925,[1] Ernst Troeltsch clearly defined and explained the German idea of liberty as contrasted with the English and the French, both similar yet a little different. If a definition is called for, Troeltsch says toward the end of the study, it will be

> an organized unity of the people based on a rigorous and at the same time critical devotion of the individual to the whole, which is completed and legitimized by the independence and individuality of the free spiritual culture [*Bildung*] (Troeltsch 1925*b*: 103).

And, if a slogan is needed, with all the risks it suggests: "*state socialism and culture individualism* [*Bildungsindividualismus*]" (ibid.).

This is a definition of central importance to us. Moreover, Troeltsch develops it and comments on it throughout his article (especially pp. 94–107). In what follows we shall take up in detail

First published in French, *Le Débat* 35 (1985): 40–50.

1. "Die deutsche Idee von der Freiheit," *Neue Rundschau*, 1916-1, pp. 50–75. The page references are to Troeltsch 1925*b*: the collection *Deutscher Geist und Westeuropa* (Tübingen, 1925; repr. Aalen, 1966), pp. 80–107. I cite other articles from the same collection. These texts are naturally inseparable from the circumstances of the war during which they appeared. German intellectuals of the day were anxious to respond to the challenge of enemy propaganda, which was considered formidable, but one is struck by the seriousness they brought to the task and the interest that this wartime literature, including among others Troeltsch's essays, holds for our purpose.

each of the two elements of the formula and the relation between them. Unfortunately the long and complex sentences of Troeltsch are difficult to translate: limiting our citations to fragments of those sentences,[2] we will try to paraphrase the rest as accurately as possible.

The first point concerns devotion to the whole. "Germans have in their blood devotion to a thing, an idea, an institution, a superindividual entity [*Wesenheit*]" (ibid.: 96). And of course their "organizational strength," their "organizability," is more or less legendary. What we first see here is a form of holism in the sense that such an attitude or tendency supposes that the whole is valued at the expense of the individual. But Troeltsch, in the very sentence just quoted, immediately insists that this devotion is "mobile, lively, full of initiative, persevering, and ingenious." In other words, the subject subordinates himself spontaneously to the whole; he has no feeling of alienation in doing so, and therefore all his personal qualities are given free rein in the fulfillment of his role. We can thus understand how Troeltsch can speak of "liberty" or of "organic liberty" as when he writes: "The thought of organic liberty poured out into a harmonious and graduated cooperation of enterprises great and small, state-run or private" thanks to "the disciplined sense of the whole and the sentiment of honor in participating in the whole" (ibid.: 97).

This spontaneous adhesion to the social whole is exactly what Toennies called "spontaneous will" (*Naturwille*), for him the characteristic trait of the community or *Gemeinschaft* as opposed to the "arbitrary will" (*Kürwille*) of the individual subject in the society (*Gesellschaft*) (Toennies 1971). As for Troeltsch, he speaks of "liberty" because he wants to counter the enemy propaganda, which capitalizes on liberty or freedom as the monopoly of the Western democracies by showing that Germany has "its own sense of liberty, which is determined by German history and the German spirit" (94). It is illuminating for us to observe the seriousness and honesty with which Troeltsch as a scholar carries out what he conceives as a counterpropaganda job and what becomes in fact a kind of comparative exercise.

Here "the individuals do not compose the whole, they identify

2. There will be some examples below of the difficulties in translation. A literal translation is often useful for grasping a writer's thought without an intermediary, although it may be inelegant, or, occasionally, hardly correct English.

with it. Liberty is not equality but service by the individual at his place in the function allotted to him" (literally an organ position, *Organstellung*) (ibid.: 94), or again, and more completely: "The liberty of the German is willed discipline, advancement and development of one's own self in a whole and for a whole" (97).

Troeltsch knows very well, and he says so, that the French or English tradition—for brevity we shall call it Western, as he does—cannot see liberty in that formulation but only autocracy, slavery, etc. (97). He simply maintains that that is how liberty is according to Hegel, and how it is expressed, one way or another, "in all the great German creations of the century" (94), and in the Socialist party as well as in the army. Troeltsch traces the origin of this disposition back to the seventeenth century (95–96). It results from the transformation of Christian submission to the patriarchal-absolutist State under the influence of the Western spirit of Enlightenment. The State was modified, and "the submissive believer turned into the freely obedient and devoted citizen, who participates in the general will by fulfilling his duty in his place and freely exercising his criticism" (95). German liberty is thus a "secularization of the religious sense of duty and, in particular, its intensification into an activity of creation in common [*mitgestaltend*]" (96). Here we perceive a recognition of acculturation: we are dealing with a traditional holism that was modified or transformed under the influence of "the spirit of liberty and independence [*Mündigkeit*]" (95).[3]

At the same time the basic underlying assumption will be noticed: far from there being incompatibility between individual development and service to the social whole, it is "in and for the whole" that the individual develops. None of these ideas is exclusive to Troeltsch; all are widely encountered in other authors.

There is no unanimity, however, and here we must dare to pose a radical question: Is all of this genuine, or is it simply a construct of patriotic intellectuals, a representation influenced by the speculations of philosophers, doubtless reinforced by the circumstances of war, but little more than a nationalistic myth unmatched by any deep sentiment in the German people itself? There is no shortage of witnesses to support such an accusation. Under admittedly different circumstances, neither the young Hegel nor the young Marx recognized the existence of this fine unison of wills. On the con-

---

3. *Mündigkeit*, lit. "age of majority." This is how Kant designated the Enlightenment (cf. the booklet *Was ist Aufklärung?*).

trary, it was the search for such a union that launched them on their careers as innovators. Troeltsch was surely thinking primarily of 1914 and the extraordinary surge of enthusiasm aroused by the declaration of war.[4] But was he not stretching the notion to periods to which it applied less aptly? Could we not argue that the powerful prewar Social Democratic party was evidence of an alienation of the working class? Troeltsch answered this decisively when he applied the formula of German liberty to that party as well as to the army. Given what we know from history, we must admit that only a small minority was truly alienated.

It is also true that such an excellent Germanist as Robert Minder was able to consider those ideas of integral devotion to the community as ideal images formed in the minds of intellectuals, but I believe that on this point he has himself succumbed to an ideal representation—the representation a Frenchman holds of the "real" society (the *Gesellschaft* of Toennies)—and that he has dangerously separated German literature from German life. Certainly Troeltsch's view represents a stereotype held as much by Germans themselves as by foreigners. In our view, however, this stereotype corresponds sufficiently to experience; Troeltsch broadly spoke the truth; and "society" is, or rather was, not exactly the same thing in France and in Germany. The difference is perhaps only a matter of the predominance of one or the other pattern (community or society), but this predominance is precisely what matters.

Incidentally, we might see here a reason for the weakness of the Weimar Republic: because of its democratic formula itself, the republic was unable to arouse the "identification with the whole" that Troeltsch stressed, and could thus be perceived as a foreign importation.

Let us return to Troeltsch. Devotion to the State, which makes a supersensible reality of it, has individualism, personal liberty, as its necessary complement, an indispensable counterweight (99). Given the narrowness of political conditions in Germany, the liber-

---

4. Cf. the article by Troeltsch himself, entitled after Plenge and Kjellen, "*Die Ideen von 1914*" (The Ideas of 1914): entry into the war created a "spiritual revolution," "the return of the nation to belief in Idea and Spirit" (1925b: 33, 37). In his memoirs Meinecke mentions the unforgettable burst of enthusiasm as one of the peaks of his life (quoted in Stern 1965: 256–57, together with Thomas Mann and Adolf Hitler).

ation of the spirit took place "essentially within the soul" (in the form of) "personal liberty, vivacity and profundity of thought, imagination (*Phantasie*) and poetry" (98). It is a perfect independence and inner liberty, which gave life first and foremost to *Selbstbildung*, that is, self-construction, self-education, or cultivation. This personal cultivation had to appropriate and elaborate Western culture and the cultural heritage of Europe, and at least for a time found a support and a yardstick in antiquity (98). That culture is broadly human or cosmopolitan, but, comparing it with that of England and France, one perceives that German humanism is basically an enrichment of German inner life in the image of the spiritual liberty of antiquity, a spiritual liberation and deepening of the people itself (98–99).

We have here what might be called German individualism, characterized by two very marked traits: on the one hand the closing up of the self vis-à-vis the external world, and on the other the activity of construction or education of the self, the famous *Bildung*, which is more or less identical with culture. Such a pattern is quite foreign to traditional holism, of course, and such a deepening of the world of interiority cannot simply result from an adaptation or internalization of the ideas of the Enlightenment or the French Revolution along the lines of presumed Germanic characteristics, as Troeltsch seems to be saying in this text when taken by itself. In fact, it is impossible not to think of Luther, and we will come back to this.[5] Let us light for a moment on what at first sight appears to be a deep separation between externality and internal-

---

5. German characteristics are not specified in our text, but in the same collection, and dealing precisely with education (*Bildung*), Troeltsch accepts Richard Benz's view that "the essential thing about Gothic man is the infinity and depth of his imagination" (*Phantasie*) (Troeltsch 1925b: 229). The relatively restricted view Troeltsch proposed here is surprising when contrasted with the fullness of his considerations of Protestantism and its developments, including Pietism, or when contrasted with his preoccupation with relations between "Protestantism and the modern spirit" (the title of one of his studies). According to the texts I have read, it seems that the discord can be explained thus: Troeltsch in general is interested in the whole movement of ideas—an internatinal set of ideas—except where he specifies national contexts secondarily; in contrast, the 1914–18 war led him or forced him to focus on what was specifically German as opposed to "Western" ideology, and in this matter he left unexpressed the broader context, the historical underpinnings, up to about 1750. However, the idea that Luther is the prototype of the *Bildung* man bursts upon us if we go back to what was said about him in the *Soziallehren*, for example (Troeltsch 1922, English trans., pp. 540–609).

ity, but is in fact a very peculiar relation between them. True, the individual is here folded back on himself; yet at the same time he knows he is, and wants to be, a German; his inwardness rests on his belonging and is actually a part of it: in this sense, this purely internal individualism leaves the surrounding holism standing. The German intellectual also turns away from external conditions but on another level, the level of what we are accustomed to call sociopolitical questions. This is seen in the contrast between German and French fiction in the nineteenth century, rightly emphasized by Robert Minder.[6] The matter immediately gets cleared up if we make use of Toennies's categories: paradoxically enough, the individualism of *Bildung* is located on the level of community (*Gemeinschaft*), which is union, cultural belonging, and has nothing to do with the level of society (*Gesellschaft*), which is division, the struggle of particular interests.

The reader unfamiliar with German culture may well feel that we are exaggerating wantonly. Let us therefore take a spectacular though by no means aberrant example. In 1918, Thomas Mann published his *Reflections of a Nonpolitical Man* (Mann 1922), in which, while identifying himself with Germany at war, he proclaimed his belief that it would have been contrary to his vocation as a German writer to interest himself in politics.

Here is a superb passage from Mann, extracted from a lecture he gave to a group of students in 1923, after his conversion to the Weimar Republic, in which he presents from the outside what had been his own attitude and sentiment some years before when he wrote the *Reflections*. We borrow the translation from W. H. Bruford, who deservedly printed the passage on the first page of his book *The German Tradition of Self-Cultivation* (Bruford 1975).

The finest characteristic of the typical German, the best-known and also the most flattering to his self-esteem, is his inwardness. It is no accident that it was the Germans who gave to the world the intellectually stimulating and very humane literary form which we call the novel of personal cultivation and development. Western Europe has its novel of social criticism to which the Germans regard this other type as their own special counterpart; it is at the same time an autobiography, a confession. The inwardness, the culture (*Bildung*) of a German implies

6. Minder 1962: 5–43.

introspectiveness; an individualistic cultural conscience, consideration for the careful tending, the shaping, deepening and perfecting of one's own personality or, in religious terms, for the salvation and justification of one's own life; subjectivism in the things of the mind, therefore, a type of culture that might be called pietistic, given to autobiographical confession and deeply personal, one in which the world of the *objective*, the political world, is felt to be profane and is thrust aside with indifference, "because," as Luther says, "this external order is of no consequence." What I mean by all this is that the idea of a republic meets with resistance in Germany chiefly because the ordinary middle-class man here, if he ever thought about culture, never considered politics to be part of it, and still does not do so today. To ask him to transfer his allegiance from inwardness to the objective, to politics, to what the peoples of Europe call *freedom*, would seem to him to amount to a demand that he should do violence to his own nature, and in fact give up his sense of national identity.

In a comparative sense, to sum up, there would appear to be two modes or formulas of belonging. One, essentially cultural, holistic, traditional even when modified or somewhat transformed by modern influences, is the German formula, both on the level of that devotion to the whole of which Troeltsch spoke and on the level of the individualistic subject and his vocation of *Bildung*. In the other mode, which is modern, universalistic in the French Revolutionary sense, the nation-state is defined not by concrete belonging but by its conformity or faithfulness to the ideal of equality and liberty of individuals; one adheres to the group as a citizen, the act of belonging operates on the sociopolitical level: one is a man by nature, and a Frenchman empirically, as if by accident, while on the other side a person thinks himself a man to the extent that he is first a German.[7]

Having clarified this point, let us now get back to German individualism as being essentially inward and keeping its distance from the external world—a clear-cut and at first sight strange break between the inner life and society. It is impossible not to see a

---

7. On the subject of education in Germany, Troeltsch cites and underlines C. Burdach: "But we are men and we feel ourselves to be men uniquely in the nature of our particular hereditary essence, and only because we feel it to be inalienable (imprescriptible?) and legitimate" (1925*b*: 225).

descendant of Luther in the *Bildung* intellectual. Not necessarily a follower—he may even be an atheist—but a descendant. Actually it is only in Luther that we can understand this dichotomy, which would appear incomprehensible if we looked at it, for example, from a medieval viewpoint. As against the Catholic Church of his day, and the scholastics whose thought nurtured his own, Luther appears as someone who has gone back to origins and defines himself, in the manner of the early Christians, as an outworldly individual[8]—or almost so. He reintroduced a gap—we might say a chasm—between the Christian's relation to God on the one hand, and to the world of social reality and of relationships between men on the other. Faith, and grace, that is, the relationship with God, are of the essence. Once this relationship is assured, it expresses itself quite naturally though secondarily in the form of love for one's fellows, and gives value to the Christian's works. The subordination of the world and the State to inner life is strongly stressed in Luther, quite explicitly and still more so perhaps implicitly from the fact that he suppressed the extraordinary power of reconciliation of the great mediator between the two, the Church. As for political institutions, they were no doubt necessary, and Luther boasted that he had exalted them more than anyone else and had prescribed obedience to the established powers, whether good or bad. But what scorn for the wielders of power! Whether Christian or not, they are nothing but rabble, and a good prince is a rare bird indeed.[9]

In more ways than one, Luther is the prototype of the German intellectual. He is so in particular as a writer, in his basic contribution to the development of the German language, but also as the *representative* of the German people in relation to the Catholic Church and hence on the world scene, as witnessed by his popularity, which means that to a great extent the Germans recognized themselves in him. This function of representative or *mediator* between the German people and the "Western" or universal culture passed on to the German writer and thinker. Troeltsch indicates or implies this, and others have noticed it, even Lukács. It comes out clearly from Thomas Mann's analysis in his war book (Mann 1922: 34–73), and the role is essential. If we are to understand it, we must reflect that in a period when there is no political but only cultural unity, the function of representative devolving

8. See the Glossary, under "Inworldly individual/outworldly individual."
9. Plass, 1959, respectively nos. 1745 ff.; 868, 1796 etc.

elsewhere upon a head of state or an ambassador quite naturally falls on a Goethe, a Hegel, or perhaps a Beethoven. Besides, the German themselves are well aware of this when, as so often, they tell us that Germans have achieved in ideas what others have accomplished on the world scene. And so did Marx. We cannot understand German literature and thought if we neglect this role of representative or mediator in the German intellectual at the height of his renown.[10]

Not only does Luther provide us with the archetype of the *Bildung* individualist, but, what is more, the historical transition from the one to the other is richly documented. As Thomas Mann subtly indicated in the passage quoted above, that transition is found primarily in Pietism, which on the one hand has spread and democratized what had remained exceptional in Luther's day—the study of the Bible—and on the other, through a complex interaction with the Enlightenment especially from 1750 onward, has assured the passage from Lutheran inwardness to aesthetics, to patriotism, to romanticism. An abundant recent literature shows that Pietism is found everywhere at the roots of the literary and philosophical movement near the end of the eighteenth century.[11]

10. It is surprising that such an eminent Germanist as Robert Minder, in his comparison of French and German literature (Minder 1962: 5–43), should have failed to appreciate this double relationship of the German intellectual: Minder sees him as being in touch exclusively with his own culture, his own people, and paints a dramatic picture of his isolation. For a start, isolation is the natural lot of the artist in our societies; it is even connected to his representativeness. It is not isolation but recognition, wherever it occurs, that might need explanation. Now in the German case representativeness has two faces to it; or, if you prefer, it is from the nature of its circumstances more two-faced than elsewhere; and without wishing to explain the pitiable funerals of Schiller or Mozart by this point, we can see in it the source of a further distancing of the artist or intellectual from his people. There is something similar about the thinkers' choice of problems. We have found (chap. 4, above) that the development of thought in Fichte and Hegel had been magnetized by the French Revolution, and we have regretted that they did not thematize hierarchy, an idea that would have imposed itself if it had been a matter of the German people alone: there too mediation was foremost: the deeper concern was to articulate one's own culture and contemporary events expressive of another culture (or rather of another variant of the same culture). At the romantic extreme, this same situation resounds in the vogue for *Gegensatz*, contrast or antithesis (notably in politics with Adam Müller).

11. For aesthetics, see for example my article on Moritz (Dumont 1982); on the political plane, Pinson 1934, Kaiser 1973. But pietistic roots can be seen everywhere, as evidenced in a symbolic fact: in what has remained the *Bildungsroman* par

We have now commented separately on the two complementary aspects of German liberty according to Troeltsch, free dedication of self to the whole and *Bildung* individualism. It remains to consider the relation between them. It should be clear by now that the two factors are less discrepant than it may have seemed at first glance, since the German individualist is no stranger to the holism underlying devotion to the State. Viewed from without, individualism lies within this self-dedication; viewed from inside, it very clearly subordinates concrete external circumstances, to the point of despising them, just as Luther's faith subordinated worldly kingdoms.

Troeltsch insists that the two tendencies he has isolated must remain united. To dissociate them would be fatal, leading either to enslavement to the State or to a sort of ethereal individuality (99). He states that the link between the two ideals is felt, and he makes no bones of the tension between them: German liberty is no more immune than its Western counterparts to degeneracy or to excesses: any idea of liberty has its internal contradictions. Yet German thought tends particularly to reconcile or smooth out (*Ausgleichen*) the two conjoint ideals—in truth, and not by superficial compromises.

We will direct two criticisms at Troeltsch. To begin with, he does not ask himself in this text about the nature of the combination he is insisting on (but only about the nature of the two factors). One has the feeling that, as so often with Germans, he is satisfied to end with an antithesis, that the contrariness he has revealed makes him feel that he has reached the actuality of life. Yet some questions arise. Has not German thought itself actually tried to rid itself of that contradiction, or to suppress it? In the course of the preceding argument, the reader may have evoked the classical period, Goethe and Schiller, and asked whether they had not striven toward a universalism without boundaries, beyond any (conscious) German specificity. It cannot be denied that *Bildung*, including its disaffection for contemporary society, then had pride of place. It was in the very process of being born, in the sense of going through its last metamorphosis.

It is noteworthy that Troeltsch's definition uses the word *liberty* in both the senses that are most often opposed to each other: the

---

excellence, *The Years of Apprenceship of Wilhelm Meister*, Goethe introduced a portrait of a Pietist lady, composed from his youthful memories, which forms a long, rather detached chapter entitled "The Confession of a Beautiful Soul."

negative freedom of nonconstraint, independence of the subject; and liberty in its essentially German concept as consisting of the acknowledgment of necessity by a rational subject (here, belonging to the whole is felt as vital and therefore accepted willingly). Since this latter sense has sent us back to Toennies's *Naturwille*, we find ourselves asking whether the "acknowledgment of necessity" is not perhaps a form under which the holism of traditional culture is surreptitiously maintained. At the very least, there is an affinity or congruence between the two attitudes.

It turns out that the evolution of Hegel's thought from his youth to maturity provides a kind of parallel to our problem. Young Hegel was looking for a religion, we may say an ideological form, which would reconcile modern individualism with the fine harmony of community as found in the Greek *polis*. Later he came to construct a philosophy that produces this reconciliation by means of levels of reality, which it organizes hierarchically, ascending from subjective spirit to objective spirit (institutions), and from this to absolute spirit (religion, art, philosophy). The latter two levels broadly correspond to the two poles of Troeltsch's formulation. Still, Hegel knew very well that, as distinct from his youthful dream, this philosophy offered reconciliation only for the benefit of educated people, in other words within *Bildung*. There is something aristocratic, or elitist as we would say today, in the result, just as there is, after all, in Troeltsch's presentation: everything indicates that the common man must be content with self-dedication while individualistic culture will be the privilege of the few. Regarding the State, Troeltsch and Hegel are remarkably similar, but Hegel is more complete. With him, individualism is given free rein on the level of civil (or bourgeois) society—which is absent in Troeltsch, while at the higher level civil society and its individualism are encompassed in the holism of the State, with which the individual subject can do no better than identify himself, exactly as in Troeltsch. The question has sometimes been raised whether Hegel, in his *Philosophy of Right*, was guilty of adapting his theory to the Prussian State of the day; he would seem, rather, to have expressed what was going to be the German reality of the matter for a century. Will it be said that the Wilhelmian State, in contrast to the Hegelian, found a place for universal suffrage? It was only a superficial concession to modern democracy, which did not cut into the monarch's prerogatives, and in the final analysis the German State essentially stayed faithful to traditional holism, in conformity with the Hegelian thesis. Here it is worthwhile to contrast the German and the Western—or, let us say, French—formulas of liberty: on the one side is a spiritual liberty going back to Luther, which leaves the political *community* intact; on the other side, another liberty, which, though also of religious origin, through the Enlightenment and the Revolution extends into the political realm to the point of appearing to be centered on it, and transforms it into a political *society*. Schematically, Luther and the French Revolution provide two variant forms of liberty in the abstract sense of the term. To some extent they are two equivalent variants, since they have managed to impose themselves in lasting fashion in two neighboring countries at the same period and in similar economic circumstances.

Let me observe once more that this trait is recognized—or almost so, we may say implicitly recognized—by German writers themselves when they contrast German inwardness or German thought to the "historical" outwardness of other peoples. Yet they most often attribute the difference to political circumstances, if not to a metaphysical characteristic of the German people, and more rarely mention what we might call the schismatic introversion introduced by Luther and generalized by Pietism.

Making this parallel between the Reformation and the Revolution seems to be fundamental for a Franco-German comparison. Thomas Mann, reflecting studiously on what is specific about German culture in his *Reflections of a Nonpolitical Man*, comes back to the point several times (1922: 242, 257, 535–77). He states among other things:

> Out of the liberty and sovereignty of the Germans Luther made something accomplished by turning them inward and thus keeping them forever out of the sphere of political quarrels. Protestantism has deprived politics of its spiritual goad and has made it a practical matter (1922: 237).

Here, in the author's own language, is a deep insight supported by Hegel and Carlyle. "Hegel said that France would know no rest for lack of a Reformation" (ibid.: 242), and Carlyle saw in the Revolution a "bad substitute" for Reformation (535–37). It is worth trying to grasp the matter more firmly in our own language and to characterize the two contrasting forms of individualism. That of Luther is located on the religious plane. It is directed against the religious division of labor and against the hierarchy: all Christians become priests and retrieve from the Church the responsibility for their own salvation. There results an internalization and the subordination of everything else to the inner life of the Christian. Politics, especially, is subordinated, the State is subordinated, and by the same token it is accepted as life and power, with its division of labor: there are specialists in government because it is of no import.

In contrast, the French Revolution lines up its forces against the sociopolitical hierarchy, against the hereditary division of labor: in the name of the Individual all citizens are equal; each is simultaneously subject and sovereign. The *community* is dissolved and becomes a *society*; we might say that the State, the nation, loses its ontological reality, as the Church did in the other instance. Ontologically there is no longer anything between the individual and the human species, the concrete global society no longer exists, has no will to live, no will toward power. All this is ideologically denied and enjoys only a residual factual existence.

We must also note that the level on which this conquest of the individual occurs, the political level, subordinates the religious level, the inner life. In both cases, that is, *the level on which the individual is emancipated subordinates the others*. There is nothing new about this in the case of the Reformation, since there the absolute continues to subordinate the rest. But it *is* new in the case of the Revolution, for here the traditional level of the absolute, namely religion, becomes subordinated—a fact of huge significance, and yet one which goes more or less unperceived.

If this is so, can we go even further and say, with Thomas Mann, that "the experience of the Reformation *immunized* people [by itself alone] against Revolution" (1922: 535), it being understood that Mann had only the Lutheran Reformation in mind, in other words, Germany? This would be a hasty conclusion, making light of differences in the political constitution itself. Even if Lutheranism has had an effect on the political constitution of Germany, it is not entirely responsible for it. The crucial fact on the ideological level— hitherto not clearly singled out, it seems—is probably the emergence in the West of the modern type of sovereignty—*territorial sovereignty*—and its absence in Germany. We shall return to this.

It might be objected here that we have strayed from Troeltsch's thought by omitting from liberty the spontaneous self-dedication to the social and political whole that he wanted to be included in it. We omitted it because, as soon as we isolate the political plane, to call liberty Toennies's "spontaneous will" would be to introduce confusion by acknowledging "liberty" in any political regime that is spontaneously accepted by those subjected to it. In fact—and that is our second criticism—we can reproach Troeltsch for having left out of his discussion the nature of the State to which the Germans were spontaneously devoting themselves, especially in 1914. However useful his analysis is, it remains fragmentary from this angle. He has taken us as far as he could, it is for us to take up the baton.

Now the State in question is a pan-Germanist State. At that time the will to dominate others was an integral part of the German conception of the State. The fact may take us by surprise, but it is there, and contemporary writings by Troeltsch himself make it clear: they suppose or imply a State which at the least should play a part in world domination, a "world power" (*Weltmacht*): this is what was at stake in the war according to him.[12] Thomas Mann too is quite explicit on the point (1922: 179, 326–29).

Against the background of this vocation of domination of the German State, the German formula of liberty according to Troeltsch, "self-dedication + *Bildung*," assumes a new meaning. Not only does politics fall outside of education and culture,[13] so that the State is left to itself and accepted in whatever form it wishes to take, but self-dedication is directed to an entity that is destined to dominate non-Germans. The political domain, finding itself here protected institutionally from the individualistic critique which has elsewhere dismantled the absolute monarchy, shelters traditions and survivals. I once wrote that traditional ethnocentrism or, better, sociocentrism survived in the modern era under different guises: universalism, naive or mystifying, on the French side, pan-Germanism, forthright or brutal, on the German side (see the end

12. In the "Ideas of 1914" we read, "It was a matter of power and life" (Troeltsch 1925*b*: 31); and at the end of this text the construction of a Central European bloc is mentioned (ibid.: 52–53). In 1919 Troeltsch wrote: "Today the Reich (of Bismarck) has toppled over, and all that remains for us is the spirit and the work" (1925*b*: 210). As if the nation were no longer herself, once deprived of her dimension of domination!

13. In contemporary articles brought together in the same collection, Troeltsch is quite categorical in the matter of primary education: "Education has nothing to do with intensification of national feeling or with the awakening of political awareness" (1925*b*: 177); and similarly for secondary education (ibid.: 220–21). Here, though contrary opinion and even practice exist, Troeltsch maintains that the school must restrict itself to the spiritual, inner development of the free man, and asks only that a German humanism—however difficult to pinpoint—should supersede the exclusively classical humanism that has held sway up to this time.

of chapter 4 above), but perhaps in this latter case there is one more survival. In the course of centuries—and Troeltsch alluded to this— the German State also had been transformed, or rather had adapted itself to modern conditions. The Holy Roman–Germanic Empire was finally succeeded by the Prussian State, and then the German State. And everything looks as if the faithful subjects, comforted to see it always referred to by the same term, *Reich* or Empire, had noticed no change and had continued to give to the latter State the sort of allegiance that the former had received in the name of universal sovereignty.

As with everything touching on the political constitution of Germany in the broadest sense of the term, things are obscured in the current accounts of historians because of their underestimation of ideology in general and, in this case, their neglect of the ideological aspect of sovereignty. Such is, at least, the provisional conclusion I have reached. The point is very important for comparison, it demands an ample discussion, but for the moment it can only be briefly mentioned. We are told constantly about the political fragmentation of Germany, which was provoked or aggravated by the Lutheran Reformation, the treaties of Westphalia, etc. The *material fact* is obvious, but its interpretation calls for caution. Very generally we are told that Germany passed in this way to a territorial political organization, and it is implied—not explicitly stated— that Germany thus achieved the same transition from universal sovereignty to territorial sovereignty that France and England had gone through. Now this is to forget the fact that this transition represents a radical transformation including an essential ideological aspect that is not found in the German case.[14] It is to forget the survival of the Empire. No doubt it had become more and more powerless, but on the *ideological level* it was in no way replaced by the particular territorial identity. Political Germany led a quartered existence between territorial belonging as a fact and universal sovereignty as a principle right down to the battle of Sadowa (1866). In my view, we have here a major fact that has hitherto been concealed by the overestimation of material aspects and the neglect

14. It should be recalled here that according to Sir Henry Sumner Maine there are only two types of primitive or traditional sovereignty—tribal and universal sovereignty. The third type, territorial sovereignty, is a modern innovation (Maine 1887: 103 ff.). This distinction is a fundamental one, and territoriality in this sense is quite obviously a major characteristic of modern ideology (Dumont 1980, App. D, sec. 3).

of the ideological dimension, together with insufficient comparison with the Western neighbors. It follows that Germany, once unified by Prussia, was Janus-headed: on the international level it was a national or territorial State among others, while at the level of internal representation it was a resurgence of universal sovereignty. Such is perhaps the deepest explanation for the will to dominate inherent in this "Empire" or, in other words, for pan-Germanism as a concomitant of the German idea of liberty as defined by Troeltsch in 1916.

6 The Totalitarian Disease

Individualism and Racism
in Adolf Hitler's Representations

It is essential that the comparative perspective presented in this book should show what it can contribute to the decipherment of the most awesome enigmas of our time, when men have wanted to take their fate in their own hands and have actually ended, with respect to wars and totalitarianism, in unprecedented monstrosities that defy their understanding. Some years ago, noting the absence of a "thorough reflection" in that regard, I stated that our sinister Hitlerian experience had not yet been mastered in thought, thirty years after the event (*MM*, 11). Are we in a notably better position today, when the literature goes on accumulating in unheard-of proportions, which is perhaps a sign that the question is felt to be important? In my view, major shifts in viewpoints are called for, and they are missing.

We propose here precisely some requisites for a renewal of viewpoints. An unpublished study of fifteen years ago has been taken up again,[1] in the light of the advances made in-between in the general ideological study and most particularly that of Germany, which added cogency to the analysis and allowed to round off the general picture. It would certainly have been better if the publication of the research on German ideoogy could have been more complete and its conclusions established on a wider basis before their being taken up, as they are here, as explanatory factors.

---

1. I was unable to really master the immense literature that has appeared in the meantime. So far as I could see, however, this literature does not put in question what should be our concern here, and the original part of the former study remains unaffected.

Instead, the two preceding monographs (chap. 4 and 5) will have, in their condensed manner, introduced the main points.[2]

The following falls into two parts: a general discussion is followed by a brief analysis of the fundamental representations of Adolf Hitler seen from the main text that we have from him, his book *Mein Kampf*.

Too much has been done using historical continuity as an explanation. The continuance of anti-Semitism since the Middle Ages no more explains the sinister invention of extermination than an undeniable continuity in German ideology explains the catastrophic episode of the Nazi degeneration. Aside from French interpreters, who have a feeling for this ideological continuity (but to feel is one thing and to reason is another), there has been a tendency either to link Hitlerism directly to German romanticism or to reject everything in German culture that diverged from the straight line of the Enlightenment and its claimed extension in Marxism as "irrational" and as automatically paving the way for National Socialism.[3] These are partisan and mutilating views, which in the last analysis show an inability to understand not just the Nazi phenomenon but German ideology itself and its necessity as a national variant of modern ideology.

The first corrective that must be applied is to acknowledge that National Socialism is a modern phenomenon, a disease, no doubt, but a disease of our own world—and not simply an aberration of a group of fanatics, the effect of various historical causes, or the going astray of an entire nation.[4] Right from the start, as Nolte (1963) has recalled, Nazism defined itself in relation to the socialist-communist movement, which it opposed. In *Mein Kampf*, Hitler explained very clearly that he designed his movement as a sort of antithetical

2. The French edition of this book did not include the present fifth chapter. The beginning of the present essay has therefore been recast and a few points made more precise.

3. Cf. for instance Lovejoy 1941 (and the pointed critique of Spitzer 1944); Lukács, 1955.

4. From this point of view, one welcomes general expressions that record the existence of similar movements in other countries, such as "fascism," much in use in the period itself and later as in Ernst Nolte, *Der Faschismus in seiner Epoche: Die Action Française, der Italienische Faschismus, der Nationalsozialismus* (1963), and "totalitarianism," which has the advantage of a wider connotation—even if the definitions are difficult. Cf. Friedrich, Curtis, and Barber 1969; Turner 1975.

copy of the Marxist and Bolshevik movement, replacing, among other things, the class struggle by a race struggle. We are here confronted with an international process. What strikes one as a modern trait in the broadest sense is a historical chain of successive outbiddings or, I would say, a kind of hubris of the will. Marx inherits the titanic speculation of the German philosophers (Dumont 1977: 117) and intensifies it: instead of interpreting the world, he is going to change it by means of an alliance between philosophy and the proletariat. Hence the "professional revolution-ary," Lenin, who goes one step farther: Russian populism has proclaimed the possibility of the Russian people's overtaking bourgeois Western civilization, which leads Lenin to the idea that the small group of conspirators who call themselves the Bolshevik party will be able to skip the capitalist stage of economic develop-ment altogether and lead Russia directly from Tsarism to Socialism (Dumont 1985a). Along comes Hitler, who rejects the Bolsheviks' ideology but picks up the instrument of power they have forged and combines their party model with a quite different ideology. What is increasing here from stage to stage is the ambition of a few men to impose their will upon history, and their actual power to manipulate people. It begins in the shadow of ambitious theories, in the shelter of widely humanitarian aims. Shedding by stages all constraint, it ends in the service of the will to power of a group or a man. In national terms we distinguish a notable Russian contribution and a still more important German contribution, both at the initial and at the final point.

Hence we return, willy-nilly, to German ideology. What is essential to understand here is that in German ideology one is never really dealing basically with Germany itself, but always with Ger-many-in-relation-to-the-rest-of-the-world. This is as true for Hitler himself as it was true of Herder at the beginning of the modern notion of *Volk* (on the latter, see chap. 4 above). It is rather strange that from any other point of view, political or economic, for in-stance, we certainly think of Germany in relation to the surround-ing world, while from the cultural point of view we isolate it as though its culture were not also in a living relationship with its environment. Here is the source of a curious lack of comprehen-sion. We have long *known* a great deal, maybe we know all we need to, and yet we do not *understand* the thing as a whole. To look closely at the matter, it is precisely the relation between Germany and its surroundings in the first place that determines the global form and historical development of German culture; the very originality of German ideology cannot be divorced from it.

The two preceding chapters will have thrown some light on the phenomenon. We shall here make use of their conclusions and attempt to complete the picture. German ideology suffered a trauma and entered a deep crisis around 1918. Until then, as a result of the labors and successes of the great writers of the period 1770–1830, it harbored both the traditional notion of man as a social being and the modern idea of man as an individual. Comparatively we may say that it embodied a claim to have transcended the contradiction between the two, to have produced a synthesis of them. But what was the real bearing of that synthesis? On which plane of social reality should it be read? Clearly not on that of the social and political history of Germany in the nineteenth century. For here the contradiction was not overcome: Germany was not unified by the National Assembly at Frankfurt in 1848–49 but ultimately by the king of Prussia, or his chancellor, "through blood and iron." German authors tell us again and again that what other peoples have lived through more or less successfully on the stage of history, the Germans have accomplished in thought. In other words, the contradiction was surmounted only in principle, on the ideological plane, in the sense that Germany (in the thought of its intellectuals) had both integrated itself into the contemporary world and by the same stroke defined itself as a unity. No wonder, then, that the intellectuals took on national importance in their own eyes. As we said above, these people were mediators between German culture and the external world. The great ones in particular were very much on the level of culture what a chief of State or an ambassador is at the political level: *representatives* of their country.

While Germany had thus come of age as a cultural community, by adapting to the ideas of the French Revolution and successfully answering its challenge in its own estimation, it reached a new, chronologically modern, political constitution by a detached, purely political process. Political unification was an empirical adaptation to contemporary conditions realized in the main by the skillful determination of the Prussian government. It is essential to bear in mind the distinctness and independence of the two processes and of the two domains, the cultural and the political. As an instance, we found it reflected in the German idea of freedom according to Troeltsch.

This being so, the major question for us may concern the

articulation or interface between the cultural configuration and the political domain. There must have been a degree of empirical congruence between German culture and the German State, although they had evolved in a largely independent manner. For explicit features, we have to look at ideology. The two preceding chapters of this book have revealed two major aspects of ideology that are relevant regarding its articulation with the political domain. We found, first, that the introverted individualism of the Lutheran Reformation had allowed the Germans to resist the extraverted individualism of the French Revolution and, second, that they had remained adepts of a primitive type of sovereignty, namely universal sovereignty. The first feature accounts for the sharp separation between culture and politics and, incidentally, for Thomas Mann's suspicion of social-political questions. The second feature explains how the Prusso-German State found support for its aggressive foreign policy among German intellectuals, as if pan-Germanism was the only—or the main—attribute of the State that German culture accepted as genuine, in other words the only—or the main—positive link between German culture and the German State. The fact may seem unlikely, or even incredible, and I cannot document it here as it would deserve; yet it is a fundamental fact, which helps us understand what a deep trauma German ideology suffered with the defeat of 1918: for many intellectuals, at any rate, suppressing the German State's vocation of foreign domination was almost tantamount to destroying that State.

Otherwise, the ideology of German individualism, with its ideal of *Bildung* or self-cultivation and of freedom in the German sense as expounded by Troeltsch—i.e. freedom in community, that combination of individualism and holism in which either principle took precedence according to the situation at hand—seems to have been remarkably stable in the nineteenth and the early twentieth centuries. Yet in another sense it was a precarious balance, which could and perhaps had to be threatened by the dynamics of individualism. For instance, there appeared as early as 1810–15 a curious figure, "Pater" Jahn, a patriot who created gymnastics societies, invented a national Old German costume and spread nationalist agitation in the universities. Jahn, a sort of fiercely anti-French German Jacobin who in many ways prefigures the Nazi type, differs mainly from his more distinguished contemporaries as thoroughly equalitarian. Might not the technical and economic development itself, which went very fast in Germany from the middle of the century, have reinforced equalitarianism and individualism in general? What is most obvious is something different, a defensive reaction, a current of dissatisfaction in the face of the development of the bourgeoisie and of utilitarianism, which appeared among some intellectuals in the last quarter of the century—an intellectual movement that Fritz Stern (1965) has called "the politics of cultural despair," a kind of holistic protest again what was seen as a Westernization and de-naturing of Germany. Finally the defeat of 1918, felt to be unbearable, should have tilted such a delicate balance. In fact, the defeat was to transform the balance into a contradiction that Hitler among many others was to inherit.

This, then, is perhaps how we may conceive of a general ideological continuity, without making philosophers or romantics responsible for National Socialism and without breaking German culture in two. As Bracher put it, it is the whole cultural patrimony (*Bildungsgut*) of national consciousness that must be put in question if we want to understand how Germany advanced to catastrophé.[5]

Moreover, this ideological continuity was in large measure perceived at the time by the Germans themselves. Such, at least, is the impression one gets today when reading the articles in which German intellectuals expressed their views during and after the First World War. Perhaps the finest example is an essay by Karl Pribram, a German-language sociologist of Czechoslovakian birth. It was published in 1922 under the title "German Nationalism and German Socialism." The following translation of the first two paragraphs will, I hope, convey something of the striking effect of the original.[6]

1. *The reinterpretation (or "transformation of meaning,"* Umdeutung) *of socialism through the national idea.*

We observe today in Germany a very particular phenomenon, indeed astounding at first sight. The spiritual fermentation of wartime and the final collapse have brought about a bewildering din in the literary marketplace. Rising from the noise more and more distinctly are the voices of serious thinkers announcing with increasing persuasiveness that Germany, without knowing or consciously willing it, may have entered the

5. Karl Dietrich Bracher, *Die deutsche Diktatur* (1972): 536.
6. Karl Pribram, "Deutscher Nationalismus und deutscher Sozialismus," *Archiv für Sozialwissenschaft und Sozialpolitik*, 49 (1922): 297–376.

path of the practical realization of socialism even before the war itself, [or] at the very least, that Germany, given her specific spiritual constitution and economic development, was capable of taking that path, and was called upon to do so, in the very near future, [or] more particularly, that the political, social and economic conception embodied in Prussianism (*Preussentum*), as opposed to the democratic ideals and the economic ethic of England, would bring the idea of true socialism to its purest expression.

Such a transformation of the traditional representations amounts more or less to pulling out the revolutionary teeth of socialism; it appears as a movement of self-defense arising from the deepest thought and will of the German people as a whole— and not only from the working class—directed against the capitalistic economic order based on individualism, while individualism itself and its conceptual and economic forms are described as disreputable immigrants from the West, which it is Germany's great mission to conquer, first at home and then in the world. According to this conception, the struggle against the capitalist order would be the continuation of the war against the Entente with the weapons of the spirit and of economic organization, and at the same time it would mean entering the course leading to practical socialism and returning to the noblest and best traditions of the German people. Obviously the affirmations presented by those thinkers in various forms but always with great and persuasive warmth are derived from ethical representations belonging to socialism. At the same time, those thinkers all reject socialism in its Marxist form, primarily the doctrine of class struggle as the motive force of social and economic development. However, any socialist exigency pretends to judge social and economic phenomena according to other norms than those in force in the spirit of the capitalist order, and thus seems to demand a transformation of the concepts formed by that spirit for the understanding of those phenomena (State, economy, economic unit, value, etc.). The affirmation that the introduction of a socialist economic constitution corresponds to the deepest will of the German people in its specific and unchanging character amounts to saying that the forms of thought of that people, its manner of understanding economy and society, contrast—even if unconsciously—with the method of thought characteristic of the adepts of the capitalist economic order.

The notes that accompany this passage offer ample evidence.

They are made up of long quotations from Lensch, Metzger and Scheler, Korsch, Spengler, to whom Kelsen, Kjellen, and Plenge among others are added later. For instance, a passage of Plenge would be perfectly in place here.[7] It must be admitted that a "national socialism" (or a "socialist nationalism") was on the national program, and that the party which took that name had in this sense its place reserved as early as 1920.

Our quotation is only the beginning of a long essay. Pribram was not content with stating the facts; he proposed an explanation. According to him, German nationalism (that is, essentially Prussian nationalism) on the one hand, and German socialism (i.e. Marxist socialism) on the other, rest on similar ideological formulas, so that a possible shift is understandable from the one to the other, or from Marxist socialism to "national" socialism. Both Prussian nationalism and Marxism were built on an individualist, "nominalist" foundation, and both claim to reach a collective being—the nation, or the social class—endowed with a kind of reality that is actually inconceivable for mere aggregates of individuals. They are supposed to have a destiny, the promise of a development, and even a will, all qualities which can be granted them only by a holistic or "universalist" mode of thought. Pribram therefore designates this mode of thought "pseudo-holism" (he says "pseudo-universalism").[8] The expression may be unpractical, but the perception is essential, and the end of the quotation shows that the author has thus characterized German ideology in general.

True, Pribram's concepts and ours are differently defined, but they are close enough for a brief summary to ignore the distance between them. It is also true that Pribram's "pseudo-universalism" can appear in the quotation, despite its name, as a species distinct from the two primitive types and not, explicitly at any rate, as resulting from their historical combination. But this is so only in the limits of our quotation, and other passages are clear in that respect.

7. "The necessities of war have made the socialist idea penetrate into German economic life, whose organization has developed in a new spirit; thus the self-assertion of our nation has produced for mankind the new idea of 1914, the idea of German organization, the popular community of a national socialism" (Plenge *1789 und 1914*, 1916: 82, quoted in Pribram 1922: 322, n. 34).

8. The term "universalism" taken in the sense of what we (now) call holism comes from Othmar Spann, more widely known than Pribram as a theoretician, but in relation to whom Pribram is careful to mark a distance (see his note 13) and adds an indispensable complement (with the "pseudo-" qualification).

Thus in his conclusion Pribram presents the modern revolution through which, first in England and later in France, individualism has triumphed over the holism of the Church and of the absolute State, adding:

> It is characteristic that the contrasts arising from the transformation in the mode of thought did not burst out suddenly in Germany as among the peoples of Western Europe, but that the synthesis achieved in the pseudo-holistic mode of thought has assumed there the role of a mediator between holism and individualism [actually: *Universalismus und Nominalismus*] (1922: 371).

Here, says Pribram, is what Marx has called a revolution in the heads ("under a skull") as opposed to the revolution in the streets in the French fashion. The thought is common to Marx and many others. The difference with Marx is that the adepts of the *Bildung* were satisfied of that state of things as defining German culture. After 1918, this ideological formula will be dramatically confronted with the political reality. Even this we find adumbrated in Pribram:

> This form of thought [*Denkform*][9] is that of the German people in its overwhelming majority, and it has not been deeply altered by the war. The rejection of the princes caused by the catastrophic issue of the war and the adoption of a democratic constitution can hardly be considered as a revolution in the strict sense of the term (ibid.).

This remarkable essay by Karl Pribram cannot here be commented on at length, as it would deserve. Pribram, in 1922, not only clearly designated in German ideology the place that National Socialism was to occupy, and anticipated my own analysis of that ideology in terms of individualism and holism.[10] He also, implicitly

---

9. Pribram says simply "mode of thought," "method of thought," for what will later be called "worldview"—an expression that Hitler uses frequently. A little further in the text (1922: 373), Pribram notes that "it is the German idealist philosophy that has built up this form of ethics," which subordinates the individual to the whole, and quotes Fichte.

10. Discovering the writings of Pribram during a stay in Göttingen in 1977, I was surprised to find that as early as 1912, in a book to which he refers in the article here quoted (1922, n. 5), *Die Entstehung der individualistischen Sozialphilosophie*

at any rate, justified in advance the study that follows, for it consists precisely in showing that Nazism was a *pseudo*-holism.

"When I hear the word gun, I reach for my culture."
—*Alexander Gerschenkron, in a seminar at the Princeton Institute, March 1969.*

I previously wrote that totalitarianism is a disease of modern society that "results from *the attempt, in a society where individualism is deeply rooted and predominant, to subordinate it to the primacy of the society as a whole*" (Dumont 1977: 12). I added that the violence of the movement is rooted in this contradiction and that it "abides in the very promoters of the movement, torn apart as they are by conflicting forces."

Such is the thesis that we here attempt to verify or to illustrate in the case of Nazi ideology or, rather, in a more limited and precise fashion with regard to the representations of Adolf Hitler himself, his *Weltanschauung* (to use his own expression), including the anti-Semitic racism he emphasized so heavily.

We shall proceed in two stages. First, we review what can be considered as already known through the literature;[12] then, by means of an inventory of traits of holistic and of individualistic inspiration, we examine the way these traits were interrelated and combined into a whole.

Before proceeding, we must dispose of some prejudicial questions. In the first place, can one become interested in such a figure? Though certainly not inspiring, to consider him is useful for two reasons: because he was the leader, and for our convenience. He was the leader, the Führer, a designation that united indistinguish-

---

("The origin of the individualistic social philosophy"), he had in large measure anticipated my study of economic ideology.

11. Inversion of a taunt attributed to Hermann Goering and widely popularized by the Nazis. A colleague assured me that in Montreal, in the late 1960s, leftist students had appropriated it as a motto under the delusion that its author was Mao.

12. It is on this point that I was not able to bring the study up to date, as I said at the start. Previously, restricting the references to what concerned interpretation and analysis, I mentioned only the work of Hannah Arendt (1958) and that of Nolte (1963). I must now add, at the very least, the excellent theoretical clarification by Buchheim (1962), the wide and invaluable inquiry of Faye (1972), and Jäckel's (1973) study.

ably a function and a person, and as such he had extraordinary importance and power. This is something to be taken seriously, especially for an inquiry which, like ours, aims at taking the fullest possible account of ideology: clearly we cannot study the regime as we would another lacking this characteristic. Furthermore, the Führer recorded his views with brutal frankness in his book *Mein Kampf*, "My Struggle," written in 1924 during his imprisonment in a fort following the failure of the putsch at Munich.[13] Here lies the convenience to us: a monograph of restricted range holds some promise. But how can we take advantage of the Führer's importance? Very generally, the popularity of this man would be incomprehensible if he had not been somehow, on some level, *representative* of the contemporary German and even more broadly of modern man, and an analysis should throw light on this point. Conversely, given his immense power, his very particularity may have put its imprint on historical facts. The most spectacular monstrosity of the regime, what has been called a genocide or holocaust, namely the systematic extermination of entire populations, particularly the Jews and the gypsies, baffles the understanding and commands the attention of historians, no doubt legitimately to begin with, as being *the* thing to "explain."[14] Now there are reasons to think that extermination issued from the will of Adolf Hitler, and that it would not have happened had the leader of the movement by an improbable chance been someone else. Indeed, it had been a fixed idea of Hitler's at least since 1919 to eliminate or exterminate the Jews, whereas in Himmler himself we can find some traces of reticence:[15] a dreadful example of the role of personality in history.

13. A second volume was added in 1926. We quote from the complete edition of 1933 (the pagination does not seem to have changed until 1939); the references we add to the American translation by Ralph Manheim ("trans.") are only indicative, as its wording has not been considered for the quotations. For Hitler, the brutality of assertion determines the efficacy of propaganda, that is why he is frank in essentials within limits to be determined. Neither can we assume that Hitler said all that he thought in this book, nor can we exclude that his views may have matured subsequently (cf. Jäckel 1973).

14. For recent discussions of this point, see Friedländer 1982, Mason 1982.

15. In 1919, letter to Gemlich (see Nolte 1963: 389–90); around 1922, Eckart's dialogue (Nolte 1963: 407; and below); 1924, cf. Hitler 1933: 772 (suggests the use of toxic gas); also Nolte 1963: 502. On Himmler, see Nolte, 1963: 614, n. 113; Arendt 1958: 375n. What we know of Himmler suggests that he may have carried out the will of his chief with maniacal precision despite a marked reticence (see Himmler 1978:

In the second place, can we speak of Nazi ideology as having been something more than a mere series of propaganda themes, not lacking contradiction and variation (cf. especially Faye 1972: 555 ff.); can we speak of a set of representations as having really been held by Hitler? It could be claimed that there was no Nazi ideology, in the sense that among those people primacy was given not to ideas but to action, while action itself was more often destructive than directed toward the realization of an ideal. In contrast to Stalinism, Nazism involved no mandatory doctrine in terms of which conflicts internal to the commanding clique were expressed; no Nazi leader was ever condemned in the name of the party's principles.[16] Some writers have suggested that there were as many different ideologies as leaders, and that those more inclined toward ideology, such as Rosenberg, were regarded with less favor than the more cynical.

All the same, a small number of interconnected notions were the object of more or less unanimous belief, and oriented the Nazis' actions. Such was the very notion of the primacy of action, or of struggle, and such the notion of the "leader," for faithfulness to the person of the one supreme leader was the ultimate reference, replacing what should otherwise have been "truth" or "reason." Now modern ideology generally entails the primacy of the relation to objects (and of "objective" truth) over relations between men. So already on this point we find the Nazis returning to the premodern (but with some changes, as we shall see).

Mein Kampf contains a precise indication of the place of ideology in the movement. In one passage, Hitler explains that violence alone is powerless to destroy a "worldview"; to succeed, another worldview must be set up against it; to bring Marxism and Bolshevism to an end, therefore, one needs an ideology working in the service of organized force (Hitler 1933: 186–87; trans. 170). It should be noted that Hitler makes great use of the notion of "worldview" (*Weltanschauung*), which appeals to him because of the relativism it implies. This passage shows the necessity and the difficulty of distinguishing between what Hitler believed or thought

---

14, 167, 204–9; Nolte 1963: 614, n. 113). Himmler proclaimed for the whole SS the principle that no task should be accomplished for itself (Arendt 1958: 409n).

16. Yet Faye notices that most of the pre-Hitler racist doctrinaires were under interdict after 1933 (1972: 168), and it might be generalizable to theoreticians in general. There seems to have been a determination to preserve the official simplifications from all contagion or reflection.

and what he wanted to make others believe or think. We should not let ourselves be fooled but should "decode," as people now say, the official ideology. The same goes for the very term "National Social-ism." Its genesis is given very clearly in *Mein Kampf*: Hitler (1933: 133; trans. 122) tells how he learned at Vienna to borrow from the anti-Semitic pan-Germanist Schönerer the general aims of the movement and from the social-christian Dr. Lueger the effective means.[17] "Socialism," in this context essentially the manipulation of the masses, is at the service of nationalism, by which one should understand a racist pan-Germanism. Coming back to the relation set by Hitler between force and the ideological justification it needed, we can say without risk of erring that he gave *ideological* primacy to force over ideas. This primacy could be followed at the level of the organization and program of the party. In Hitler himself, a set of ideas and values can be identified—what we will call an ideology on the social level.

It is clear that racism in general and anti-Semitism in particular play a central part in that set of ideas and beliefs. What does the literature tell us? We have already noted that race has in Nazism a role homologous to that of class in Marxism, the aim being to replace the class struggle by a race struggle. Nolte also says that the Nazis combined all existing forms of anti-Semitism, but he adds that Hitler's anti-Semitism is essentially racial (Nolte 1963: 408). The transition from religious anti-Semitism to racial anti-Semitism is clear-cut, and Hitler himself insists on it. Thus in the dialogue recounted by Eckart and published in 1923, Hitler objects to a text by Luther that to burn down the synagogues and Jewish schools will serve no useful purpose so long as the Jews continue to exist physically (Nolte 1963: 407). In *Mein Kampf*, Hitler insists that a purely religious anti-Semitism is insufficient, mere idle chatter (Hit-ler 1933: 387–98; trans. 360–61). Moreover, the political leader must avoid the domain of religion; the mistake of the Austrian pan-Germanist party in making war against catholicism is criticized at length (Hitler 1933: 124 ff.; trans. 113 ff.).

Racism was generally, as in Gobineau, a pessimistic or negative ideology. Hitler made anti-Semitic racism into a positive doctrine: according to him there is a Jewish race, and it is the embodiment of

17. According to Werner Maser (1970), the account given by Hitler of his youth in Vienna is very inaccurate; on the present point, however, it is immaterial whether or not Hitler reconstructed his experiences after the event.

evil, the cause that from Moses on has intervened time after time to pervert the normal course of things, the antinatural factor in history. So it is enough to intervene—this is the "positive" aspect—for matters to return to their natural course. Furthermore, one thus finds a single cause behind all evils and all contemporary enemies— Marxism, capitalism, formal democracy, even Christianity. This view sits well with what Nolte (1963: 359) called the infantile and monomaniac character of Hitler himself: the cause of all evils is simple, unique; and, what is more, all historical causation is incarnated in a human agent: everything that happens results from someone's will—in this case the hidden, hence real, will of the Jews (Hitler 1933: 54, 68; trans. 51, 64). To what extent was Hitler thinking truly or solely along these lines? The question is a thorny one, but we have no need to ask it. For us it is enough to know that Hitler was certainly inclined to this kind of explanation and just as certainly believed that such explanations were the ones that appealed to the masses.[18] Thus assured of their effectiveness, he could indulge them without qualms.

All these remarks taken from the literature are no doubt correct and throw some light on the phenomenon. The reference to "nature" in history is to be borne in mind, for it makes us glimpse the likelihood of an action that will claim to be "scientific," the artificialism of mass killing—if need be, in gas chambers. This killing obviously represents the climax in the extension of the methods of war to political and social relations in general that has often been noticed in Hitler: what the Nazis call the "final solution" of the "Jewish problem" was equivalent in Hitler's mind to the opening of a new front against the unique and eternal foe. The autobiography shows the young Hitler arriving at his explanation of social democracy and the workers' movement by postulating that the former was inspired and the latter manipulated by the secret will of the Jews, and forming a resolution to build a similar but opposed movement, with his own will as its soul. Hitler may here have antedated in his book what was actually a later decision; at any rate the moment did come when he engaged in what he saw as a mortal duel between the Jews and himself.

In an attempt to see Hitler's *Weltanschauung* as a unity, we

18. One should never designate more than one foe at a time to the masses, and "it behooves the genius of a great chief to make even distinct enemies appear as belonging ever to a single category" (1933: 128–29; trans. 118).

shall begin by making a double inventory from *Mein Kampf*: on the one hand the holistic traits—whether nonmodern or antimodern—and, on the other, traits that are individualistic or at first approximation "modern."[19]

If looking for a reaffirmation of the holistic mode of thought, one should pay particular attention to two terms: *Volk*, literally or roughly "people"; and *Gemeinschaft*, or "community," which the sociologist Toennies neatly opposed to *Gesellschaft*, a society made up of individuals. National Socialist Germany resounded with the word *Volksgemeinschaft* or "community of the people"—but also, let us not forget, "community of culture," and above all, for the Nazis, "of race." The word occurs in *Mein Kampf* less often than we might expect from what was to follow and, one is tempted to say, without any particular accent. It enters, for example, in the discussion of class relations between employers and workers. There the author, setting up as an essential goal of the party the reconquest of the workers, who had been won over to the class struggle, speaks readily of "nationalizing" them. A little later, the collectivity to which the Aryan willingly sacrifices himself is called *Gesamtheit* (entirety, totality), or *Allgemeinheit* (generality, universality), as well as *Gemeinschaft* (Hitler 1933: 327–28; trans. 298–99).

In fact, it was very difficult to merge *Volk* directly with "race." True, one of the chapters is entitled "The People and the Race," but beyond a few racist generalizations it contains mainly a contrasting portrait of the Aryan and the Jew, and concludes with the assertion that all the woes of the Aryan come from the Jew and from the failure to recognize this situation, in other words from the neglect of the "racial interest of the people" (Hitler 1933: 360; trans. 328; Faye 1972: 532).

We may note in passing that it is the Aryan who creates all civilization (*Kultur*) thanks to his capacity for sacrifice, his idealism. Even his work is altruistic, and "this state of mind, which subordinates the interests of the ego to the conservation of the community, is really the first premise for every truly human civilization (*Kultur*)

19. Our terms may here appear specious, but in fact they are merely somewhat simplified. We define individualism and holism at the level of global values. These terms can therefore not apply rigorously to isolated features. Yet we may speak of features that have been otherwise recognized as belonging to one or the other type of system, or which evoke it or can be traced to it—at the risk of erring if we use such associations too loosely. This is what is meant here.

(Hitler 1933: 326; trans. 298). Thus holism, or rather a morality based on holism, is presented as the attribute or monopoly of the sole Aryan race. Unfortunately, there is no Aryan race except by opposition to the Jewish "race"; the German *Volk* is not racially homogeneous. Thus the chapter on the State (bk. 2, chap. 2) says that "our German *Volkstum* unfortunately does not rest on a single racial nucleus [*sic*]" (Hitler 1933: 436–37; trans. 395–96). We may note the use of the abstract *Volkstum*, in the German language the Germanic duplicate of "nationality," which is very frequent in *Mein Kampf*.[20] The same passage explains that there are several, in fact four, "fundamental racial elements" juxtaposed within the Reich, the race called Nordic being only one of them, though the superior element among the four. Elsewhere it is said that the "racist world-view" (*völkische Weltanschauung*) sees the meaning of humanity in its original racial elements (Hitler 1933: 420; trans. p. 383). This lack of coincidence between the *Volk* and the meaningful "racial elements" perhaps explains how racism takes refuge under a word that is slightly different, the word *völkisch* that we just encountered, which was in heavy use at the time.

With respect to this word we can benefit from a wide-ranging but precise investigation by Jean-Pierre Faye, who has undertaken to put National Socialism back into the contemporary welter of antidemocratic groups, splinter groups, and movements that were teeming in Weimar Germany, while putting great stress on their vocabulary. Simplifying somewhat, we can say that the word spread from the end of the nineteenth century as a Germanic equivalent of "national," permitting "national" to be thought about in good German rather than by means of a word of Romance origin. Adopted by the pan-Germanists, the word was colored by a pronounced racism or anti-Semitism (what was a cultural community for Herder had now become something like a "race"); and it had still another facet or association—a slight tinge of socialism. Thus, during the Weimar period Germans could not say "national" in good German without calling to mind "people" and thence, both "race" and socialism. Finally, the meaning of the word according to Faye (1972: 161) was "the unity of conservative nationalism and of

---

20. "Nationality, or better race, precisely does not lie in the language, but in the blood" (Hitler 1933: 428; trans. 389). *Volkstum* also designates "the set of the living expressions of a people *(Volk)*" *(Der neue Brockhaus*, 1938, s.v. "Volkstum").

the self-styled German socialism—in the 'racial sense.' " A brilliant confirmation of Pribram's thesis.

Faye devotes a whole section of his book to the racist (*völkisch*) tendencies that were present in the environment of the National Socialist movement (1972: 151–99), and later he returns to the notion in connection with Hitler and *Mein Kampf* in particular (ibid., pp. 531–36). As we just saw, "National Socialist" says the same thing as *völkisch*, except that it leaves racism implicit. The party's newspaper was called "The *völkisch* Observer." In his book, however, Hitler attacks at length the *völkisch* agitators before adopting the term for his own use, as could be expected. Why? *Mein Kampf* deals with the question twice. First at the end of book 1, and then, as if the discussion was deemed insufficient and a complement was needed, a second time near the beginning of book 2.

In book 1, the term is too vague, "too difficult to grasp," says the index; the word has too many senses, and two many dreamers parade it, people unable to act, in love with Teutonic antiquities or with monarchy. Against all this, and to evoke implacable fight, Hitler has chosen to call the movement a *party*, the National Socialist German Workers' Party, to be precise—in order to keep at a distance those *völkisch* visionaries who incline to what is "religious" or "spiritual." The underlying notion will become explicit in book 2: "religious" anti-Semitism must give place to racist anti-Semitism, which alone, in the hands of a resolute leader, will afford a solid basis for the party's struggle. Book 2 insists on the necessary transcription of the "worldview" into a battle organization and on the role of the leader who, by simplifying the doctrine, ensures the transition from the one to the other.[21] Moreover, *völkisch* in the Hitlerian sense substitutes race for the State: the State is not the creative factor, but only a means in the service of race (1933: 431–34; trans. 391). Here we see Hitler doing for race what Marx did for class: subordinating the State to it (cf. Nolte 1963: 395), a proposition which was not self-evident in Germany—witness the development in the book's index of the entry *völkischer Staat*. In sum, what Hitler does here is to impose on *völkisch* a univocal meaning, that of subjecting the State to racist anti-Semitism.

To sum up, we have been looking for a holistic assertion of the community or people and we have found something notably differ-

---

21. As Nolte has it (1963: 395), the role of the leader is to "narrow down" and to "harden" ideas in view of action.

ent: namely, that this community was subjected to (or confiscated by) a racist antagonism, although the unity of the "race" in fact only existed in the anti-Semitic antagonism toward another "race." We already can see here a structural function of anti-Semitism: suppress it, and Germany will divide itself into "four primitive racial elements." More deeply, it remains for us to find out whether, at the level of the conceptual framework of the whole system, there is a reason for the subordination of community, both in its national and social aspects, to race. Here the holistic community is dissolved, a fact that seems by and large to have been overlooked by commentators. Given, among other things, the functional homology between Hitlerian race and Marxist class, we can presume that the leaven for this dissociation was modern individualism, and we shall verify this later.

For the time being, let us pursue the holistic or nonmodern features in *Mein Kampf*. In general, and under diverse aspects, Hitler rejects the modern primacy of the man-nature relation and reasserts the primacy of the relation between men. He thus categorically refuses to admit that mankind in our day has become the master of nature. He argues that man has only succeeded in dominating other living beings by grasping some of the laws or secrets of nature (1933: 314; trans. 287). There is something uncanny about this formula, for the expression "other beings" might designate humans as well, in which case one might read this less as a rejection of modern artificialism than as a desire to intensify it by applying it to humans — and that in effect is what we find with eugenics and the extermination camps.

We perceive the same rejection of the primacy of the relation of man to things when Hitler protests the generally admitted preeminence of economics. Here, he says, is the kind of belief that has led Wilhelmian Germany to ruin. The attack is aimed at liberalism as well as Marxism. Hitler himself actually encompasses economics in politics (relations between men) (1933: 164–67; trans. 150–53). He has somehow perceived that only a certain type of political organization not only makes economic development possible but also allows the economy to be isolated as what Nolte calls a "philosophical" phenomenon (Nolte 1963: 616 n. 7; 520). Here we must refer to Karl Polanyi (1957a), who has shown that Nazism represented a decisive crisis of modern liberalism or, better, the systematic exploitation of the crisis of that world which had believed in economics as an absolute category, independent of the political. On this point, contrary to what is often maintained, I believe the Nazis were true to their 1920 program in spirit if not in the letter: they encompasssed economics in politics and maintained a truly hierarchical relation between the two.[22]

Hitler's attacks on formal, parliamentary democracy, which he condemned as impotent and as opening up the way for Marxist domination, are well known. Equalitarianism was a Jewish weapon for the destruction of the political system. What strikes me, however, on reading *Mein Kampf* is, paradoxically, the limitations of that critique of equalitarianism. Just think about it: the French Revolution is nowhere frontally attacked. Along with Marxist phraseology and traditional phraseology (see below), so also the phraseology of the rights of man is occasionally employed (the rights of man thus amount to the rights of the superior race!— 1933: 444; trans. 402). We shall see that all equalitarian aspects are not in fact absent from Hitler's representations.

There are distinctly holistic features. At first sight we are still with Adolf Hitler within the German tradition where man is a social being. Once he had left Austria for Germany, Hitler figured as a petit-bourgeois patriot who enrolled at the mobilization and served bravely all along the war; and according to him, as we have seen, the Aryan is prepared to serve the community to the point of self-sacrifice. Things are more complicated when we consider his early years in Vienna, but Hitler then was primarily a pan-Germanist, and we know that pan-Germanism can be regarded as a corollary of German holism. We may say that Hitler's dedication was addressed to a people called to domination. Nonetheless, the word *Aryan* should again remind us that the holism present here, according to Hitler, is limited to a "race," subordinate to "race." Here is a strange novelty, important for our purpose: in Hitler's view, I am either dedicated to the collectivity or, on the contrary, egoistically closed in upon myself according to the "race" to which I belong. The Aryans are capable of self-sacrifice, "idealists," in our terms holist, while the Jews are just the opposite, what we call individualists.[23] It is true that this latter term is not used, and it is also

---

22. We seem here to contradict the judgment, based on solid evidence, of Franz Neumann (1942). Actually we don't ask the same question as he did. Our question is whether in Nazi practice the political commands the economic, or the reverse. Neumann's viewpoint is clear in Ayçoberry's summary (1982).

23. Hitler did not reserve the word *individualism* for Jews. He wrote of the

true that the Jews are charged with many other defects or misdeeds, but I believe it is legitimate to isolate this single feature from among the mass of turpitudes that Hitler attributes to his chief enemy. Already in Eckart's dialogue, Christianity—that is, Paul's equalitarian preaching, which succeeded—had been presented as a kind of bolshevism produced by Jews. In *Mein Kampf*, the Jews are responsible, if not quite for capitalism and modern society in general, at least for everything in them that is decidedly bad, such as the transformation of land into a commodity, joint-stock companies, and the destructive orientation of the workers' movement (1933: 338–58; trans. 308–27).

There are first of all two very clear pages where Jews are characterized by "conservation of the individual," "egoism of the individual." Like animals, they assemble at the time of danger and disperse as soon as the danger has passed. Collectively, they know only the "gregarious instinct," which is at bottom but a circumstantial manifestation of the conservation instinct. We shall have to remember this imputation. To anticipate: I shall submit that Hitler projected onto the Jews the individualist tendency he felt within himself as threatening his "Aryan" devotion to the community.

There is a certain respect for religion in *Mein Kampf*, especially for the Catholic Church. In part it is tactical (to succeed, one must concentrate the attack on the Jews alone, at least at the beginning),[24] and in part it bears on the power and stability of the Church as an organization—a distant model for the party—rather than on the Church as a community of believers.

To what extent do we find in Adolf Hitler the hierarchical dimension of holism? Theoretically we should distinguish between hierarchy as an expression of values, and power, and in the nature of the case it is most difficult. Yet we may say that, granted some really hierarchical features, what predominates is the use of traditional phraseology to express or to mask new relationships. Consider the motto that Himmler gave the SS: "My honor is called faithfulness" (*Meine Ehre heisst Treue*). Here are words that evoke feudal aristocracy but actually refer to the great Nazi parade in

---

"hyperindividualism" of the Germans, meaning the extreme regional particularism in Germany (1933: 437; trans. 390).

24. On 8 February 1942, Hitler, angered at the ministers of the Christian confessions, promises to liquidate them within ten years, for "the lie must be exterminated" (Trevor-Roper 1973: 304).

which each human atom marches past in goose step and where the Führer, the sole object of each one's faithfulness, vociferates from above as in a trance where each one's anxiety is transmuted into numberless force. The word "atomisation" recurs often in the best works on Nazism and well expresses this dialogue between mass and chief, so far removed from the medieval network of honor and faithfulness to persons.

Mein Kampf makes several references to "nature's aristocratic principle" (1933: 69, etc.; trans. 65), but it expresses what we would call Hitler's social Darwinism. The strong defeats the weak, and there lies the measure of values. As Jean-Pierre Faye puts it, it is "the equivalence between good and strong, bad and weak" (1972: 535),[25] a relationship of force made into a moral principle, that is to say, an *inversion* of the "aristocratic principle." The struggle of all against all is here disguised in traditional language. But let us ponder for a moment what is essential: force set up as value. Rauschning was much criticized in the literature following his *Revolution of Nihilism*—an early diagnosis that has been invaluable for some of us[26]—for defining Nazism as power for itself, power resting only on itself. The critics maintained that Nazi power served certain ends. If we ask what the essential ends really were, Hitler answers precisely in this passage and elsewhere: power, that is, domination as producing or manifesting the highest value. If we leave aside intermediate goals and consider only this concept of Hitler's own, Rauschning was not wrong. Thus, the debacle of the Nazis has judged them according to their own criterion; the leaders understood it perfectly.

In conclusion, our search for holistic features in *Mein Kampf* has in the main delivered appearances rather than realities, and has for the most part led us to an intervening heterogeneous element, which must now be identified.

We now turn to the individualistic (or "modern") traits in Hitler's worldview. They generally pass unexamined, but it is these traits we must emphasize in order to understand the phenomenon.

25. According to Faye (1972: 522 and note), Hitler had very early come across the phrase "*völkisch* thought, the aristocratic principle of our times," in a Viennese anti-Semitic publication.

26. I am referring to a French translation (Rauschning 1939) that appeared just before we went to war.

Given that Hitler mistrusted ideals and ideologies, considering them vehicles of hidden interests, and given his admission that a doctrine was needed, first and foremost, to subject the masses to force, we may well ask ourselves whether there really was something to which he was genuinely attached, in which he undoubtedly believed. The answer is that there was at least one such thing: *the struggle of all against all*. A struggle for life, for power or domination, for interest—this was where the ultimate truth of human life lay for Hitler. The idea is at the heart of *Mein Kampf*. Here, in a 1928 speech, is a complete formulation of it:

> The idea of struggle is as old as life itself, for life is only preserved because other living things perish through struggle. . . . In this struggle, the stronger, the more able, win, while the less able, the weak, lose. Struggle is the father of all things. . . . It is not by the principles of humanity that man lives or is able to preserve himself above the animal world, but solely by means of the most brutal struggle.[27]

We have here something of the greatest importance. We note first that such a state of mind, skeptical, disillusioned, even cynical, and such an ultimate belief are certainly very widespread in our time at the commonsense level, both in Germany and elsewhere. Here then is a basic point through which Hitler could be representative of his time and country, able to reproduce, so to speak, in a form intensified by his monomania, the reactions and representations of masses of people from various social backgrounds. This may be why he flattered himself that he alone could arouse the enthusiasm of an intellectual audience as well as an audience of workers with the same speech (Hitler 1933: 376; trans. 342; Faye 1972: 533). He felt himself to be deeply representative, even though he depicts himself in *Mein Kampf* as poorer, more of a "worker," than he had in fact been in his Viennese days (Maser 1970) in order to bring himself nearer the condition of the workers whom he then wanted to win back from the Marxists.

Moreover, among the Nazi leaders Hitler is no doubt rightly considered as the one who had the ability, or the audacity, to follow through on his ideas, to pursue with implacable logic the principles

27. Speech of 5 February 1928 at Kulmbach (Prange 1944: 8), quoted in Bullock 1963, 1: 24.

he had set himself. Yet, his contemporaries have been bemused by apparent contradictions in his action; and the historian who takes those contradictions as deliberate still confronts the problem of bringing to light the principles that might account for them. But here, openly proclaimed, we have *the* supreme principle that should explain everything. As we have just read, it is simply the principle of "the most brutal struggle." Only it must be understood in a hierarchical way, as the primacy of *the struggle to the death* over everything that appears to contradict it: peace will be a continuation of war by other means, legality a means of setting legality at naught. The theory is not spelled out in *Mein Kampf*, though it is quite compatible with what is written there—for example, the State is not an end in itself, but a means serving other ends. It is Hitler's *practice*, once he had achieved power, that teaches us. In internal politics Hitler had learned that he could not do without legal channels. So he coupled them with what they were supposed to exclude, extralegal forms of action that are the usual tools of conspirators but were made the more formidable, and at the same time unpunishable, by this camouflage. Thus in 1933, one month after the solemn accession to the chancellorship, the Reichstag fire allowed the Communists to be outlawed and the first concentration camps to be created. Likewise on an altogether different level in 1938, hardly had the "appeasement" been obtained from Chamberlain and Daladier at Munich than the Nazis went into anti-Semitic terror with the "Crystal Night."[28] This is how, when one could no longer do without legality or peace, one took care to encompass them in "the most brutal struggle" (cf. Hitler 1933: 105; trans. 96). This breaking of the social contract, of the basic distinctions on which modern social life rests and in which everyone places his confidence, appears in its recurrence to be a hidden method, a clandestine strategic principle that makes institutions into slaves of violence and, by deceiving or disorienting the masses as well as the enemy, no doubt contributed greatly to Hitler's continued success.

28. Historians are still discussing whether the Nazis or the Communists ordered the Reichstag to be set on fire. On the other coincidence, Ernst von Salomon tells in his memoirs how a colleague of his, a writer, thought it inept to have a pogrom follow the Munich peace agreement. These two facts show how efficient the Nazi camouflage was. Yet von Salomon's friend, bewildered by the event, finally glimpsed the dreadful truth: "You know, I believe he is wicked!" (Salomon 1953: 372).

To further the analysis, we must also ponder that, in this "struggle of all against all," in this social Darwinism so common among our contemporaries, the real subjects (or at any rate the main ones) are the biological individuals, and that, moreover, the same struggle clearly goes on in every society. Here, then, individualism is present at the level of the most basic representations. This basic individualism is enshrined at the heart of Adolf Hitler's worldview, surviving all attacks and all skepticism directed at equalitarianism, democracy, and ideology in general. We have already encountered this individualism, or rather its effects, for it is the factor at work in Hitler every time the holistic tendency is halted, deviated, or warped. First of all it is this individualism that destroys the community experienced in social life and finally reduces it to race—as I shall later attempt to demonstrate.

There are other individualistic traits, equalitarian traits, for example: hostility toward royalty, the traditional nobility,and any notion of hereditary rank. The very pretension to the role of "leader" on the part of a common man calls for equality of opportunity, at the very least. (It is true that Hitler presented himself at the outset merely as the "drummer" or propagandist of the movement.) Later on, to join the "elite," to be promoted in the party, achievement was the sole criterion, and rivalry among leaders was even favored by the Führer-chancellor, who was often seen to entrust identical or similar tasks to different lieutenants—much beyond the well-known duality of state and party. Such rivalries could well compromise the material outcome, and in a matter as crucial as the war economy the attitude conclusively indicates the subordination of objective reality to human relationships—in contrast with the modern trend. The individualist valuation crept in also through other channels. Thus Marxist artificialism ("to change the world"), socialism—partly the heir to bourgeois individualism, and Bolshevism are not exempt from these modern characteristics, and one cannot "imitate and outdo" them (Nolte 1963: 395) without unconsciously and implicitly making this individualist stress one's own, a stress that in truth is ubiquitous in the contemporary world. Hitler outbids Marxism by making a copy of it; just as Marxism demystified bourgeois ideology, Nazism will demystify Marxist ideology. This is how it will be done: more real than "relations of production," we are told, are the actual men who enter into those relations. Here we are, then, with man as a biological individual, a sample of the race. No doubt this transposition was called for, for Hitler himself, because he saw race as an obvious fact, but it seems once again to contain a characteristic mixture: on the one hand, human relations were more real than the relation with things implicit in "production," but on the other hand—and this is probably more important—the human relations were logically preceded by the men who entered into these relations. This is the well-known sophism that does away with relation in favor of substance and builds up the metaphysical individual. For Hitler, the real thing hiding behind the Marxist construction was the will of individuals, of the Jews.

The foregoing inventory of holistic and individualistic features in *Mein Kampf* is surely very imperfect. It is merely a piece of rather crude detection. What is essential is to see how all of this combines or articulates, and which of the two major principles subordinates the other, if this is indeed the case. This is the task to which we now briefly turn.

The central notion is a double one: the struggle of all against all as the final truth of human existence, and the domination of one man over another as characteristic of the natural order of things or, rather, of societies. The equalitarianism that runs counter to this reputed natural "order" being presented as a Jewish weapon of destruction, one might believe—and it seems that analysts did most of the time believe—that we are in this respect no longer in the modern individualistic world. But that is merely an appearance. Not only do we find individualistic and undeniable equalitarian traits in Adolf Hitler's worldview, but the idea of domination as resting only on itself, without any other ideological basis than the affirmation that "nature" wished things to be so, is nothing but the result of the destruction of the hierarchy of values, that is to say of human ends, by equalitarian individualism. No justification is left for subordination in society—necessary as it is, and uniformly acknowledged in Germany—but the brutal fact of the domination of some over others. The very marked stress on the struggle for life (and for domination) precisely expresses the individualist valuation and the individualist negation of collective beliefs.

To better understand what happens here to modern ideology, we may go back into the past. Subordination was always problematic in this context, and with Hitler it suddenly appears to be asserted in an absolute manner. This seeming reversal obscures what is actually a continuity. Let us only remember how, in the Natural Law theories of the seventeenth–eighteenth centuries, two contracts were most often needed to transfer men from the state of nature to the social and political state: not only a contract of association, but also a second contract, the political contract or contract of subordination. It is clear that subordination represented there a special difficulty. It was therefore founded on a contract especially conceived to that end. We measure the distance covered in the intensification of individualism when we see that Hitler, wanting first of all to construct a war machine, and addressing a people for whom subordination was more or less taken for granted, found no other ground for it than nature—no longer social, but physical nature. (And surely our ethologists would see nothing wrong here!)

The reader may object that domination, or power, only appears to be an end in itself here, and is in fact at the service of a value, namely race. But it is just the case that *the emergence of race as a value has to be accounted for*. Now, it is the struggle of all against all—and hence individualism—that is at the root of race, and not the reverse. For the struggle of all against all is obviously at work everywhere; it must in particular tend to weaken, even to destroy, the idea of the global society or national community. To further penetrate Adolf Hitler's representations, we may ask what conception of the German community is going to be in a position to resist this disaggregation of his. The normal modern form of global society is the nation, and the external conditions of the moment were favorable to the affirmation of the German nation and of its cohesion. However, although the epithet *national* alone, or combined with another, was used abundantly in labeling different parties and movements (cf. Faye's list), the "nation" remained something more or less external or superficial. Deeper associations went with the equivalent, *Volk*. For Hitler himself there were additional reasons for not using the idea of nation as a basis. At the time, the nation was being vigorously attacked by the internationalists. Later, it is true, Hitler glorified in having broken the traditional socialist internationalism of the proletariat, but in general his tactic was not to attack frontally a position held by the socialists but rather to circumvent their critique. Thus, one did not say there was no class struggle, but that the true struggle was the one between races. Moreover, as Faye's book reminds us throughout, not only National Socialism but the whole movement within which it developed tended toward uniting and merging the two poles, the national and the socialist. Everything suggested that this was to be done around the notion of *Volk*. But what could possibly be Hitler's feeling, at bottom, about this notion and that of a "community of the people," of which Nazism was subsequently to make so much use?

Let us take a parallel case. To express the community of thought within a society, the French sociologist Durkheim spoke of "collective representations" and even of a "collective consciousness"; there was a lively reaction from the Anglo-American empiricists, who asked, in effect: "Have you ever met a collective representation on the street corner? There are only men of flesh and bone." Obviously Hitler, believing in the struggle of all against all, must have reacted in a very similar fashion to the idea of a collective social entity, a cultural community of the "people."

This seems confirmed by the relatively limited use in *Mein Kampf* of the vocabulary based on the word *Volk* (*Volksgemeinschaft, Volksseele or* "people's soul"), except for *Volkstum*, "nationality," and the "little word" that Faye emphasizes, *völkisch*. As hinted at above, this derivative word allowed Hiter, after abandoning the cultural or religious "musings" attached to it, to work the transition to race, *die Rasse*. The only residue that his grim—and hidden—individualism could tolerate under the heading of community was the "race": people think the same and—ideally at least—live together because they are physically, materially identical. (No doubt the slippage from "people" to "race" extended far beyond National Socialism alone, but let us stick with Hitler himself.) "The goal of the State is to maintain and develop a community of living beings who are physically and morally *gleichartig*," that is, similar because members of the same species (*Art*) (Hitler 1933: 433; trans. 393). Elsewhere Hitler exulted in the idea that after a few years his men had apparently all become physically identical (Arendt 1958: 418, quoting Heiden).

To conclude this point: a very widespread notion of modern individualistic common sense, the "struggle of all against all," forced Hitler to see in race the only valid foundation of the global society and virtually the only cause in history. Racism results here from the holistic representation of community disintegrating under the action of individualism.

We may note that Hitler's idea of race is relatively weak in its functional role as a substitute for Marxist class: after all, it merely juxtaposes individuals as such, who cannot have even the solidarity in daily life that members of the same class can have—for example, workers fighting for their demands. But the really active racist notion is anti-Semitism, which alone can introduce the common man to the abstract idea of "race." Only anti-Semitism can "racially" unite the German population, otherwise divided, we are told, into four "racial elements," i.e. four different "races." In this sense, as Rauschning said, the Jews were indispensable to Hitler. If he nonetheless carried with him the idea of eliminating them, and finally decided to exterminate them, it was not only because he saw them as representing the antinatural factor that deflected history from its normal course—perhaps a mere speculative rationalization—or even because he wanted to intensify his war on all fronts.

At a deeper level we can see a parallel between two opposites. For Hitler the struggle, we have said, was between the Jews on one side and himself alone on the other—a struggle to the death. He wanted to systematically set his will against their supposed will. He saw in them agents of destruction, individualists who were the carriers of everything he hated in modernity—anonymous and usurious money, democratic equalitarianism, and the Marxist and Bolshevik revolution. Yet we have seen that Hitler himself was infected with that poison he pretended to be fighting. The individualism implicit in the struggle of all against all dissolved in his mind that which he had wanted to believe in and the Germans had to believe in: the "community of the people." It is hence very likely that, because of the symmetry that set them in opposition, Hitler projected onto the Jews the individualism that was tearing him apart. At bottom, the extermination of the Jews appears as a desperate effort on Hitler's part to rid himself of his own basic contradiction. In this sense it was also a part of himself that Hitler tried to annihilate.

I want to add an observation. Elsewhere I pointed out the parallel between Hitler's conception and the obsession with "power" in contemporary political science (Dumont 1977: 10). Having followed the logic of deviance through to the end, we can see that from this viewpoint Hitler only pushed to their utmost conclusions some very common representations of our times, be it "the struggle of all against all," a kind of commonplace for uncultured people, or its more refined equivalent, the reduction of politics to the raw notion of power. Once such premises are admitted, and with Hitler's example at hand, one cannot see how the man who has the means to do it can be prevented from exterminating whom he will, and the horror of the conclusion demonstrates the falsity of the premises. Universal reprobation shows agreement on values, and political power should be subordinated to values. The essence of man's life is not the struggle of all against all, and political theory cannot be a theory of power but should be a theory of legitimate authority. Moreover, it must be clear at the end of this analysis that the recent generalization of the notion of "violence," which disregards the fundamental distinctions of the modern world (between public and private, etc.) is totalitarian in spirit and threatens us with barbarity (cf. Dumont 1977: 13–14).

In conclusion, is it possible to set up a general perspective? It can only be schematic and speculative, for we shall have to mix, often in approximate terms, hypothetical judgments with conclusions that are better established or more likely. Uncertain as the result may be, it should be not without interest, given the present state of knowledge.

In terms of the interplay of ideologies in the world, Nazism is part of a process of intensification and overbidding which is linked to the interaction between the dominant, individualistic ideology and the particular cultures it dominates. From that viewpoint, Nazism is part of the interaction of Germany with the world, a point that may be obvious but should not be forgotten.

On the plane of Germany itself, we noticed that the political constitution of the Wilhelmian era resulted not from the systematic application of an ideology but from a traditional political system having been modernized, modified, or adapted *empirically* to modern conditions (hence the alloying of archaism and modernity on which historians are fond of insisting). Once the system had been swept away by defeat, the democratic parliamentarian constitution of Weimar was felt as an alien imposition by the tenants of the traditional ideology—Thomas Mann's conversion being probably an exception.

At this point, everything looks as if Germany was called upon by her historical situation to invent a model of political constitution in keeping with her ideology, in order to defend her national identity against external pressure. We learned from Pribram that the form sought for would necessarily be *a* national socialism ("socialism" being taken in the sense of global organization). We have thus a double determination: a causal one (the given conditions) and an ideological one (reintroduction of a holistic aspect), but both together give us only one aspect of reality, not National Socialism as it has existed in fact. It should be noted, furthermore, that the problem has not been solved. The Nazis did not build up a political constitution, and it has even been said that, strictly speaking, there has been no Nazi State. This is not a matter of chance: racism allowed the problem to be bypassed, and Hitler had warned as early as *Mein Kampf* that the State would be merely a means in the service of race.[29] From what we ascertained above regarding the survival of universal sovereignty in German ideology and the corresponding vocation of the German State to external domination, something else has also become clear: that, in the absence of any deep transformation of the ideology, the dimension of external domination was a sine qua non for any successful attempt to restore German identity.

The kind of question we are now faced with can, at best, be formulated in the abstract, speculatively: Was the major role played by racism contingent, or, on the contrary, was the political problem insoluble, so that racism imposed itself of necessity? On the individual level, in Hitler himself, we saw the abstract or theoretical racism as resulting from the individualist disintegration of the holistic representation of "community." The proposition could well be generalizable, not only to the *völkisch* circles but, much more widely, up to someone who is often placed at the origin of racism in Europe, the Comte de Boulainvilliers, whose racism might be said to have issued from a crisis of the holistic and hierarchical representation of the "orders" or "estates" of the kingdom (nobility, clergy, third estate).

Given the fact that, once translated into German culture, the nation becomes the *Volk*, was the shift inevitable, at the collective level, from the *Volk*, people or culture, to "race"? Let there be no mistake: we are not supposing that the German people became racist, in its majority or otherwise, under Hitler, merely that it fell under the power of a racist clique. Let us admit that the ideology of the *Volk* was not racist, at least predominantly, before 1918. We have noted that until then it responded only to very limited social desirata. After 1918, that ideology found itself summoned by history to answer a new, a properly political desideratum, namely a

29. Ernst von Salomon wrote after the war: "The only aim of the great national movement, after the collapse of 1918, should have been a renewal of the conception of the State, which would have been revolutionary in its methods but conservative in nature," and he called the "attempt to shift the decisive stress from the State to the people, from authority to totality," an infamous betrayal of the true aim (1953: 618).

"renewal of the conception of the State." Did this probably immoderate command finally bring Hitler to the chancellorship, and did it thus tip Germany into racism? The question is somewhat rhetorical at this point. Yet it serves to remind us that national consciousness has its problems, in Germany and elsewhere.

Part 2

Comparison Made Radical: The Universal Viewed Anthropologically

7 Marcel Mauss

A Science in Process of Becoming

Professor Lévi-Strauss wrote an "Introduction to the Work of Marcel Mauss," which is important and, I believe, indispensable for understanding the impact of Mauss's ideas upon the questions of present-day anthropology. I am not going to follow the criticism of some sociologists who claim that Lévi-Strauss turned Mauss's thought unduly in a structural direction, for my experience is that, from the point of view mentioned, the author is right, and true to Mauss's deepest inspiration. Others have said that Lévi-Strauss made Mauss more philosophical than in fact he was. Coming after him, and because the most obvious aspect of Mauss is indeed his concrete tendency, could I not adopt a more modest approach, and content myself with trying to show you Mauss's interest in the concrete? I asked a few friends, his former students, because I wanted to bring you more than a mere individual opinion: they agreed and helped in making the idea more precise: Mauss was a philosopher, a theoretician, who had turned to the concrete, who had learned that only in close contact with the facts can sociology progress. It is about that one basic aspect that I am going to speak: I

Conference given at Oxford in 1952, in a series of university lectures on the history of sociology in France. David Pocock helped me prepare the English version. The references, which are kept to a minimum, are mainly to the collection of essays entitled *Sociologie et anthropologie* (1950), edited and introduced by Claude Lévi-Strauss, and to the invaluable three-volume edition of (the other) *Oeuvres* by V. Karady (Mauss 1968–69). The latter has the great merit of giving the substance of the numerous reviews by Mauss dispersed in the volumes of *Année Sociologique*.

want to show you how, with Mauss, French sociology, or rather sociology in France, reached its *experimental stage*. The expression may seem a little excessive. I shall try to justify it.

Mauss's concrete tendency is quite characteristic if we compare him with Durkheim, who, although he himself turned to facts to a certain extent, may nevertheless be considered the last in a line of thinkers in the abstract; Durkheim laid down rules for the study of facts, he wanted such studies and initiated them, but it was with Mauss that concrete knowledge began to react upon the theoretical framework. I regard Durkheim as still a philosopher. But for Mauss himself, Durkheim was primarily the founder of sociology, and the label of "philosopher" he reserved for Lévy-Bruhl. On the other hand, writing of Hertz's working methods, Mauss says that Hertz's plan became modified in light of the facts, "and the facts were not there as illustrations, for he was not only a philosopher but a scientist" (1922: 58).

This difference, almost a contradiction, between Mauss's craving for concrete data and Durkheim's theoretical tendency, struck Mauss's students most forcibly, and they were astonished that it was not expressed in theoretical divergences. One reason for this was Mauss's sense of solidarity in collective work and his devotion to Durkheim's memory; he was pledged to him as his disciple and heir, and he wanted to keep alive what had been their common inspiration rather than to stress some minor disagreement. Durkheim had provided a theoretical framework whose value for research purposes Mauss took every opportunity to emphasize. This side being secure, Mauss's primary concern, especially in his more elementary lectures, was for facts. But it is quite obvious that he expected the facts to react upon the theory. If he ever complains, it is about the circumstances that did not permit scholarship to develop as quickly as the *Année sociologique* group dreamed it would to fill up the gaps, to put flesh on the dry bones of classification and improve it. The idea that factual knowledge should change previous theories is so ingrained in him that he cannot help expressing some disappointment when reviewing the third edition of the *Golden Bough*: the facts, he says, have accumulated, but they have not modified the ideas; the cask has grown to monumental proportions, but it contains the same wine.

This being so, one wonders what is meant by a remark I heard recently, that Mauss failed to build a system. Of course he did not build one, but he did not want to, and it would be wrong to judge him as though he did.

Mauss was a fascinating personality. It is impossible to speak of the scholar without recalling the person. Probably the secret of his popularity among us was precisely that for him, unlike so many academics, knowledge was not a separate branch of activity. His life had become knowledge and his knowledge life; that is why he could exert, on some individuals at least, as great an influence as a religious teacher or a philosopher. And this confronts us with many a paradox.

For instance, his elementary teaching was simply intended to enable students to observe and record things correctly. As presented in the *Manuel d'ethnographie* (Mauss 1947), which was composed from auditors' notes, this teaching may seem to consist of a catalogue of facts, together with instructions that are often of such a general character as to amount to useless tautological commonplaces. We were told, in effect, that there was much of *this* and *that* to be observed, and that many valuable human ideas and ways were waiting everywhere to be recorded. We had just to go and look at things. Of course we should know what we were looking for, and know at the same time that everything is in everything—very easy and very difficult indeed. Was that all? Not quite: a medical student who had taken ethnology as a secondary subject told me how he once discovered, when traveling on the platform of a bus, that the relation he felt to his fellow travelers had changed on account of Mauss's lectures. Of course, you may say that this had nothing to do with science but was a matter of art. True enough. Anyhow, with Mauss, everything, even the most inconspicuous gesture, was made meaningful for us. He boasted that he could recognize an Englishman in the street by his gait (his "Techniques du corps" in Mauss 1950). With Mauss, the narrow classical culture in which we had been educated burst into a wider, more real humanism, embracing all peoples, all classes, and all activities.

You went to him at the close of a lecture, and he left you two hours later at the other end of Paris. All the time he had been walking and talking, and it was as if the secrets of far removed races, a part of the archives of mankind, had been unraveled for you by an expert in the guise of ordinary conversation. For he had been round the world without leaving his armchair, identifying himself with the people he read about. Hence the kind of phrase so common with him: "I eat . . . I curse . . . I feel . . . ," meaning, according to the context, the Melanesian of such an island eats, or the Maori chieftain curses, or the Pueblo Indian feels.

For if Mauss knew everything, as we used to say, it did not lead him to complicated explanations; on the contrary, it was, and it is still, a major difficulty with him that his knowledge was so real, so personal, so immediate, that it often and most deceptively took the form of commonsense statements. Here is an example. I went to him to ask about the custom of couvade. It was early morning; he finished his physical exercise on his balcony and took his breakfast, saying that bread-and-butter came from the Belgae (ancient Belgians), and so on. He asked: "Do you know how the British recognized that Joan of Arc, clad as a warrior as she was, was in fact a woman? Well, she was sitting down, and someone threw walnuts on her lap, and to try to catch them, instead of bringing her knees together, she pulled them apart, as if to tighten the cloth of the gown she was used to wearing." (This is from Mark Twain!)

Finally I succeeded in uttering a few words about the object of my visit, i.e., the couvade, patriarchy and matriarchy, etc. "It is much simpler than all that," he replied. "Birth is no small affair. It is quite natural that both parents are involved." I left quite unsatisfied, loaded with a big book and this enigmatic reply. I thought, like many others in similar circumstances: "He is great, but isn't it a little too simple? What does he mean?" After a few days I understood, and appreciated the difference between a certain kind of pedantry and Mauss's knowledge. But this is just to support my contention that Mauss had received the special blessing of being a fieldworker without leaving his armchair.

The active career of Marcel Mauss, from the competitive examination called the *agrégation de philosophie* in 1895 (he was twenty-three) until his retirement in 1940 (at the age of sixty-eight), may be divided into three periods. The first extends to 1914. At that time Mauss was a specialist in the study of religion, mainly Indian and primitive, and was taking an important part in the *Année sociologique* movement under the direction of his uncle, Emile Durkheim. It was a time of enthusiastic teamwork, of brilliant and numerous publications. By 1900 Mauss had studied Sanskritic and comparative philology, the history of religions, and anthropology, with such scholars as Meillet, Foucher, and Sylvain Lévi in Paris; Caland in Holland; and Tylor and Winternitz at Oxford.

In 1901 he was appointed to teach the History of Religions of Noncivilized Peoples at the Ecole des Hautes Etudes. At the same time, and from the beginning, he was in charge of the second section of the *Année*, that of the sociology of religion, in which, with the help of Hubert, he published annually the most detailed and enlightening reviews of all publications of any importance. Unfortunately I cannot dwell at length on that too often neglected part of Mauss's writings (perhaps 1500 pages). I did, however, read it again while preparing the present paper, and I doubt very much whether anything of the kind can be found elsewhere: every work reviewed is summarized with great care before being praised, criticized, corrected, or supplemented, and then only from the point of view of the progress of knowledge. Nowhere do sociological theories appear as anything more than tools, albeit indispensable tools, for research. The whole history, the research results, and problems of the speciality during the period are summed up in masterly fashion in those pages (see the source note to the present chapter).

As to his own publications, two well-known facts are worth recalling: Mauss never published a book, but only articles, some of them extensive, generally entitled *"Essay"* or *"Outline."* Moreover, almost all were written in collaboration with another scholar, mostly the historian of religions, archaeologist, and technologist Henri Hubert, and sometimes Durkheim, or Fauconnet, or Beuchat. This has been interpreted in various ways, as showing either that those scholars realized the ideal of collective work, or that Mauss was unable to publish by himself, for the volume of his publications was to decrease markedly after his friends and co-workers had been torn from him by death.

World War I took a heavy toll among that group of sociologists and some of its best hopes, as for instance Hertz, author of *La prééminence de la main droite* (The Preeminence of the Right Hand) and the discoverer of the custom of double funerals. With the death of Durkheim in 1917, Mauss's second period began. It was a period marked not only by his mourning for the colleagues he had lost and by devotedly preparing for publication the works they had left, but also by extended responsibilities. He had succeeded Durkheim as director of the *Année*, and that meant covering not only religion but also sociology at large. The charge was further increased with the creation in 1925 of the Institut d'Ethnologie, where Mauss gave his "Instructions" for field study year after year. He attached much importance to that elementary course, obviously because he saw it as the way to future developments. It should be noticed that, although Mauss trained his students primarily with a view to monographic, largely sociological fieldwork, he never neglected the problems either of cultural diffusion and borrowing or of material culture. The work of Leroi-Gourhan for instance, which has been considered as founding ethnographic technology as a separate discipline, rests entirely upon the development of Mauss's systematic classification of techniques as given in his lectures. On Mauss's influence and posterity, I refer you to Lévi-Strauss's report on French sociology (Lévi-Strauss 1947). In this period, apart from numerous shorter contributions, Mauss produced only one large-scale study, but it is perhaps his masterpiece, the *Essai sur le don* (Essay on Gift, 1925). The point I want to make here is that Mauss did not choose to extend the field, already vast, to which he had committed himself at the beginning into the endless arena of sociology and ethnology in general. This was forced upon him, for he had pledged himself to Durkheim's memory and to the development of the studies they had initiated together.

We may perhaps consider that a third period began about 1930. Hubert in his turn had left his fellow worker, and Mauss published his two volumes about the Celts. Mauss was elected to the Collège de France, and for ten years he was to lecture some eight hours a week, in three different institutions. At that time he seemed required by Destiny to stand bravely, alone, or almost so, in the place of the whole team of scholars with whom he had originally worked. Still, he did so with ease, sustaining the role of encyclopaedic scholar as if the material basis of knowledge had not enormously increased in fifty years, keeping contact with history, with psychology, with philosophy, with geography. This, together with his respect for facts, probably explains why he published relatively little during that period. Yet surely the ideas he generously scattered in the pages of the "Techniques du corps" or of "La notion de personne" would have sufficed to establish the reputation of any other scholar. He had too many ideas to express any one of them in detail.

Then came the Second World War, which was to repeat with heightened cruelty the trials of the first. This time Mauss's reason did not survive the ordeal. His memory wandered from time to time, and he had lost his powers of reasoning, perhaps as a result of affective as well as intellectual overstrain, by the time he died on 10 February 1950.

We can now follow Mauss's career with a view to emphasizing the concrete aspect of his thought. Our main concern will be to identify the role played in research by the anthropologist's ideas on one hand and by the data he studies on the other.

In 1897 Mauss wrote a long article about Steinmetz's *Studies in the Early Development of Sanction* (Mauss 1968–69, 2: 651 ff.), which attempts to show that sanction developed out of private revenge. While highly praising the method, Mauss made one fundamental objection and was led to sketch the subject as he saw it. The author, says Mauss, does not define; he merely classifies according to commonsense ideas ("Il ne définit pas, il classe selon les notions communes"). Only recently, continues Mauss, has the word *sanction* taken on the rational, utilitarian character that is familiar to us. This is a very particular notion, and, in order to exist, sociology demands something more general. Mauss believes primitive societies have more in common with our own, and he wants a definition common to both. He says that Steinmetz, failing to define sociologically, has missed the common element that underlies all criminal law. Sanction is any punishment falling upon one who has violated law and custom. In archaic societies, transgression provokes a religious reaction (although not always), and it was from that reaction that criminal law developed: not only do our modern laws contain remnants of primitive private revenge, but the original type of juridical reaction contain something like the germ of our penal system.

The main point here for our argument is that a sociological definition is meant to express what we have in common with primitive societies. Mauss says "If one restricts oneself (as M. Steinmetz does) to the study of noncivilized people, one loses sight of the function and even of the functioning of sanction." This clearly implies, it seems to me, that it is through our own culture that we can understand another, and vice versa.

But the possibility of such a general definition rests upon an assumption about the unity of mankind, and we may ask whence this assumption in turn derives. Steinmetz had written that ethnology should be established upon two principles: the principle of evolution, and the principle of social consciousness (*Völkergedanke*). Mauss argues that the latter may suffice, as the bearing of the evolution principle is purely negative: it just means rejecting any difference in nature between races as well as the explanation by diffusion: to deny that races are irreducible is to affirm the unity of mankind. To throw aside the historical (diffusion) explanation is to restrict oneself, in the present case, to the anthropological method, which postulates the fundamental unity of the human mind:

> Nier l'irréductibilité des races, c'est poser l'unité du genre humain. Ecarter la méthode historique, c'est se réduire, dans le cas présent, à la méthode anthropologique" (1968–69, 2: 653).

"L'unité du genre humain" is an idea seen throughout the development of sociological thought in France. The historical role of the early English anthropological school was fully recognized by Mauss in the first volume of the *Année*:

> The facts previously studied in classical history, or comparative philology, or folklore, are illuminated by constant comparison with the facts of primitive religions. Thus it appears that those three orders of facts—primitive religions, religions of ancient civilized peoples, and survivals of beliefs and rituals in the local usages and traditions of Europe and Asia—are fundamentally identical (1968–69, 1: 110).

Yet anthropologists themselves started from evolutionary premises. We may reject evolutionism today, but we should not forget that it was evolutionism that fused the "we" and the "others," civilized and barbarians, into one species. The idea of evolution has worked like a preliminary scaffolding to unite discrete sets before they could be incorporated in a single whole. Now we find that whole is rather shapeless, and we demand a study of differences, as Mauss did again and again. But it would not have been possible to study differences before the basic unity was established.

In his inaugural lecture on assuming the History of Religions chair in 1901, Mauss presented his methodological principles. First, strictly speaking, there are no "uncivilized people," there are just peoples with different civilizations. Australian society is neither simple nor primitive; it has a long history, as our own has. But just as among animals we find living species which, although as old as the mammals, are simpler and more akin to the species of earlier geological eras, now extinct, in the same way Arunta society is nearer than ours to the primitive forms of society. For instance, although Arunta totemism is in a state of advanced decay, birth is not a mere biological fact for them; it is also a magico-religious event, for an Arunta belongs to the clan of the totemic spirit that is believed to have entered the bosom of his mother, and this leads us back to really primitive ideas: "It will be one of our main and most delicate tasks to keep examining to what extent the facts we study show us back to the really elementary forms of phenomena" (1968–69, 1: 490–91).

We see that evolutionist ideas are not absent here. But this is not the only reason why a careful analysis of the data is required. For if ethnographical facts, some of them authentic, are plentiful, if, thanks to modern techniques and training, we have better information about the Hopi ritual than about the Levitic sacrifice, not to speak of Greek sacrificial ritual, that still does not mean that all documents have the same value, and "we shall have to exercise in common our critical faculty" by detailed examination of the documents. "We shall have to search for all the critical aspects necessary to discover . . . the real fact that is being spoken of" (1968–69, 3: 365–71).

There are difficulties, which are common to all observation of social phenomena. First, all information comes from the natives, and nothing is more difficult, even for us, than to say what our institutions really are. As a missionary from Korea says: "Custom, as well as language, is a property of which the owner is unconscious." That is why the ethnographer has to dig beneath the best native information to the "underlying facts, which are almost unconscious because they exist only in collective tradition. But these are the real facts, the *things* [cf. Durkheim!] that we shall try to reach through the documents."

"If it is as social phenomena that religious facts are to be observed, it is even more important that they should be accounted for as such. . . . We shall arrive at hypotheses which, though of course temporary, will nevertheless be rational and objective." The intellectualist and psychological approach is over and done with. "For instance, the fact with which mourning rites are directly connected is family organization; they depend upon that, not upon vague and imprecise feelings." We have to "keep to the solid ground of religious and social facts, to search only for immediately determining causes, and to renounce universal theories which explain only the possibility of the facts."

That is what Mauss taught in 1901. The method is firm, there is no theory-for-itself. Much stress is laid upon the intellectual analysis necessary to transform the data into well-established facts. This Mauss went on doing for almost forty years in his seminar, in which, in the late 1930s, I witnessed the study of some of Malinowski's texts. Here Mauss, thanks to his knowledge of Melanesia and Polynesia, could attain a view of the Trobrianders which differed notably from that of their observer. Such a scientific achievement, where comparison brought a deeper insight—as Malinowski recognized on one occasion—was only made possible by Malinowski's publication of a large corpus of data, a method growing rare in our day.

On the subject of explanation, Mauss was just as unswerving. In a review he says that "a rigorous philology, a scrupulous sociology understand, they do not interpret." And in his last lectures on Sin and Expiation he still repeated: "Sociological explanation is completed when one has seen *what* it is that the people believe and think, and *who* the people are who believe and think that." A recommendation that is perhaps not entirely out of date.

The *Essai sur le sacrifice* was published in 1899, two years before the second edition of the *Golden Bough*. No doubt the large gap that separates the two works, one of which now appears as fresh as the other is antiquated, was produced by the Hubert and Mauss's adoption of the sociological method. The *Essai* was intended as Hubert and Mauss's first step in a systematic study of religion. Their approach is stated in the preface to the *Mélanges* of 1908. The method consisted in starting out from a typical, crucial fact, and sacrifice was chosen for that reason. Through it, Robertson Smith's ideas about the sacred and the profane were tested and developed. If time allowed, I wish I could praise at least the Indian part of the *Essai*. Everything here is amazing, the quality of the work, its peculiar situation in Indian research, and, not least, the fact that it did almost nothing but order the data, for the fruits of Indian thinking were there, ripe and ready for plucking. Only they looked unconvincing to philologists, and a sanskrit-reading sociologist was needed to harvest them.

The year 1901 brings the article "Sociologie," written in collaboration with Fauconnet in the *Grande Encyclopédie*. It is remarkable that obligation, although discussed here as a characteristic of social facts, is not retained in the end, and the emphasis is rather on "institutions" defined very broadly. Still more clearly later, mainly in 1908, Mauss departs from Durkheim's definition, especially with respect to religion: "For us, obligation is not a characteristic of social facts."

In 1903, in collaboration with Durkheim, the article "De quelques formes primitives de classification," with the subtitle "Contribution à l'étude des représentations collectives," opens a line that was to be pursued, although incompletely, and probably represents one of Mauss's major interests. Hubert was later to study time, Mauss substance, Czarnowski space, and so forth. Important as it is, this article seems to be surprisingly loosely connected with the idea of the sacred. It is possible that the connection was established only through Frazer's *Origins of Totemism*, a quite unexpected contribution. Moreover, I perceive a touch of disdain in the approach to primitive ideas, which was quite foreign to Mauss's factual and sympathetic outlook, and which one is inclined to attribute to the philosopher Durkheim.

In 1904, the line opened by the *Essai sur le* sacrifice was continued by the "Esquisse d'une théorie générale de la magie," completed by a part of its critical basis: "L'origine des pouvoirs magiques." Exceptionally here the object is not concrete, as in the *Essai*, but more abstract and also not geographically limited. Though all that is justified in the introduction, it may be the reason why it is not one of the most successful writings. The question of *mana* is posed here, on which I refer you once again to Lévi-Strauss's Introduction.

1906 saw the publication, in collaboration with Beuchat, of the *Essai sur les migrations saisonnières des sociétés eskimo*. Here again the choice of topic issued from the search for a typical case, this time regarding the interrelation between morphology and physiology within society. I mention only in passing the beginning, about a hundred pages, of a work on prayer, privately printed in 1909 and apparently discontinued, and the minor writings, which were still to increase in numbear.

In 1925, Mauss publishes the *Essai sur le don* ("Essay on Gift"). Here again the subject matter is largely concrete, and geographically circumscribed in the initial stages (Northwest Coast Indians, Melanesia). Here again Mauss searched for and, indeed, found the typical fact, "le fait privilégié," what he here called *a total social fact*. It was one of his leitmotivs that the aim of research was to study not bits and pieces but a whole, a total, something with an internal consistency one can be sure of. How is this to be found? In a sense, society is the only "whole," but it is so complex that however scrupulously we reconstruct it, there is doubt about the result. But there are cases where consistency is found in less extended complexes, where the "whole" can be more easily kept within view, and this is one. The whole society is present, as condensed, in the potlatch. Here lay that "typical fact," the scientific study of which would be sufficient to establish a law or, rather, as I think we should more exactly say, a fact which compels the observer—at least when the observer is Mauss—to transcend the categories through which he approaches it. These are our commonsense or economic ideas of gift and exchange, as the title indicates. They are confronted with a corpus of data, and from this confrontation results the scientific category of potlatch or "total prestations of competitive character." This, taken from Mauss himself, is an example of a process to which we shall have to return.

As to the idea of a "whole," seductive and enigmatic, perhaps all too concrete, Mauss never categorically answers the question, What does characterize a "whole"? Still, he often emphasizes the importance of differences and separations; he says that the taboo of contact, the rules which separate one kind of thing from another, are as important as the identifications, the contagions, what Lévy-Bruhl called participation. We may say that Mauss came as near as possible to defining a "whole" as a structure, i.e. I submit a combination of "participations" around one or more *oppositions*. Here it is difficult to escape Lévi-Strauss's structural developments, and I refer you to him once more.

We noted earlier how Mauss dealt with general problems. A long paper about classification, entitled "Divisions et proportions des divisions de la sociologie" (1927), is quite characteristic of his attitude to Durkheim's legacy and of his own tendencies, as well as of his respect for the knowledge brought by other specialities, and of his awareness of the requirements of research. He explains what corrections and adjustments the old framework of the *Année* would require. Essential, in my view, is the recognition that all those categories of religion, law and morals, economy, etc., are after all "fixed by the historical state of the civilizations of which our science itself is the product." "It is not certain," says Mauss, "whether we would have been able to separate religion and morals, for instance,

if the distinction had not already been made in our civilizations"
(1968–69, 3: 220). Finally all those categories which seem to enter
proudly and as of their own right into science are anything but
objective; they belong exclusively to our own common sense; they
are no scientific sociological categories, but just practical contriv-
ances, necessary evils. (This is a schematic, somewhat forced
rendering, but see for instance 1968–69, 2: 178–79, 202–4.)

Still, Mauss thinks the old framework should be kept, but with
what satisfaction he introduces, as a supplement and a correction to
it, another classification, the division into morphology and physiology, form and functioning, the latter subdivided in turn into representations and practices, i.e. ideas and actions. He celebrates the
advantages of this division: it does not involve any preconceived
idea, but takes the facts as they are, because it is concrete
(*concrete!*). After he has shown how usefully the two divisions may
be made to cut across one another, he insists as usual on the
necessity for reconstruction after analysis: "After cutting up more
or less arbitrarily, one must sew things up again." You will observe
that in these simple words we are presented with the same thing that
some people nowadays more pretentiously call the social function
of this or that. Mauss is even more rigorous, because he does not
rely upon the categories used for analysis.

One more remark: Mauss used to say of his work with Hubert:
"There were two oxen to pull the plow, one was the mythologist,
the other the ritologist, and now that only one is left, the work is
more difficult." No doubt this is why Mauss affirms as a fact of
experience that the division into representations and practices is
useful and practical. He also justifies it by an insightful comment:
"Very often," he says, "collective representations [say, myths]
have more affinities, more natural connections among themselves
than they have even with the various forms of social activity that
correspond to them particularly, one to one [*i.e.* rites]."

A later article of the same kind, the "Fragment d'un plan de
sociologie générale descriptive," also shows comparatively the
range of Mauss's open-mindedness. On the one hand, social cohesion, authority, discipline, tradition, education do not constitute
the essence of sociology—as they do in functionalism—but are
merely its general aspect, and on the other hand they are only a
part, the intrasocial part of the "general social phenomena," which
also comprise the intersocial facts (peace and war, civilization).
Mauss defined civilization in a communication of 1929 in which he

also gave a definitive judgment about the contributions and the limits of the Culture Morphology and the Culture Circles schools of ethnology. In fact, Mauss never separated the study of exotic societies either from the study of our own or from the study of culture.

Since it was in the last period that I enjoyed some—too few—of Mauss's lectures, I would like to offer two examples to show the degree to which he carried his respect for facts. In 1937, he entitled one of his lecture series in the Collège de France, "On the greasy pole, the ball play, and some other games of the periphery of the Pacific Ocean." He began with New Zealand and was then caught in Maori cosmogony, with which he was familiar. But one day he arrived at his lecture quite excited. "You must always reread the sources, he said. There is one thing I had overlooked in White's figure (at the end of the first volume). It is even simpler and more extraordinary than I had thought. We have to begin again." That year he did not go farther than New Zealand.[1]

Another example: Mauss lectured for years on "Sin and Expiation in Polynesia." At first he wanted to complete and publish Hertz's research on the matter, and then he developed and improved it year after year. It was almost done, when he received a valuable manuscript from Hawaii which was to confirm and enlarge the study. The course of lectures was expanded again—and never published. It is a great pity. A scholar might possibly devote himself to their publication, but it would be no easy task, for these lectures that were so illuminating for the audience lie at the limit of shorthand and esoteric knowledge:[2] to really understand Mauss, you have to reconstruct the whole movement of his thought—an exercise that is not always possible.

We might describe what went on in the mind of that great scholar as a kind of short-circuit: accustomed to move in his own idiom from one people to another, or from one level of abstraction

1. (1984 *note*.) Alas! I am sure of the "fact," and yet something is wrong in my rendition. What was in question was the interpretation of *tiki*. It is clear, from Mauss 1968–69, 2: 156, 160 that in 1934—that is, some three or four years before the scene I recount—Mauss discovered in the British Museum Library that the notes taken by himself and Hertz in the 1900s were grievously incomplete. If Mauss was as excited as I perceived him to be, it was therefore not because the discovery was recent—as I wrongly imagined—but because it was so important and in a sense so shocking for him.

2. (1984 *note*.) Mauss's own notes having not been recovered, I tried in vain to reconstruct the lectures from several of the auditors' notes.

to another, he took less and less care in communicating his experience by translating it at length in scientific language. What had begun as a science finished largely as an art; the balance was not kept between personal identification and rational expression. Mauss had largely transcended by concrete experience the categories with which many sociologists are still satisfied. He had not transcended them for the most part scientifically. Among other reasons for this was his extraordinary concrete versatility, which made not only for his greatness but, by multiplying the problems, for his failure. He had gone too far ahead for his voice to be easily heard.

After what was said above of the choice of subject matter in Mauss's writings, of his notion of the "typical fact," the "whole social fact," of theory as a preliminary condition—classification and definition allowing for an adequate transformation of raw data into sociological fact—we could perhaps already speak of an experimental spirit. But the relation between theory and data, between the observer and the observed, between subject and object, needs to be discussed a little more. We can do it conveniently by asking whether there is in Maussian anthropology anything like what is called *experiment* in the natural sciences and, if so, in what it consists. Not to ask this question, I think, would be to miss the main point, not only with regard to Mauss's place in the development of sociological thought, but also with regard to the general attitude of anthropologists at the present day and the relation between anthropology and general sociology.

If anthropology were to give a definitive classification of societies or enunciate laws like those of natural science, it would first have to have at its disposal definitive concepts and principles. Mauss, however, felt very strongly the temporary and imperfect character of its present conceptual tools. Having drafted a plan of general sociology for concrete purposes, he ends the discussion with these words:

> There is not much use in philosophizing about general sociology . . . when there is still so much to do in order to *know*, and then so much more in order to *understand* (1968–69, 3: 354; my italics).

We saw what is meant here by *to know*. But what is meant by *to understand*? Is it only to see the interrelations or, better, to reconstruct the real fact, the "whole" fact which has been, necessarily but more or less arbitrarily, broken into elements by analysis? There is probably something more in the term "to understand," something we already encountered and which is always implicit with Mauss— understanding from the inside, that remarkable faculty which springs from the unity of mankind, by which we are able to identify ourselves, under certain conditions, with people living in other societies, and think in their categories, that faculty by which, as Lévi-Strauss says, the observer becomes a part of the observed. On this point we shall consider another of Mauss's conclusions, the importance of which could easily be missed because it is expressed in a deceptive form: "The Aristotelian categories are not the only ones which exist. We have first of all to make the largest possible catalogue of categories."

There is little doubt, for those who know Mauss, that "making a catalogue" means nothing less here than experiencing the categories, getting into them, elaborating them into sociological facts. Of course, we are close to the idea of fieldwork as practiced in England and the theory of it as set down by Professor Evans-Pritchard. To see how "understanding" and "making a catalogue of categories" are essentially the same thing, let us take one more example, a quite unpretentious one, after those of the sanction and of potlatch. By applying our category "father," Morgan found it impossible to understand what he called the Malayan system of kinship terminology. He *interpreted*, he explained away this difficulty by an elaborate theory of previous group marriage, etc. But when it was afterward admitted that the native category could be *understood*, the explanatory theory, having become useless, was rejected, and a new category appeared, that of "classificatory father," which is scientific just as far as it subsumes our commonsense category and that of the natives.

If I am not mistaken, scientific anthropological categories are only engendered that way: out of a contradiction between our categories and others' categories, out of a clash between the theory and the data. I submit that this is the reason why Mauss did not want a philosophy (that is, a speculation with unsatisfactory concepts) but an inventory of categories (equivalent to the building of scientific concepts).

I conclude that we are thus justified for speaking of an *experimental stage* of sociology. Here the two processes of experimentation and conceptualization are not apart. If there is a difference between this and ordinary experimentation, it is that in anthropology the experiment does not only test a hypothesis but reacts on the concepts themselves—contributes, in fact, to the building of scientific concepts. As a result of the identification of the observer with the observed, the experiment springs into the observer himself.

What has just been said contains, it is not to be denied, an element of personal interpretation. But I think I have merely given precise form to something which pervaded Mauss's thought, which he did not express precisely because it was self-evident for him (as custom for the native). Coming from a different point of departure, we meet Lévi-Strauss here on one of his points. It seems impossible to do otherwise if one wants to show how Mauss went beyond Durkheim. Experimentation here involves the subject in the object, as is obvious from the work of many anthropologists, and scientific objectivity demands that this be recognized. It would seem that the nonanthropologists among French sociologists have not appreciated the importance of that fact, which makes perhaps for the particular value of anthropology as among other sociological disciplines.

It may be argued that by reintroducing the subject we are doing away with science and breaking with the whole tradition of the Enlightenment and of the French speculative sociologists, whose efforts aimed at extending science to society. But this does not follow. It so happens that some of the conditions of a science of society have just been discovered. We need neither continue automatically as though that had not happened, nor switch over to another mode of thought, but must simply continue the development in a new stage by recognizing the new conditions and working accordingly.

Now it is possible, as a conclusion, to review in what I hope to be a Maussian perspective the main attitudes of anthropologists at the present time. First, on the vexed question of whether anthropology will one day attain universal truths, we may perhaps say that, although it is very doubtful whether it can ever formulate a universal knowledge of the same kind and in the same form as do the natural sciences, some universal value has already crept in and is contained in every concept by the help of which the anthropologist passes from one society into another. If not a science-in-itself, it is already in that sense a science-in-the-making. True, we have to recognize that if on the one hand the general value, which is often sought in vain in laws and general statements, is in fact present immanently in the tools anthropology uses, on the other hand it is very unequally distributed thus far and still often in an embryonic state. It has to be developed, which brings us to a second point.

Intellectual development, the process of better conceptualization, is perhaps the core of anthropological progress, much more so than the mere accumulation of data. This is shown by the really accomplished monographs, those in which the facts really bring with them their adequate conceptual elaboration, typified by Evans-Pritchard's *Nuer*. But when this is not recognized, when, in Mauss's terms, it is thought that there is no need, once we *know* things, for a slow and painstaking process in order to *understand* them, when this understanding is not conceived as taking place in time, but as either instantaneous or impossible, then certain tendencies appear which are, I believe, unscientific.

One is a kind of chronic disappointment. Once what I call commonsense concepts are taken at their face value for scientific ones, then it becomes hard to understand the present imperfect state of the discipline. People forget the prodigious progress of the recent past, and are about to despair; they want to build a science of man as rapidly as a skyscraper, they take to complicated modes of calculation, or search for new topics. Or else the double intellectual effort of identification and abstraction is despised, the present state of things is made into an ideal, and we are told that we should be satisfied with studying facts without assuming or trying to discover their consistency, as if our mind were not a part of society even more strictly than it is a part of nature at large. All this suggests a very low opinion of man as an object, for his discovery is certainly worth more labors, as well as subject, for certainly the anthropologist is able to think more accurately than he does at present.

Now if we are asked what will happen to anthropology once economic progress has made all archaic people into modern citizens of the world, we may perhaps answer that by that time anthropology will have progressed enough for us to be able to build our own sociology, something that would probably have been impossible if the existence of different societies had not forced us to get out of ourselves and look scientifically at men as social beings.

In that enterprise, I do not think that Mauss's part will have been negligible. Through his personal genius and historical position he could conceive better than many the conditions to be fulfilled.

True, he was unable to raise the art of understanding to the level of a science by his sole exertion, but he himself certainly never thought it could be an individual enterprise but only the work of generations of diverse callings. His legacy is one of widened reason and deepened optimism.

8 The Anthropological Community and Ideology

This paper offers some general views which a series of circumstances had led the author to make somewhat more precise and systematic. Whatever may have been the achievements and advances and the recent development of anthropology, its present situation and its future—particularly, but not exclusively in France—remain for many of us, no doubt in different ways, a cause for concern. It is hoped that the following reflections, in principle purely theoretical, will assist in clarifying the situation and hence, if possible, in strengthening the unity of the discipline.

1. The Discipline in Its Relation to Ideologies

Confronted with such a problem, it is natural to turn toward the past and in particular toward the recent development of our studies. If I consider the perspective which I thought twenty-five years ago I had been able to derive from Mauss's teaching, I can still maintain its

This paper was first presented at my seminar at the Ecole des Hautes Etudes en Sciences Sociales (EHESS) and then at the Department of Anthropology of the University of Chicago. I should like to thank the audiences for their often extremely useful observations. Since then, the first part has been developed, though in certain respects it still remains most summary. The intention was to offer for the consideration of anthropologists a principle expounded with sufficient explicitness, together with some indication of the consequences entailed. In all but the essential matters, there appeared to be no inconvenience attached to the use of approximate language. Thus, all systems of ideas and values, whether in the stricter or the broader acception, are referred to as ideologies or, in the American fashion, as culture, or even as society; no distinction is made between social anthropology and cultural anthropology. As my intent is constructive and not polemical, I have in the first part omitted general tenor, but I should need to temper my somewhat juvenile optimism of the time and correct the assertion of a problem-free continuity with regard to the ideal of the Enlightenment.[1] There is indeed a problem, one which is crucial for us at the theoretical level, and which furthermore corresponds to a cardinal problem of modern civilization. One would need only to examine Mauss in greater depth to perceive it.

In considering the anthropology of the last thirty years, one may feel glad in the first approximate assessment, at the generally increasing place assigned within the discipline to the systems of ideas and of values or ideologies. By way of complementarity, this fact at once suggests a reflection on the ideology of the anthropologist himself, in the double sense of the ideology of his speciality and that of surrounding society—I mean the modern society of which we as anthropologists form part, whatever may be our nationality, our place or culture of origin, etc. This will be my first theme.

A moment ago, I said "in the first approximative assessment." The development of anthropology appears, in fact, to be suffering from a chronic discontinuity which leads one to wonder whether each step forward is not followed by a step back. In the second part of this essay, I shall give an example relating precisely to the study of ideologies. It would seem that a feverish impatience is driving us headlong to forget or swiftly compromise our most valuable acquisitions. This is a trait which may have come from the United States, where transitory fashions rapidly succeed each other in an ideological and institutional climate of competition which favors overbidding (see the last part of chapter 7 above), but it is a fact often encountered in modern thought, though the intensity may vary. It is true that the succession of predominant theories, from functionalism to structuralism and "symbolic analysis," is often presented as an ordered sequence of developments each of which was ephemeral because incomplete in itself. I suspect there is some complacency in such a view and, at the risk of myself exaggerating, I shall say that we are living, according to all appearance, in a

---

references bearing on controversial aspects and have not provided a formal bibliography.

This article was first published in French in *L'Homme* 18, nos. 3/4 (1978): 83–110. The translation, by Alan McConnell Duff in collaboration with the author, was published in *Social Science Information* 18, no. 6 (1979): 785–817.

    1. Cf. chapter 7 above.

permanent revolution. In the alternation of phases that Thomas Kuhn detected in the history of the sciences, one—the "structural revolution"—appears to be permanent in anthropology, while little room is left for the calmer, less ambitious phase of "puzzle-solving" when, in between two revolutions, everyone is agreed about the general framework.

The weakness of the scientific community in the social sciences can be explained as deriving from the very character of these disciplines. It is, in fact, in their nature to be the most directly exposed to the surrounding ideology. Now, this ideology is not only fundamentally opposed—in my opinion, because it is individualistic—to the principle of anthropology and all sound or thorough sociology, it is also split up into diverse tendencies. Consequently, it cannot but weaken the consensus one would expect from the scientific community in a period of stability. Conversely, it is clear that the weaker the consensus the less able the community will be to resist the pressures, or even incursions, of the general ideology.

The lack of consensus within the profession is best seen in another trait: the proliferation of more or less conflicting tendencies within the discipline, which now seems on the point of splitting into an indefinite number of anthropologies, each one bearing its particular qualifier. This, however, is a sweeping statement, and a more precise formulation is needed. I shall therefore define three levels: (1) specialized activities, each concerned with a more or less well-defined field of study within the domain of anthropology proper or in areas bordering on other disciplines; (2) rival approaches, relating to the same global domain, but more or less mutually incompatible; such rivalries there have always been, and, while it may be true that they are increasing in number, they still in principle spring from the same ideal and acknowledge the same scientific criteria; (3) approaches or would-be approaches, which have recently been multiplying and which, in the guise of a specific anthropology, are in reality intent on subjecting anthropology to nonanthropological concerns. There is good reason for attentively observing the transition from (1) and (2) to (3), since it leads to the substitution of an imported dogma for the basic tenets of anthropological research. Generally, it is at level (3) that the pressure of the ideology of the environment makes itself most directly felt in the form of various "activisms."

The anthropological community, institutionally at least, is weaker in France than elsewhere. A recent symposium organized with the intention of remedying a notorious deficiency in the profession by laying the basis for a French anthropological association, left the impression (on one who, it is true, was unable to follow the entire proceedings) of extreme confusion, due in part to the development of tendency (3) among the emerging generation. It is clear to the present writer that there can be no hope of uniting anthropologists in an association which would propose acknowledging these pseudo-anthropologies, which are in fact so many anti-anthropologies. This said, I believe we have to do here with more than a surface phenomenon, something that is not unrelated—merely falsely related—to the true nature of anthropology. Under different forms, occasionally caricatural ones, personal commitment, which is total by definition, demands the sacrifice of anthropology as a scientific, specialized-activity discipline subject to its own rules and bound to an international community of specialists. What gives rise to confusion, inasmuch as anthropology is concerned, is the scope of its ambition, the promise it tacitly holds of in some way transcending the specialties, and giving access to a seamless totality, a promise that legitimately attracts the young, and that one should not like to deny, even though one must sharply circumscribe it. I have used the vague word "totality." Our contemporaries readily confuse totality and totalitarianism, or rather, totalitarianism involves a confusion regarding totality. It is necessary, therefore, to specify what totality is involved, to show not only that it is compatible with specialization but also that the promise of anthropology requires that the individual should agree to distinguish between his absolute convictions and his specialized activity as an anthropologist. I do not know if I shall succeed in bringing this out, but I believe that what follows is relevant to the issue. I have the feeling that here we are touching upon the ground where many present misunderstandings are rooted: misunderstandings about the relation of anthropology to the modern world, about the kind of (limited) totality anthropology legitimately aims at, and about the place it may—or may not—give to the concrete social totalities which are its primary objects. All in all, misunderstandings as to the necessary and limited sway to be allowed to both modern and nonmodern constraints. Our profession is not a form of mysticism, nor is it an art of entertainment or conversation.

What is called for is a definition of anthropology that illuminates its ideological bearings by revealing their principle.

Marcel Mauss has given—as early as 1900—what is in fact a definition of social anthropology. First, to say "anthropology" is "to posit the unity of mankind." Then, "in order to provide a scientific picture one must consider the differences, and to do this one requires a sociological method" (*HH*, 324, notes 1 and 2). All is said there; one need only draw the implications of these two succinct statements. We shall do so by degrees. With the affirmation of the unity of mankind, we find ourselves within the modern system of ideas and values, citizens of the world together with our contemporaries and in particular with our colleagues in the other "human sciences" and the exact sciences: in essence, there are only individual men at one end, and the human species, often called the "society of mankind," at the other. But that is not all: the consideration of "differences" leads us, if only we will give it its full weight, into quite another mental universe: together with Rousseau, we posit that men are men only by virtue of their belonging to a specific, concrete global society, and from this point of view the "society of mankind" just mentioned appears to be an ideal abstraction, as Rousseau said in what was in fact a reply to Diderot.[2]

But should the recognition of difference be taken so far? It will be objected that our view is not generally held, and that it must surely be possible to operate at a lesser cost since many do so in practice—not to say all of us most of the time; on the one hand not everybody pays allegiance to the global approach, on the other there exist a few categories applicable to all societies, a few social universals, and that is enough for differences to be transcended, and talked about.

Now, the development to which I alluded at the beginning has, on the whole, rehabilitated the indigenous ideologies as against our own, and, correlatively, made apparent the ethnocentric—or as I prefer to call it, sociocentric—character of many of our naive or pretended universals. The radical thesis I am putting forward has the heuristic value of the limiting case. It also has other merits. For instance, it corresponds to various formulas by means of which the situation or function of the anthropologist is often expressed: social facts are, and are not, things; the anthropologist must "translate" one mentality into another; he identifies himself with the observed while still remaining an observer; he needs to see things both from within and from without, etc. At the heart of all these formulas is hidden our opposition, and this is what gives them their full mean-

2. In the first version of the *Contrat Social* (Rousseau 1964, book 1, chap. 2, p. 287); cf. chap. 2, n. 27, above.

ing: on the one hand, we have the modern individualism cum universalism, in which alone anthroplogy's ambition is grounded—I beg that this fact be given its due weight; on the other hand, we have a society or culture closed in upon itself and identifying humanity with its own specific form (while subordinating man to the society as a whole, which is why I speak of "holism"). Here it is that anthropology begins. It modifies and combines the two terms of this encounter. The point must be underlined.

We sift, so to speak, the discourse that comes to us from the society we observe (supposing it to be a nonmodern one).[3] We accept the claim of those people to be men, but we reject their claim to be *the only men*, that is the naive devaluation of the outsider. In other terms, we reject the exclusivism or absolute sociocentricism that accompanies every holistic ideology.

At the opposite pole, our own universalism itself undergoes a modification in two aspects at least: between individual and species it agrees, roughly speaking, to interpose a middle term, the society. That is to say, individualism is maintained as the ultimate value, but not as a (naive) mode of describing society. That this last statement, incontrovertible as it is, encounters an obstinate resistance within the social sciences themselves should warn us—if need be—of the strength of collective representations, and of the absolute necessity of not antagonizing the common (modern) consciousness by presuming to teach it what even specialists find offensive. On this point, we may well imagine that anthropological specialization corresponds to an avant-garde that is necessary in the movement of ideas. From this first aspect there follows a second: we ourselves are made to look back on *our own modern culture and society as on a particular form of humanity* that is exceptional in that it denies itself as such by its profession of universalism.

Of course, this modified universalism is open to all, and in particular to the other human sciences, but it characterizes anthropology in the sense that it springs from the heart of our practice. Seen from without, it represents a mixture, indeed a somewhat subtle mixture, of modernity and tradition, universalism and particularism.[4] In principle, neither of these two poles, the univer-

3. In a modern society, sociocentrism would not be absent but it would be mediatized. I have chosen the more typical situation.

4. Supposing one wished this professional point of view to be matched by a political attitude in the broadest sense, it would be dominated by the idea of the world as a unit in the process of becoming, which would seem—contrary, perhaps, to

salist and the "diferential" can be challenged. But if one refuses the combination proposed here, if one alters, in one way or another, the balance of the ingredients, one ends up with one or another of the contemporary errors or misunderstandings. When, for example, setting out from the fact that a modern society can be studied anthropologically by a person who was born in another culture, in which he remains partly situated, one draws the conclusion that there may be a multiplicity of anthropologies, i.e. as many as there are distinct cultures, then one quite simply forgets the universal reference. In reality, there is no symmetry between the modern pole, where anthropology is located, and the nonmodern pole. I hope the point will become clearer in what follows.

So much for the normative level. Now, at the factual level, the view proposed is valuable, I think, as a principle of integration. The different varieties of anthropology as practiced at present can be located in relation to this principle. It is not a particular viewpoint that would exclude others, but a perspective of sufficient scope and precision to bring together the scattered parts of a common effort. For instance, the simple description, the *complete* ethnographic monograph, so excessively decried in our time, recovers here its legitimation. Moreover, the difficulty of realization is in general so great that it is natural for one to resort most often to compartmentalizations or simplifications which, having emerged in the course of development, combine the universal and the specific in a variable and incomplete way. One may regard these simplifications as temporary landing stages, the merits of which must be estimated at each particular moment in relation to the global aim. Ours is a science in the process of becoming, which, to a large extent, progresses by means of approximations that are successive and/or simultaneous (cf. chapter 7 above).

Finally, I believe that the place of anthropology thus characterized in the world of yesterday, today, and tomorrow emerges clearly, in contradiction, perhaps, to certain more or less widespread prejudices.[5] While maintaining the full distance between the

---

widespread ideas—to require a dose of progressiveness (and not jealous conservatism) for nonmodern societies, and a (certain) conservatism (the opposite of the "flight forward") for modern ones. (Cf. note 5 below and further on in the text.)

5. A humanitarian society recently launched a campaign against the "sexual mutilations" inflicted by certain societies upon "millions of young and adolescent girls" (Vichniac 1977). The practices concerned are linked to the initiation of girls.

two, one perceives a general consonance between the definition and the future of our discipline and the foreseeable or desirable evolution of the world. Without prejudicing the originality which one would like each culture to retain, it is clear that the nonmodern cultures are going to weigh more and more heavily in the making of the common civilization of the world (Dumont 1975b: 159). Now, this process presupposes a reciprocal action between the universal and the specific, similar to that which we saw at the core of our profession. This, it is true, raises a formidable question, a question which today dominates the world scene—and, in fact, all the more restricted political scenes—a question which cannot be passed over in silence, even if it does extent well beyond our domain, and even if it still cannot be more than most imperfectly formulated. Let me therefore confine within a parenthesis the gross statement that must be made. The great contemporary challenge to modern values results from the claim—or the problem—of human solidarity on a world scale, and of justice, particularly at the economic level, in the relations between peoples and states. Condorcet already foresaw in 1793 that inequality would completely disappear between peoples, and only there. No doubt, in relation to the present state of affairs, the World Movement (le Mouvement Mondialiste) seems, for all one knows, to have little advanced its thinking, and one can well see why. But perhaps it is running up against the same contradiction around which the present reflections center. It may well be, then, that anthropology has a contribution to make in the matter.

Thus far, I have done no more than state a principle. Can it be realized, and how? Here, German thought will serve, both positively and negatively, to guide us. We may see our immediate ancestor in Johann Gottfried Herder, who described the cultural community (rather than the strictly social community) as *Volk*, people. In *Another Philosophy of History* in 1774, he staked a claim

---

As it does not lie within my competence, I shall leave aside the details, the alleged particularities, and the errors of interpretation, in order to raise only the general issue. Here is, surely, a case in which anthropology is brought directly into question, one in which we can neither reject outright the modern values underlying the protest, nor simply endorse the condemnation pronounced, which would amount to authorizing interference in the collective life of a population. Ideally then, we are bound to consider the particular configuration of each case in order to state the forms and limit under which modern universalism may be justified in intervening.

for the original and specific value of every cultural community (see chapter 4 above). This was a passionate protest against the universalism of the Enlightenment, particularly in France, which Herder accused of being superficial and vain, of impoverishing the complexity and rich diversity of cultures, and, as such, of acting as a force of oppression—at least implicitly—when confronted with the vital unity of a particular culture, such as that of Germany. I should stress that Herder perceived forcefully at the outset the opposition between the two conceptions—which we might call individualist universalism and cultural holism—even though later, like many others after him, and without great effect, he tried to transcend the quarrel. I would like to add one remark: a reaction such as that of Herder is likely to appear whenever a particular culture feels itself threatened by modern universalist culture. Herder exerted a profound influence on the emergence of nationalism among the Slavic peoples (including the Czechs); moreover, the impact of modern culture on India, where no Herderian influence has been detected, has produced a similar reaction. One can generalize hypothetically for the present and the future.

Another German thinker, from whom Herder was by no means independent in this respect, offers us a model that fits our needs: I am speaking of Leibniz and his system of monads. Each culture (or society) expresses the universal *in its own way*, as does each of Leibniz's monads; and it is not impossible to conceive of a procedure—complicated and laborious it is true—which would enable one to pass from one monad or culture to another through the intermediary of the universal taken as the sum integral of all known cultures, the monad-of-all-monads, present on everyone's horizon (for a bipolar comparison, see *HH*, 218; for possible simplifications, see Dumont 1975*b*.).

In passing, let us acknowledge and salute an achievement of genius: it is from the mid-seventeenth century that what is doubtless the only serious attempt to reconcile individualism and holism has been passed on to us. Leibniz's monad is at the same time both a whole in itself and an individual in a system that is unified in its very differences—let us say the universal Whole. The closing off of the monad with regard to the exterior—a point often misunderstood—expresses this double requirement. And here we have not only a model suited to our basic problem, but also one which, it so happens, exerted great influence over German thought in its more specific aspects. The fact may be of great profit to us, and it is actually the study of this thought that led me to conceive clearly the thesis I propose. But it is also a reason for prudence, for one quickly realizes that the successors of Leibniz are often less precise than he himself was on one essential point: in their thinking, the incompatibility of individualism and holism is more often forgotten than recognized. They rather postulate the contrary. It is part of the inordinateness of this thought, its *hubris*, its pretension to build on contradiction at every turn, which is encountered egregiously in the Great Conciliator, and which should keep us on the alert.[6] We shall put to use the profound perceptions of the Germans, and avoid the inherent danger by taking Leibniz's model not as justification for an imaginary identification but as an ideal to guide our work, a regulating idea in the Kantian sense.

Modern culture is made up of national subcultures concerting with each other. In that concert, the interest of German culture for us is in the relative strength of the holistic component. Social science of the French tradition owes perhaps more to it than is usually seen. In this respect, there is a curious contrast between two of the founders of sociology. Durkheim, insofar as he stressed collective representations, sets out from the social whole, while Max Weber starts with the individual. In relation to the predominant national traditions, there is an inversion involved here. The case of Weber can be explained through the evolution of ideas in Germany during the second half of the nineteenth century (the eclipse of romanticism and Hegelianism, the predominance of neo-Kantism, and the growing influence of positivism). As for Durkheim, the German influence was decisive in the formation of his project. This influence was subsequently blurred, and in turn exaggerated by others; it has been precisely assessed by Steven Lukes (1973: 92–93). Now a third figure emerges appropriately to complete the picture: the great figure of Tönnies. Unlike Weber, Tönnies is in direct continuity with all German thought: his *Gemeinschaft*, or community, corresponds to the holism of Adam Müller and the romantics. His merit lies in having reanalyzed and distinguished the two components that Hegel, after he had succeeded in isolating them, then forcibly combined, and Marx confused. This, to my mind, is the reason for the fertility of Tönnies's antithesis. One knows the curious apparent inversion of meaning between the

6. On German thought, see chapter 4 and 5 above.

view of Tönnies and that of Durkheim in his *Division of Labor.*[7] Durkheim says "mechanical solidarity" where Tönnies says "community," and "organic solidarity" where Tönnies says "society." The inversion derives from the fact that Tönnies is considering the level of representations, and Durkheim, here, that of material facts. The two views complete each other, provided Durkheim is placed within Tönnies. What held Tönnies back in the exploitation of his contrast was that he brought his reflection to bear on the juxtaposition of the two elements in all societies without concentrating on the hierarchy between them in each case. One has only to add the dimension of relative value for Tönnies' distinction to provide the basic tool required for the comparison that, as we have seen, the very situation of the anthropologist demands.

It is easier to maintain a distinction between *Gemeinschaft* and *Gesellschaft*, holism and individualism, than to attempt to unite or to subsume them in some way. These two views of man and society, even though in a given society they are present empirically at different levels, are directly incompatible.

In truth—and we have already alluded to the fact—this incompatibility is perceived in a most unequal manner. Maybe some colleagues feel it very strongly and find this a reason for not accompanying us in a dangerous exercise in which one is in their judgment too much torn in two directions. On the other hand, it often happens, no doubt more often, that the incompatibility is not perceived or not acknowledged. Perhaps an Aristotelian outlook has contributed toward blurring the issue, as when Marx, recalling the *zoon politikon*, adds that man is "an animal which can develop into an individual only in society," or when, today, Charles Taylor, in seeking a formula for distributive justice, tempers the fundamental equality of individuals according to their relative contribution to the common good. As for myself, I would maintain that modern thought becomes singularly impoverished and loses one of its essential dimensions if one does not consider it in the light of this incompatibility, up to and including the cases where it is ignored, turned away from, or censured.[8] If this is the case, how is one to go about establishing a constructive relation between the individualism from which we originate and the holism which predominates in

7. See above, beginning of chapter 2. Werner J. Cahnman has compiled the reciprocal commentaries of Durkheim and Tönnies (Cahnman 1970: 189–208, with the original texts; Cahnman 1973: 239–56, in an English translation).

8. On Marx, cf. *MM*, 164; Taylor, unpublished; see also chapter 2 above.

the subject of our study? I have proposed the model of Leibniz. Better than a conciliation of the two principles, it presents a complex hierarchical combination of them which I shall briefly describe for our own use.

At the first or global level, we profess of necessity universalism. Only we want to look at the human species no more as an entity devoid of all that is particular to some or other societies, but as the sum integral of all those social particularities—a sum that we postulate to be real and coherent. Here we are taking up again the Germans' ambition. Our mankind is like the garden of Herder, in which each plant—each society—has its own beauty to offer because it expresses the universal in its own way. Or again, as for Schiller, "the whole lies before us again, no longer confused, but illuminated on all sides."[9]

At a second level, where one is considering a given type of society or culture, the primacy is necessarily reversed, and holism imposes itself. Here the modern model itself becomes a particular case of the nonmodern model. It was in this sense that I wrote that a comparative sociology, i.e. a comparative view of any society, is necessarily holistic. The watchword of this approach might be: "Society as a concrete universal."

Thus, by establishing a hierarchy both for the levels of consideration and, within these levels but in two opposite ways, for our two principles, we overcome—ideally—the incompatibility we have recognized and respected. On reflection, one will recognize, I think, that in this task it is impossible to attach another relative value to the two principles, impossible in particular to subordinate universalism entirely without destroying anthropology, and one will relegate to their due place the dreams of a multitude of anthropologies corresponding to the multiplicity of cultures.

This solution of an anthropological problem is by no means irrelevant as regards the world order as considered above, and, moreover, it is open to an analogy which might, in the long run, lend it some general interest. It may well be that our formula presages the solution of the other major political problem of modern societies—I mean the totalitarian threat that hovers over democracy. If totalitarianism represents a collision between individualism and holism (*MM*, 12, 107–8, etc.), if it is a disease of modern democracy to

9. Quoted by E. M. Wilkinson and L. A. Willoughby, in Schiller 1967: 234.

which it succumbs by a sort of irresistible sliding down once it loses sight of its limitations, strives to perfect realization, and, checked by the facts, ends up divided against itself, if this is so, then we are—as history should teach us—locked in a circle. The Rights of Man must certainly be claimed against established totalitarianism, but by themselves they are not able to break the circle, as the Terror of 1793–94 will testify. In the long run it will presumably be perceived that the solution consists in giving to each of the two contrary principles its legitimate field of supremacy from the modern point of view: individualism will rule, but will consent to be subordinated *in subordinate domains*. Different levels, therefore, perhaps a great number of them, will have to be distinguished, mutatis mutandis as was done above, or as was the case in the ancient *polis*. The complication will be great, for individual consciousness in the first place and then, no doubt, for the institutions as well—and who could be surprised at this?—but the major clashes will be overcome. An adequate analysis of modern society would in fact show that such a reversal of values is at present implicit in the practice: as Tönnies realized, *Gemeinschaft* and *Gesellschaft* are present one after the other in experience. Consequently, it would suffice if this reversal became conscious in hierarchical form and was generalized. This would be a decisive and difficult progress of general consciousness, to which anthropology would have contributed in its fashion.

Having enunciated a principle, I shall now mention a few of its corollaries or applications. Let us begin by considering some likely objections. Is not the model proposed unilateral, does it not ignore all sorts of phenomena and preoccupations which rightly command the attention of our colleagues today? What becomes of the animal, technical, and economic determinisms here and, more generally, of the study of cause and effect, of the interaction between social strata as distinguished in modern society, and between distinct societies or cultures? What becomes of history, diachrony, social change, and the genetic or generative aspect? What becomes of the individual, and the person?

I shall not reply to all these questions, which are of very unequal importance in terms of the real acquisitions which correspond to them. We have only sketched a framework or global orientation, without specifying all that might enter into it, whether it be what we have referred to above as intermediate landing stages, which are useful in the otherwise abrupt confrontation that has occupied our attention, or else additions which do not alter the principle, such as the interaction between a society and its human environment. In fact, there is no objection to giving back to the monad doors and windows once the principle of its separate existence as a distinct whole has been granted, and one can isolate monads at different levels, for example, that of a regional culture as well as that of the societies (or subcultures) which it includes.

The question of history will detain us for a moment. To start with, let us note that the model of Leibniz replaces, as a unitarian scheme, the Victorian model of a unilinear evolution by substituting difference for a supposed continuity (*MM*, 182ff.). Furthermore, nowhere did we claim that a society should be considered or compared solely from the synchronic aspect, to the exclusion of its own diachronic continuity or dynamism. What we need to know is whether, in this model, the process of becoming, or the laws thereof, are the same for all monads—which would bring us closer to the Victorian model or to the philosophies of history in general—or whether each social type has its own form of becoming. The question is best left open; besides, it cuts across the question of interaction.

On one important point, there is exclusion, for the Individual is actually excluded here as a universal reference coordinate. The Individual, by which I mean the human individual as a value, appears only in the ideology of modern societies. This is the reason for its exclusion and for that of its many concomitants. I shall go on to justify this point, but first I must express a reservation, possibly even overstressing the point, in order to leave nothing obscure.

The anthropologist should not, I feel, forget the limits that may result from his own experience. In my generalization, I took India as my starting point, and until now I have opposed modern society to traditional societies, in the sense of the great, richly differentiated societies that have embodied the superior civilizations. Here I am generalizing again from "traditional societies" to "nonmodern societies." But can one maintain that the simpler, less numerous, and less extensive societies, which have been the chief object of anthropological study, can be opposed to the modern societies in the same way as those previously considered? In short, there are doubts concerning some of these societies. Let us take Melanesia, or, more precisely, New Guinea: what is known about it, and the failure of both substantialist and structuralist theories to this day in that field would seem to indicate that we have not discovered—or that, by comparison with other cases, we have not discovered *at all*—the ideological axes which would provide a relatively coherent and simple formula. One would then advance the hypothesis that these societies use forms of differentiation *different* from those to which we are accustomed elsewhere. In terms of our present interest, these differentiations would lie beyond or outside the opposition individualism/holism, with the result that they would be as badly described from one point of view as from the other. It may prove that one should use another axis in comparing them to modern societies. For the moment, this axis or these axes are not to be seen. Their discovery would certainly have consequences with regard to what we have taken as established elsewhere, and we should be prepared for an "agonizing reappraisal," as is always the case when a whole is not completely known.

This having been said—and to return to what is better known— in addition to the logic proper to the scheme, two arguments would justify the exclusion of the Individual: (1) it is when the Individual is accepted as an ideological fact that, in my opinion, the sociological, or comparative, discovery of modern societies begins; (2) individualism and its implications have been, insofar as they were naively imported, the main obstacle to the study and understanding of nonmodern societies (this fact will emerge with increasing clarity as the implications are better revealed; cf. *MM, passim*). Consequently, whenever one is protesting against the "oversocialized conception of man" in contemporary sociology, or whenever one declares that in the final count, and beyond all abstraction, one is concerned with living men, i.e. living individuals, all I can see there—from the point of view I hold—is a protest of modern ideology against a true sociological perspective. We are engaged in the discovery of a *dimension* of man that is in fact obscured, scotomized among the moderns. This discovery is a long-term task for this very reason, and one which opens up a totality, but, as was said at the beginning, these are a specialist's task and a special totality. We are not dedicated to the "integral resurrection" of anything but societies and cultures. From the point of view of the Individual, this specialty has the same status as the others.

It is clearly on this issue that one can expect the utmost tension between the surrounding ideology and anthropology or truly sociological thinking in general. This tension is evidenced today by attempts to import an activist attitude into anthropology, by which I mean an artificialism based on personal commitment which is here just as implausible and preposterous as it is ill-timed. Indeed, if there is one thing we have learned, in spite of the excesses and limitations of functionalism, it is surely that social facts are far more interdependent than it appears at first sight. It is strange, therefore, at a time when the protest against the disruption of natural equilibriums has for the first time in public opinion placed a check on modern artificialism, that one should need to remind people who claim to be anthropologists that social environments, which in this respect are also part of nature, are just as delicate. It is true that one respects and even defends nonmodern societies. It is for our society that a more or less arbitrary intervention is reserved. Doubtless, then, our own society is no society at all? Some people will add that in order to understand society one must be committed to its transformation. Here the contradiction between Marxism and anthropology is patent. Let us turn then to those pretended technico-economic determinisms which buttress a form of activism. Let us recall that from the outset they have formed part of the hypotheses which were intended to permit an "explanation" of the idiosyncrasies of societies and to reduce their diversity to unity. The least that can be said is that these ideas have not been confirmed: we know that we do not know, and this negative knowledge is not a negligible result. A recent book by Marshall Sahlins seems to me to have drawn admirably the conclusions of this long experience and to have provided a decisive explanation with materialism in all its varieties.[10] Some people may, in spite of everything, wish to take up again these worn-out ideas as hypotheses while modifying them. Very well. The trouble is that what is presented here as a hypothesis is the very same thing as the dogma which elsewhere serves to destroy societies to the profit, in the last analysis, of the will-to-power of certain persons, the very same thing as here permits one to pay obedience to the surrounding ideology and, while claiming the authority of anthropology, to neglect for personal convenience its main acquisitions, be they positive or negative.

Let us return to anthropology proper. If its nature and its objectives are such as have been stated, certain of its aspects may be readily

---

10. *Culture and Practical Reason* (Sahlins 1977*a*) is courageous in its broad design and meritorious for the meticulous precision of the discussions. It also acquires singular appeal from its author's personality and the evolution his ideas have undergone. It is completed by a critique of sociobiology (Sahlins 1977*b*).

understood. Thus, it has occasionally been regretted that most of the time we have reached only an "intermediate level of abstraction." This is the ransom we pay for our attachment to the difference, to the concrete; it is, then, the ransom of our dignity. The same goes for the heaviness and complication of our surest methods. There can be no doubt, either, that our instruments are for the most part imperfect and need to be improved. But it would be unwise to reject them, as though they could immediately be replaced by perfect instruments, for the complex nature of the task precludes such a hope. Let us take the category of "kinship." In the present state of affairs, this category combines, imperfectly no doubt, universalism and concrete difference, and as such it is not entirely devoid of value (see above, p. 198).

The anthropologist's task is by nature such that his work is characterized by a deep-rooted tension, which accords both with the rigor and with the ambition of the discipline, and determines its progress. Upon reflection, one perceives that many contemporary attitudes—which are not new, although they may have found favor in the emerging generation—express a rejection, often an unconscious one no doubt, of this tension. To verify this, one would need a whole book; but it may be that the destiny of anthropology is here at stake: will it succeed in maintaining its vocation and its unity, or is it already succumbing to the multifarious pressures of the very same modern ideology which gave it birth?

The rejection of this tension can be seen immediately, whenever an arbitrary choice is made in a situation that is essentially ambiguous or uncertain (e.g. a partisan rather than a scientific attitude), whenever one of the two poles present is eliminated, arbitrarily suppressed, prematurely or definitively effaced to the profit of the other. Thus, since our habitual thought patterns resist the transmutation required of them by the culture under study, one can imagine two opposing ways of refusing to confront the difficulty. One is to become converted to the exotic life, breaking all ties with the discipline of "translation": there may be complete personal experience, but there is no contribution here to the research community. The other way of avoiding the issue is to reduce the distance by taking people close to oneself for one's first field of study—a difficult task and better entrusted to research workers who have gained experience elsewhere; this choice avoids the traumatic experience of *dépaysement* but contains the risk of remaining superficial. It is true that the "privilege of distantiation," which we claimed for our profession, is now not only denied from without but also contested from within—a sign that either the power of the mere technique of research is being overestimated or else that conformity is gaining ground on us. Indeed, the votaries of this smooth way will most likely be led imperceptibly down the slope toward technocracy; and yet our predecessors are occasionally reproached, with a thoughtlessness that is incredible but revealing, for having placed themselves at the service of the powers that be or of "imperialism."

Let us now apply the above consideration to the relation between anthropology and its social environment—here French society—and in particular to the question of the possible introduction of anthropology into pre-university education. We shall begin by clearing the ground. A triple issue is involved: the purpose of education, its content, and the foreseeable consequences. One can popularize only what has already been established, and the lack of consensus within the profession will make it difficult to confine oneself to this. Moreover, what is taught does not depend only on the syllabus, but also on the tendencies dominant among those by whom the instruction is given. One may therefore expect a rough and ready materialism to flourish. And there is worse for, in the absence of a general theory, relativism runs a good chance of becoming the main conclusion that will be drawn from an elementary education. One would certainly wish to combat racism, and one would be most surprised if it were discovered to have been encouraged. This is the kind of problem that has demanded the attention of our English colleagues.[11] All those who imagine that they can with impunity relativize contemporary values at a level which is no longer that of a specialist activity but that of the common consciousness should be reminded that the society in which this process was taken the furthest was undoubtedly the German Weimar Republic, and we know what followed, without it being necessary to see this as the sole cause. In other terms, an elementary education in anthropology will be possible only once our relation—our corporate relation, I should say—to modern values has been elucidated and clearly posited. Otherwise, one would lapse into irresponsibility or into something which would have nothing of

11. RAIN 1976; nevertheless, the project seems to be underway (RAIN 20, 1977: 14).

anthropology to it but the name. (It should be mentioned in passing that one cannot touch upon racism—as regards France—without mentioning the situation and the treatment of "immigrant workers"; it presents anthropology with a formidable challenge, which one would like to believe it capable of meeting.)

Now, it so happens that our model corresponds perfectly to the need we have just described. To my mind, it corresponds to the highest humanist ambition and hence *in principle* is invested with the highest educational value. In principle only: for, apart from the fact that numerous anthropologists will probably challenge it, those who may or do accept it will agree that it is a heavy burden for the specialist himself to carry and one which it would not be possible to impose on young minds still unripe. We conclude, then, that the proposition is premature, that it requires more thorough study than appears to have been believed, and above all that the community should put some order into its ideas. This is certainly not an encouraging conclusion, but the evidence cannot be gainsaid.

One final point: according to an idea that is perhaps vague yet fairly widespread, anthropology, although it may not yet be considered a science in the strict sense, should as it progresses draw closer to this ideal, and perhaps attain it in the end. Now, in the light of what has been said here, one is led—not without hesitation—to cast doubt upon this idea. It would certainly seem that imitation of the "hard" sciences should be a means of ensuring a certain degree of rigor and continuity in anthropology. But is it really so? If one sorts out the real contributions from the borrowed trappings, one will find that the influence of the exact sciences is positive, but the imitation of them negative. It would certainly be desirable for all anthropologists to have a basic training in these sciences, but it is a fact that mathematical formalization is frequently accompanied by rudimentary thought or that it dissimulates real and soluble problems.

Let us then take up again the thread of our argument. We have several times detected an uneasy relation between anthropology and modern universalism. In rejecting unreflecting negations and facile elisions, we have in the end reached the idea of an enlargement of this universalism, first as a method and then, in the end, as the result of a regulated combination of it with its opposite at the level of social values; and finally we have brought this process closer to that of the possible future of world civilization. We now come to another aspect of this modern universalism. Normatively speaking, the universal is rationality, and scientific laws are commonly given as the sole nontautological propositions that are truly universal. Our problem is to locate our position in relation to this rationality. An absurd question, one may say: there is only one reason, and one cannot evade it without becoming strangers to the truth. But it is not in fact a matter of evading rationality in itself; and the question is less absurd than it might seem. There are by and large two—not to say three—sorts of motives which command reserve in the face of scientific rationality.

First of all, men did not begin thinking when they invented, in Greece, what the classicists call a "consistent discourse." The invention must have consisted of a *decomposition*: the different dimensions of existence were separated out, each in a distinct sequence of discourse. Rational discourse says one thing at a time, while the myth or the poem makes allusion to all in one sentence. The one is flat, the other is "thick" (cf. Clifford Geertz's "*thick description*"). The myth is coherent thought, but its coherence is rooted in its multidimensionality, it is thus of a different type than discursive consistency or "rationality." We cannot, however, allow it to be relegated to the "irrational" identified with incoherence.

This is not all, for the decomposition has been continuing. Philosophical rationality still aims at totality, even if this is a totality stripped of its thickness, so to speak. Scientific rationality, which predominates among the moderns, aims each time at a slice of totality. It is essentially instrumental (relating means to ends) and specialized in the sense that it operates within compartments that are not rationally but empirically defined (*MM*, 20). One of the results of the rationality of science is that the complexity or "multiplexity" of human experience, which was presupposed and collected in the myth, is now dispersed. We do not each take part in science in the same way as we participate or participated in myth. Here one observes a notable reversal (cf. Tönnies-Durkheim): the normative subject is the individual, but knowledge is not wholly present except in the diversified social body. I believe, furthermore, that anthropology can help to rediscover or to reveal the principle of the unity of the culture in which science predominates.

A second reason for reserve: this scientific decomposition of the universe of man has no doubt shown overwhelming power, but it has not passed without raising a wave of protest in our own culture. For example, the destruction of the hierarchical cosmos, the object/subject division, the establishment of a hierarchy of qualities as measurable (primary) and nonmeasurable (secondary), have been felt as attacks upon man. We know of Goethe's hostility, in the name of the sense of human life and of living totalities, toward the mechanistic and atomistic science of his time. Lévi-Strauss himself has raised an echo in defense of sensory qualities, and this fact underlines the continuity with the nonmodern cultures of this current of protest, which is certainly submerged but by no means negligible.

There is a third argument that could be drawn from the development of science itself. I mention it only as a confirmation and as an index of convergence, for here the layman risks committing serious errors. Let me then remain intentionally vague and say simply that there is a crisis in the model science, physics.[12] Heisenberg's principle of uncertainty would no doubt have been exhilarating and confirmatory to Goethe, while to us it recalls the familiar relation between the observer and the observed.

From these two or three sorts of reflection, we may conclude that science, a science of the type of classical physics, is not coextensive with universal rationality. The success of science is incontestable, and there can be no question of rejecting it, but all the same it is unilateral and insufficient on its own, like that of the society by which it is borne, and the two taken together are pregnant with conflict and danger, for at one and the same time they require a complement and reject it.[13]

This situation bespeaks both the interest that our efforts can hold and the prudence that is dictated to us. Just as at the level of social values we found in the above that it might be possible to so dilate modern universalism that it can encompass its opposite, so here we can try to reconcile the "flat" universal with the "thick" universal or, as we called it in speaking of societies, the concrete universal. But this is possible only in an inverse perspective: just as the simple regularities of classical physics appear as particular cases

12. I have had access to the communications prepared by Daniel Bell and others for the Aspen-Berlin seminar (September 1975) entitled "The Critique of Science" and organized by the International Congress for Cultural Freedom.

13. I must be brief, but here the reader will surely be thinking of social artificialism. *1984 addition*: Here, a grave objection is expected, and should at least be mentioned. In the above, we speak of science without touching on mathematics, the queen of sciences, which is in itself pure rationality, by no means instrumental, and whose statements are necessary, universally valid. Let us admit all this, provisionally. The fact remains that the world had to be decomposed before it could be mathematized.

in a broader perspective, so too the abstract universal of science may appear as a particular instance of the concrete universal. If our task is really, as we just described it, to work at reintegrating the scientific culture among the other human cultures, what a paradox there would be in wanting at all costs to fashion anthropology after the exact sciences, which are, moreover, increasingly less sure of their foundation!

One would be far more inclined to see the purpose of anthropology, as a fundamental social science, in an inverse and complementary approach to that of (classical) science and of modern ideology in general: to reunite, comprehend, reconstitute what has been separated, distinguished, and decomposed. Not to mention possible parallelisms between certain procedures in anthropology and in modern physics, one may be permitted to observe that an approach of the kind suggested is already to be found in our undertaking such as it is, or rather such as it is becoming. Is it not, in fact, in turning away from the sciences of nature, from causal explanation, from prediction, from application, etc. that our endeavor has recently achieved its most notable advances?

It is true that the task thus seen is immense, and will even seem insane if one matches it with the present state of the profession, which is disunited and split into widely divergent tendencies. One is always brought back to the need for improving the scientific community. For, as long as there is no live consensus, no conscious unity, our highest destinies will remain but vain shadows.

I shall conclude here, and it will be said that it is here that I should have begun: Is reform possible? What should be done? I will be content with three statements: (1) the anthropological community must define itself in its nature and function in relation to modern ideology; (2) the principle of unity lies in a comparison of the concrete universals in an universalist perspective; (3) one understands, then, that many contemporary practices are destructive to the community. Everyone can examine his or her own practice and improve it in this respect.

2. Where Equalitarianism is Not in Place

I should like to demonstrate the relevance of the foregoing discussion to contemporary practice through a precise example of general import.

For communication within a research community, universal

concepts are required. Now, the recent development that emphasizes the specific character of each culture destroys or weakens, sometimes no doubt thoughtlessly, the universals which we have hitherto been employing. It would therefore be useful to identify at least some sound or sufficiently durable universals of anthropological discourse. Earlier on, we outlined a comparative procedure which introduces a universal principle at the global level. But can we assert the presence in every culture of universal components? For lack of substantial elements, these will be types of relations. We have the distinctive opposition. It is clearly a fundamental acquisition. I shall demonstrate through an example that to this opposition must be added a second type, hierarchical opposition or the *encompassing of the contrary* as the relation between an ensemble and its part. As I have introduced this opposition elsewhere, I should willingly have left to others the task of carrying out a fairly obvious application. But this has not been done. One must perforce believe that the surrounding ideology has made hierarchy decidedly unpopular (but see note 18 below). I therefore propose here a defence and illustration of the hierarchical opposition based on a case where the distinctive opposition is insufficient.

This is also an occasion for providing an example of the discontinuity that is so frequent in our studies. One can consider the classic work of Sir Edward Evans-Pritchard on the Azande as a reply to Lévy-Bruhl. The author had taken a lively interest in Lévy-Bruhl, and in this book he went beyond him by showing that the judgments Lévy-Bruhl qualified as "pre-logical" were linked to certain situations and could not be generalized as characteristic of a "mentality," as though the same people did not know how to resort to logic in other situations. The concern to distinguish different sorts of situations, whether it be in connection with beliefs relative to causality (Azande) or with the conception of a "segmentary system" (Nuer), appeared twenty-five years ago as an important and definitive acquisition. Will it be said that it is still so today? At any rate this concern is seriously lacking in one type of studies, and this discontinuity is the more striking if detected in Evans-Pritchard's own immediate entourage. We know that it was owing to his impulsion that, by means of English translations or otherwise, all that part of the heritage of the Durkheim school that had not been adopted by Radcliffe-Brown was reinstated in a place of honor. Thus, after having translated Hertz's two great essays, Rodney Needham prepared, beginning in 1962, at the same Institute of

Oxford over which Evans-Pritchard presided until the time of his retirement, and with his encouragement, and later published in 1973, a collective work entitled *Right and Left: Essays on Dual Symbolic Classification*.[14] This is an important work, which begins with Hertz's *Essay* of 1909—it opens with a photograph of him—and contains no less than 18 contributions, old, recent and new, including two essays by the editor, not to mention an introduction in which he presents the panorama he has assembled. It must be made quite clear that I have not picked on Rodney Needham in order to address a personal criticism toward him : I take this book as representative of a type of analysis and, additionally, as a work that poses a problem of continuity. In relation to the classic works of Evans-Pritchard, the interest here has been shifted toward the system of ideas and values, a "symbolic" or ideological system, considered in itself, more or less independently of social morphology. Hertz has been rediscovered. What is curious, given the circumstances, is that the Evans-Pritchard distinction of situations should have been neglected, for, in a somewhat different form, this distinction would have made it possible to further or renew Hertz, instead of doing no more in fact that illustrating him, most richly at that. This, at least, is what I shall strive to show.

On the whole, one has discovered, or rediscovered, or set in the foreground, the fact that man thinks by distinctions and that the oppositions resulting from this fact in a certain way form a system. This has led to presenting lists of oppositions, more or less homologous to one another, and "binary classifications," as a sort of dualist grid constituting the essential of the indigenous "symbolic system," or at least an important aspect of it. Since the question is familiar, I shall immediately present the matter in abstract form. Let there be a series of oppositions: a/b, e/f, i/k, o/p, which will be presented in

14. Needham 1973. A small historiographic point to complete one of Needham's developments (pp. 13–14); Hertz had been forgotten in Oxford when I mentioned him in my talk on Mauss in 1952 (above, chap. 7), which attracted the attention of Evans-Pritchard as is seen in his Introduction to the translation of the *Essai sur le don* (Mauss 1925) published in 1954. He had been unaware that Hertz's *Mélanges* were in the Institute Library (Radcliffe-Brown fund) and immediately got hold of it (cf. his reference to Hertz in Needham 1973: 95 and n. 10). His memory betrayed it when he claimed (ibid.: 9) to have spoken of Hertz at Oxford from the outset. He was more accurate in 1960 when he wrote "for a number of years" in his Introduction to the translation of Hertz (Hertz 1960). This detail is relevant both as an illustration of discontinuity in anthropology and as evidence of the usefulness of the exchange of scholars between countries.

two columns: a, e, i, o next to b, f, k, p. At the very least, one will have found in a particular context that there is a homology between the first two oppositions: a/b = e/f; likewise, in another context, e/f = i/k, etc. It is stated (Needham 1973: xxvii–xxviii) that each of the oppositions should be taken in its context, or rather that each of the homologies between two of these oppositions be taken in context. But it is clear that in the two-column presentation of the table, all contexts are confused or elided. In short, the distinction of situations ceases to be considered as pertinent at the moment we pass from elements to the set as a whole, as though each situation were in itself independent of the "mentality" as a whole, though it should be evident that the very distinction of situations depends on the mentality in question. I do not retain the objection according to which Evans-Pritchard's distinction is purely empirical or external, not ideological; yet it is true that the ideological aspect is more stressed here: the distinction becomes that of levels in the ideology.

Such simplifications are doubtless widespread when a new perspective is launched. Has this one been improved elsewhere? I shall be corrected if need be, but nowhere do I discern a systematic presentation of the situations as classified, and therefore defined, in the ideology under study. On the contrary, it is assumed rather, that the ideological system is all of a piece—monolithic. Thus, my interpretation of the caste system has been criticized for admitting two sorts of situations defined in relation to the ideological system: value situations and power situations. The critics have required that all situations should be regarded as being of the same kind, which would amount to perfect agreement between the ideological and the empirical (and I myself, moreover, may have in places left open such a possibility). With reference to the same example, if one objects that there are on the contrary more than two sorts of situations, I should not exclude the hypothesis a priori, but should rather recall the sophism of Zeno concerning Achilles and the tortoise: the hierarchical disposition entails that the successive distinctions possible are of rapidly decreasing global significance; in fact, as we know, Achilles catches up with the tortoise.

It may just be the case that the aversion toward hierarchy plays a role here. If the distinction of situations requires the consideration of values, i.e. the introduction of hierarchy, and if the modern research worker runs away from it, he may tend to reject or neutralize an epistemological "situation" of this type. At this point, I must propose a definition. I shall use the opportunity to widen slightly one previously given. (Dumont 1971*b*: 72–73). What I call hierarchical opposition is the opposition between a set (and more particularly a whole) and an element of this set (or of this whole); the element is not necessarily simple, it can be a subset. This opposition is logically analyzable in two contradictory partial aspects: on the one hand, the element is identical to the set in that it forms part thereof (a vertebrate is an animal); on the other hand there is difference or, more strictly, contrariety (a vertebrate is not *solely* an animal; an animal is not *necessarily* a vertebrate). This double relation—identity and contrariety—is stricter when a proper whole is concerned than when a more or less arbitrary set is involved. This double relation is a logical scandal, which is both an explanation for the disfavor it finds and a reason for the interest it deserves: every relation between an element and the set of which it is part introduces hierarchy and is logically inadmissible. Essentially, hierarchy is the *encompassing of the contrary*. Hierarchical relations are present in our own modern ideology—as I have begun to show (*MM*, see index s.v. Hierarchy) and shall continue to do—but they do not present themselves as such. This is probably what happens whenever a value is concretely stated: it subordinates its contrary, but one refrains from mentioning the fact. In general, an ideology hostile to hierarchy must obviously dispose of a whole battery of devices for neutralizing or replacing the relation in question. I shall single out two of them in relation to the present discussion. The first consists in avoiding the point of view in which the relation would appear. Thus, in taxonomies, we are accustomed to considering each level separately, and thus avoid bringing together an element of the first order, call it *A* and one of the second order, *a*. In connection with this separation, the criteria of distinction can be quite different from one level to another (animal/vegetable; vertebrate/invertebrate; mammal, etc.). We thus produce sets, not wholes. A second and very important contrivance lies in the absolute distinction we draw between facts and values.[15] Hierarchy is thus exiled from the domain of facts, and the asepsis prevailing in the social sciences guards us against hierarchical infection. The situation is clearly exceptional from a comparative point of view, as is seen in modern ideology itself from the tendency to reunite yet again and to confound "is" and "ought to be," a tendency which, as

15. An observation made by Daniel de Coppet stressed the point and led to its subsequent development.

we know from our experience in Europe, opens up the way to totalitarianism, as Leszek Kolakowski recently insisted (1977).

Let us now apply the hierarchical principle to binary classifications, or, more precisely, to the opposition between right and left which serves as their emblem. The problem, as found in the literature and in the work cited, is essentially epistemological. The opposition is uniformly treated as a distinctive opposition, a simple "polarity" or "complementarity." But in actual fact the two terms or poles *do not have* equal status: one is superior (generally the right), the other inferior. Hence the problem as it has been historically posed: how is it that the two opposites which we (groundlessly) assume to be equal are not equal in reality? In the language of Hertz, why is "preeminence" given to one of the two hands?

What is lacking here is the recognition that the right-left pair is not definable in itself but *only in relation to a whole*, a most tangible whole, since it is the human body (and, by analogy, other bodies). The fact is familiar to the physicist, who sets up an imagined observer in order to be able to speak of right and left. How can "symbolic analysis" ignore this fact?

In saying that the right/left opposition refers to a whole we are saying that it has a hierarchical aspect, even if at first sight it does not appear to belong to the simple type in which one term encompasses the other and which I have referred to above as "hierarchical opposition." We are accustomed to analyzing this opposition in two component parts, as though it displayed at its base a principle of symmetry more generally encountered and, superadded unto it, an asymmetry of direction to which the value would be attached. This, it should be noted, is a manner of separating *fact* (the assumed symmetry) and *value* (the added asymmetry). Concretely, however, right and left *do not have the same relationship to the whole of the body*. They are differentiated at the same time both in value and in nature. And as soon as different associations and functions are attributed to them, this difference is *ipso facto* hierarchical because it is related to the whole. Thus, the function of the right will be more important in relation to the whole than the function of the left— more essential, more representative, etc.

One notices, moreover, that writers on this matter vary greatly in their sensitivity to this aspect. In his study of the symbolism of the spear among the Nuer, Evans-Pritchard presents it as "an extension of the right hand"; he writes that the spear "is a projection of the self and stands for the self" and that "as an extension of the right arm, it represents the whole person" and even, beyond it, the clan (Needham 1973: 94, 100). An example to the contrary is found in the same volume in an article altogether very tendentious by Brenda Beck. The article deals with the castes of a small region in South India as recognized or assumed to belong to the right hand or to the left hand. Here the author succeeds in eliminating all reference to the whole, to the point of claiming against all likelihood that the left-hand castes are such by reason of their being outsiders to the village system of division of labor.[16]

It must be concluded that the preeminence is not here contingent, but necessary, because it results from the differentiation of the two terms in relation to the whole. It might be objected that in saying this we are doing no more than shifting the problem: what advantage is there in admitting that a difference of status is necessary here if one still needs to know why most of the time one term—and in rarer instances the other—is preferred? To begin with, we shall answer that by substituting an asymmetrical or ordered opposition for a symmetrical or equi-statutory opposition that does not exist, we are drawing closer to the thought we are studying. It is clear that other oppositions, bordering on this one in our binary lists, are also hierarchical (man/woman, etc.), and, in principle, such must be the case in "dualist organization" since here too a relation to the whole is involved.[17] (In passing, I should point

16. See Beck 1973. In her book *Peasant society in Konku* (1972—the region is in fact called Kongu) this author takes care to explain from the start (p. 14, n. 7) that she has omitted reference to the hands (present in local speech and general in the literature) because the word *hand* refers also to the arm and to the side of the body. The result is to omit reference to the body (and with it the inevitable question: *whose* body?).

17. A recent example is so illuminating that it prompted me to add this note. I found it in a paper by Christopher Crocker (Crocker 1977). Let us admit that just as the relation between element and set is hierarchical, conversely a hierarchical relation between two terms to the exclusion of all others will indicate a totality composed of these two terms. Here, each Bororo clan is associated with a pair of hierarchized *aroes*, each of which presides over a subclan. Crocker says that the connection between the two "terms of the pair is not essentially one of resemblance but of metonymy: larger, smaller; older, younger; high, low; first, second; etc." (p. 164). The substitution of "metonymy" for "hierarchy," inescapable as the latter is here, is most suggestive: will the fashionable use of tropes in turn enable us to evade what is disturbing us? Has it already begun to do so? (Another anomaly in this passage: "nominalism" for "realism" in the philosophical sense, belief in the reality of ideas). The expression "metonymy" conceals the homology with the relative situation of the two Bororo moieties, which is classed as "metaphor." The author

out that in an early study I too approached hierarchy in an indirect fashion, beginning with the sole distinctive opposition. Cf. Dumont 1970.) In proceeding as suggested here, we simply get rid of a difficulty which we ourselves had needlessly added and which stems from the requirement that facts (or ideas) and values should be kept separate. This separation thus appears to be illegitimate in the case.

That is not all. There is an immediate practical advantage to be drawn from our effort. By definition, a symmetrical opposition may be reversed at will: its reversal produces nothing. On the contrary, the reversal of an asymmetrical opposition is significant, for the reversed opposition *is not the same as* the initial opposition. If the reversed opposition is encountered in the same whole in which the direct opposition was present, it is evidence of a *change of level*. In fact, it announces such a change with maximum economy, using only two hierarchized elements and their order. (Do we have here the perfect antithesis of those taxonomies in which we use a new criterion for each level?) Here, the unity between levels and their distinction are both indicated: we are dealing with a whole and not just with a set, and it is highly probable that one level is contained within the other (encompassing the contrary, hierarchy in the strict sense).

No finer illustration of this disposition could be conceived than that provided by Pierre Bourdieu in his description of the Berber (Kabyle) house. (Bourdieu 1972: 57–59). Once the threshold has been crossed, space becomes reversed, the cardinal points are interchanged; as though the threshold were the center of symmetry or rather of similitude (*homothétie*) between the exterior space and the interior space of the house, which is reversed in relation to the former. But let us go beyond this physical image to say rather that the interior space is qualitatively different to the exterior space, something other while still the same. We are made aware that in crossing the threshold we have passed from one level of life to another. This is a distinction that will doubtless be encountered again in other forms in this culture and that is probably far more pronounced here than in cultures where no such reversal is present

---

says very little about moieties, and it is Lévi-Strauss who, in the subsequent discussion, seems to have asked him to deal more precisely with their asymmetry. After emphasizing the strength of identity in Bororo society (p. 158), the author misses its principle: that all that is real is manifested in the form of a hierarchical pair. A "dyadic totality" (p. 169) is necessarily hierarchical.

and where the exterior space is quite simply continued into the house, where, finally, the house is not expressed as a spatial whole, subordinated or superordinated to the exterior space.

Classic examples may be found to verify that the same holds true for reversal of right and left. Let us take a society in which the right is generally accorded preeminence. If this preeminence is then reversed within an element classed as left, this is an indication that the level encountered here is clearly distinguished from others in the indigenous ideology, and this fact must in turn be recognized as an important feature of the global ideology. One is therefore surprised to find Rodney Needham, in his study on the Mugwe, avoiding expressing such a case as one of reversal and, in a footnote, declining to pursue the theme of reversal as being too extensive (Needham 1973: 117–18, 126, n. 26). Yet one would expect that all reversals, whether they occur between ritual action and ordinary action, within ritual itself, between the world of the living and the world of the dead, etc., would have this function in common, and that they could all be illuminated through being set together. Further on in the book, in speaking of Nyoro symbolism, Needham seems inclined, particularly with regard to diviners and princesses (306–8), to take advantage of reversal, but he does not pursue the issue not does he systematize.

We have found that the hierarchical grasp of an opposition such as that between right and left referred us to the distinction of levels within the ideology as a whole. Now, while in the binary classification the distinctive opposition used in its pure form both atomizes the data and renders it uniform, the hierarchical distinction unifies the data by welding together two dimensions of distinction—between levels and within a single level. Thus, in the study of castes the hierarchy once recognized led to a distinction of levels being made. More generally, if for each culture one agrees to seek out the preeminent value-idea by which it is animated, or, as Marx said, the ether which lends its color to all things, one will perceive at one stroke—at any rate, from a comparative viewpoint—the main lines of organization of the ideological whole, the necessarily hierarchical configuration of levels.

This hierarchy of levels derives from the very nature of the ideology: to posit a value is at the same time to posit a nonvalue; it is to organize or constitute a datum in which some of the elements will remain insignificant. Now, the ideology requires for its self-justification that this insignificant residue should be limited, and made inconspicuous. What happens in fact is that it is gradually covered over with progressively diminishing grades of value. The hierarchy of levels is therefore hypothetically one of the universal traits we were searching for at the start. But there is no doubt that it varies greatly in its degree of complexity from one ideology to another. And it is a serious shortcoming of binary classification to say nothing of this and to reduce to the same form—too simple a form—both the simplest and most complex of these hierarchies.

Altogether, binary classification is inadequate from two points of view. As regards the oppositions themselves that it considers, it is wrong in looking on oppositions that are not of equal status as though they were; it claims to grasp the anatomy of ideas independently of the values that are indissolubly attached to them, and it errs therefore through a misplaced equalitarianism which voids the idea of its value. Secondly, it uniformly confuses contexts or situations which may or may not be distinguished in the ideology under study.[18] This aspect occurs in another form in *Right and Left*. In fact, the question has been raised by Rodney Needham and others whether the binary table extracted by the analyst is or is not present in people's minds. T. O. Beidelman, for his part, has provided, along with an extensive global list, two more restricted clusters, which he says are really present in the mind of the Kaguru (Needham 1973: 154). In general, it may be said that this book approaches the issue somewhat as though everyone were Chinese. Traditional China, as Needham says in his Introduction (p. xxxiii), does in fact draw a classificatory distinction between two classes of symbols under the rubric of *yin* and *yang*. But in this case this is not all, and one should not stop here. It is abundantly clear, from the fine study by Granet in this same work, that Chinese etiquette resorts intensively to reversal in a complex set of oppositions and homologies, and thus succeeds in differentiating, one might say, each situation from all others, and in reducing to naught the residue of insignificance left by the ideology. We hinted above at the possibility that, in quite another way, the future of our own culture might lead to a similar complexity.

I should like to conclude with a remark on the relation between

18. 1984 note: I formerly noted in this context that a short diploma paper by M. Serge Tcherkézoff had offered a criticism of binary classifications very similar to this one and quite independent from it. I can now refer to the same author's book: *Le Roi Nyamwezi, la Droite et la Gauche*. Révision comparative des classifications dualistes. MSH-Cambridge University Press, 1983.

ideas and values. We have observed that in a given case the separation of these two was fallacious. There is a general reason for this: it is that the degree of diffentiation and articulateness among ideas is not independent of their relative value. The correlation is not a simple direct one. There is, doubtless, little chance of finding elaborate ideas in matters of little interest, and, conversely, differentiation occurs at the same time as value is stressed. But everything looks as though beyond a certain degree, value concealed what normally it reveals: the fundamental idea, the mother of all others, often remains unexpressed, but its location is indicated by the proliferation of value-ideas in the very zone where it is hiding (*MM*, 19–20).

By not making an a priori separation of ideas and values, we remain closer to the real relation—in nonmodern societies—between thought and act, while intellectualist or positivist analysis tends to destroy this relation. But is not this to contradict what was said above concerning the modern tendency to confuse "is" and "ought to be?" Quite the contrary: the difference between the two points of view brings us back to the general perspective as outlined in the first part of this study. From a comparative point of view, modern thought is exceptional in that, starting with Kant, it separates "is" and "ought to be," fact and value. The fact has two consequences: on the one hand, this specific feature demands to be respected in its domain, and one cannot without serious consequences presume to transcend it within modern culture; on the other hand, there is no need to impose this complication or distinction on cultures which do not recognize it: in the comparative study one will be considering value-ideas. This will be applied even to our own culture considered comparatively, that is to say, one will be able to search for the underlying link in our customary distinction; here one will encounter, for instance, the Weberian set of problems (the relation between *wertfrei* and *Wertbeziehung*, "value-free" and "relation to value").

If uniting through differences is at the same time the aim of anthropology and the characteristic of hierarchy, they are doomed to keep company.

9 On Value, Modern and Nonmodern

I saw Radcliffe-Brown only once, in this very room. In my memory I can still see him today, though somewhat hazily, delivering the Huxley Memorial Lecture for 1951 (Radcliffe-Brown 1958). I must have made it to London for the occasion, from Oxford where I was a new, if not that young, lecturer. As I listened to him, he seemed to have made one step in the direction of Lévi-Strauss, and I felt comforted in my recent structural allegiance. In fact it was only a limited, passing convergence.[1]

In those days I was busy learning a good deal from him, and from British anthropology at large, which had reached unprecedented heights partly under his influence. Yet I must confess that, for one whose imagination had been initially fired by Mauss's

Radcliffe-Brown Lecture in Social Anthropology, 1980, "On Value," *Proceedings of the British Academy*, 66 (1980): 207–41. Thanks are due to Alan Montefiore, who kindly suggested some improvements in the English.

1. Actually, Sir Raymond Firth tells me that such developments were habitual in Radcliffe-Brown's teaching, from early days onwards (in Autralia in the thirties). Radcliffe–Brown said in the lecture "*the kind of structure* with which we are concerned is *one of* the union of opposites" (Radcliffe-Brown 1958: 123, my emphasis). It was thus a particular case, not the application of a general principle, which required speaking of "oppositions." Cf. Leach 1976: 9. Accordingly, my first and limited attempt at structuralist analysis (Dumont 1953*a*) drew shortly afterwards a magisterial rebuke from the aging Radcliffe-Brown (Radcliffe-Brown 1953; my reply Dumont 1953*b*). My paper was a piece of that "Parisian heresy" which, as Sir Edmund Leach said (Leach 1976), was mostly ignored in this country for ten years or more. Yet, let it be said for the record that Radcliffe-Brown's strictures did not alter the friendly protection and non-committal encouragement of Evans-Pritchard, who, of all colleagues, showed most understanding for the effort at a systematic retrieval of affinity.

genial humanism, Radcliffe-Brown's constricted version of Durkheimian sociology was not very attractive.

Today, one feels the need to insist, beyond all divergences, on continuity on one basic point. Reading his *Natural Science of Society*, one is struck by Radcliffe-Brown's decided holism.[2] Whatever the shortcomings of his concept of "system," the point—should I say the importation?—was probably decisive in the development of anthropology in this country, and it made possible the dialogue with the predominant sociological tradition of the French.

There is relatively little about values in Radcliffe-Brown's writings.[3] Yet the expression was very much in the air in British departments of anthropology in the last years of his life. My impression was that it figured largely as a substitute for "ideas," which stressed the relation to action and was therefore less unpalatable to the empiricist temper. No doubt the situation is quite different today. But to state plainly the reason for my use of the term, preferably in the singular, and for my choice of topic: I have been trying in recent years to sell the profession the idea of hierarchy, with little success, I may add. I thought of making another bid, this time by using the professionally received vocable, which I had instinctively shunned heretofore, I suppose because of the forbidding difficulties the term seems to present. May the attempt

2. Sir Edmund Leach has discussed at length (Leach 1976) this posthumous presentation of Radcliffe-Brown's widest views (Radcliffe-Brown 1957). In it the positive aspects of Radcliffe-Brown's teaching appear clearly, together with what appears to us now (or to me) as its shortcomings. In retrospect, he is seen to have gone in the right direction, but not quite far enough. Yet his articulate holism (pp. 22, 110, etc.) coupled with the consequent stress on "relational analysis" and on synchrony (pp. 14, 63), and, remarkably enough, with the downgrading of causality (p. 41, cf. n. 43 below), appears very meritorious if one looks at it against the background of the nominalism which permeates his own thought and the predominant orientation in British ideology. In this perspective, it is not surprising that Radcliffe-Brown's holism remains narrowly functional, that the distinction between "culture" (somewhat reluctantly ushered in, p. 92) and "social structure," sound in principle, in fact reduces the former to a mere means of the latter (p. 121). Also Radcliffe-Brown did not—probably could not—perceive that relational analysis demands that the boundaries of the "system" be rigorously defined and not left to arbitrary choice or expediency (p. 60), and that such analysis is incompatible with the primary emphasis he put on classification or taxonomy (pp. 16, 71) (See Leach's early dismissal of "butterfly collecting," 1961). I shall refer to a few other points in the following ("natural kinds of systems," n. 42 below; fixed equivalences in exchange, n. 35 below).
3. See Radcliffe-Brown 1957: 10–11, 119, 136–40 (economic value).

be taken as an effort to come closer to the Radcliffe-Brownian heritage.

In fact, my intention is solely to offer an observation bearing on the relation between ideas and values, or rather to comment on that observation and draw some consequences from it. The modern type of culture in which anthropology is rooted and the nonmodern type differ markedly with regard to value, and I hold that the anthropological problems relating to value require that the two be confronted. We shall start from the modern configuration, which represents an innovation, then introduce in contrast some fundamental features of the more common nonmodern configuration, and finally return to the modern predicament with a view to setting it "in perspective" and to thus, it is hoped, throwing some light on the position and task of anthropology as a mediating agency.

The modern scene is familiar. In the first place, modern consciousness attaches value predominantly to the individual, and philosophy deals, at any rate predominantly, with individual values, while anthropology takes values as essentially social. Then, in common parlance, the word, which meant in Latin healthy vigor and strength and in medieval times the warrior's bravery, symbolizes most of the time the power of money to measure everything. This important aspect will be present here only by implication (cf. *MM*).

As to the absolute sense of the term, the modern configuration is *sui generis* and value has become a major preoccupation. In a note in Lalande's Philosophical Dictionary, Maurice Blondel said that the predominance of a philosophy of value characterizes the contemporary period, following a modern philosophy of knowledge and an antique and medieval philosophy of being (Lalande 1968: 1183). For Plato the supreme Being was the Good. There was no discord between the Good, the True, and the Beautiful, yet the Good was supreme, perhaps because it is impossible to conceive the highest perfection as inactive and heartless, because the Good adds the dimension of action to that of contemplation. In contrast we moderns separate science, aesthetics, and morals. And the nature of our science is such that its existence by itself explains or rather implies the separation between the true on the one hand, the beautiful and the good on the other and in particular between being and moral value, what *is* and what *ought to be*. For the scientific discovery of the world was premised on the banning as secondary of all qualities to which physical measurement was not applicable.

Thus for a hierarchical cosmos was substituted our physical, homogeneous universe (Koyré 1958). The value dimension which had been spontaneously projected on to it was relegated to what is to us its proper locus, that is, man's mind, emotions, and volition.

In the course of centuries, the (social) Good was also relativized. There were as many Goods as there were peoples or cultures, not to speak of religions, sects or social classes. "Truth this side of the Pyrenees, error beyond," noted Pascal; we cannot speak of the Good when what is held as good on this side of the Channel is evil on the other, but we can speak of the value or values that people acknowledge respectively on one and the other side.

Thus, value designates something different from being, and something which, while the scientifically true is universal, is eminently variable with the social environment, and even within a given society, according not only to social classes but to the diverse departments of activity or experience.

I have listed only a few salient features, but they are enough to evoke the complex nexus of meanings and preoccupations to which our word is attached, a tangle to which all kinds of thoughtful efforts have contributed, from the romantic complaint about a world that has fallen asunder to the various attempts at reuniting it, and to a philosophy of despair, Nietzsche's, contributing to spreading the term. I do not think that anthropology can disregard this situation. Yet it is no wonder that there is something unpleasant about the term. Being comparative in essence, it seems doomed to emptiness: a matter of values is not a matter of fact. It advertises relativism, as it were, or rather both the centrality of the concept and its elusive quality, to which a considerable literature testifies. It smacks of euphemism or uneasiness, like "underdevelopment," "methodological individualism," and so many other items in the present-day vocabulary.

Yet there is a positive counterpart, modest but not insignificant, for the anthropologist: we have at our disposal a word that allows us to consider all sorts of cultures and the most diverse estimations of the good without imposing on them our own: we can speak of our values and their values while we could not speak of our good and their good. Thus the little word, used far beyond the confines of anthropology, implies an anthropological perspective and invests us, I think, with a responsibility. But of this more later.

We begin with a few introductory remarks about the study of values in anthropology. The prevailing use of the word in the plural—values—is indicative not only of the diversity of societies and of the modern compartmentalization of activities but also of a tendency to atomize each configuration that is in keeping with our culture in general. This is certainly the first point that requires attention. In a paper published in 1961, Francis Hsu criticized some studies of the American character for their presenting a bare catalogue of traits or values without bothering about the relations prevailing between those items. He saw conflicts and inconsistencies between the different values listed, wondered at the lack of serious attempts to explain them, and proposed to remedy the situation by identifying one fundamental value and by showing that it implied precisely the contradictions to be explained. The "American core value," Hsu suggested, is self-reliance, itself a modification or intensification of European, or English, individualism. Now self-reliance implies contradiction in its application, for men are social beings and depend heavily on each other in actual fact. Thus is produced a series of contradictions between the level of conception and the level of operation of the main value and of the secondary values derived from it or allied with it.

I, for one, cannot but applaud both the search for a cardinal value and its identification in this case as some form of individualism. One also notes that Hsu implies, if he does not state it explicitly, a hierarchy between conception and operation. Yet in the end Hsu's distinction between the two levels is still insufficient. He uses a classification of Charles Morris (1956), who had listed three uses of value or sorts of value, among them conceived and operative value, and he goes some way toward ranking these two levels. Finally however, he speaks of "values" for both, and thus lumps them together again in the same way as the atomizing authors he had begun by criticizing. In fact, the two levels should be firmly distinguished. For we have here a universal phenomenon. Surely all of us have encountered this characteristic complementarity or reversal between levels of experience where what is true on the more conceptual level is reversed on the more empirical level, a reversal which bedevils our attempts at unifying, for the sake of simplicity, the representation and its counterpart in action. Whatever the peculiarities of the American case, the end cannot be its own means: either what is called "operative values" are not values at all, or they are second-order values that should be clearly distinguished from first-order values or values proper.

In general, there is perhaps a surfeit of contradictions in contemporary literature in general. An author belonging to a different era or *milieu* will frequently be taxed of contradicting himself simply because a distinction of levels obvious to him and therefore implicit in his writings, but unfamiliar to the critic, is missed.[4] It will be seen later on that where nonmoderns distinguish levels within a global view, the moderns know only of substituting one special plane of consideration for another, and find on all planes the same forms of neat disjunction, contradiction, etc. Perhaps there is a confusion here between individual experience which, while crossing different levels, may be felt as contradictory, and sociological analysis, where the distinction of levels is imperative in order to avoid the short-circuit that results in tautology or incomprehension. Apart from Clyde Kluckhohn, the late Gregory Bateson is one of the rare anthropologists who clearly saw the necessity of recognizing a hierarchy of levels.[5]

There has been in the history of anthropology at least one sustained attempt at advancing the study of values. In the late forties, Clyde Kluckhohn chose to focus attention on values and to concentrate efforts and resources on a vast cooperative long-term project devoted to their study, the Harvard "Comparative Study of Values in Five Cultures." There seems to have been in the United States, at the end of World War II, a wide renewal of interest in social philosophy and in the understanding of foreign cultures and

4. Arthur Lovejoy sees in some passages of Plato a contradiction between the Good (or God) being self-sufficient in its perfection and its being the ground and source of this world: the same entity cannot be both complete in itself and in any degree dependent on something else. (Lovejoy 1973: 43–50). But Lovejoy comes to this contradiction by erasing the philosopher's progress and flattening its result. In a first step one must turn away from the world to come to grasp the Idea of the Good (and True and Beautiful). In a second step, once the Good is correctly understood— as limitless generosity or irrepressible fecundity—one finds that it explains and justifies the world as it is. These two conclusions are not at the same level: on an inferior level God is absolutely distinct from the world, on a superior level the world itself is contained in God; the Good transcends the world and yet the world has no being but through it. The world depends on God, God does not depend on the world. The crux of the matter is that Lovejoy stops at the inferior level. He does not and probably cannot accept hierarchy, or transcendence. He looks at Plato with egalitarian eyes.

5. Gregory Bateson 1972: 271–78 (double bind), 336, and *passim*; cf. Kluckhohn 1951 "what appear superficially as incompatibilities are seen on closer examination to be functions of different frames of reference" (p. 399 n. 19); the difference is between seeing things-in-themselves and seeing things-in-relation, i.e. within a "frame of reference."

values.[6] Kluckhohn may have found in the circumstances of the time the occasion to develop what was undoubtedly a deep personal concern. In the late forties, he launched his project, which assembled a number of scholars and issued in an imposing array of publications over the next decade. Today this considerable effort seems largely forgotten. Unless I am deeply mistaken, it has not left a deep mark in American cultural anthropology. Is this one more example of those fashions that disconcertingly displace one another in our discipline, particularly in the United States; or are there internal reasons to the discredit, and, in the worst case, are values a mistaken focus or a "nonsubject," something I could hardly believe? I am not able to answer this complex question. I shall only try to draw from Kluckhohn's endeavor a lesson for our benefit. There must be such a lesson if we believe with him that values are a central problem. For Kluckhohn was not naïve: he was obviously a man of wide culture (with a German component, I suppose, as is the case with several of the early American anthropologists), and, moreover, he anticipated much of what I shall have to say here. Yet, whatever contributions the project may have brought to the knowledge of each of the particular groups or societies studied, the results seem disappointing as regards Kluckhohn's main aim, namely the advancement of comparative theory. How can we account for the fact?

Clyde Kluckhohn was closely associated with Parsons and Shils in the symposium that was published as *Toward a General Theory of Action* and to which he contributed an important theoretical essay which can be taken as the chart of the Harvard Project.[7] It is clear that Kluckhohn developed his own position while agreeing on the broad "conceptual scheme" of the symposium. He dissented only from the rigid separation between social and cultural systems.[8] To be brief I shall mention only three main points in Kluckhohn and two of his main associates. First, that (social) values are essential for the integration and permanence of the social body and also of the personality (p. 319)—we might say with Hans Mol (1976) for their identity—is perhaps obvious, but it is in practice too easily forgot-

6. Cf. Northrop 1946 esp. p. 257; Lepley 1949; Clyde Kluckhohn himself alludes to the circumstances (1951: 388–89).

7. Kluckhohn *et al.* 1951: 388–433. Kluckhohn reiterated his basic position in a number of papers.

8. See the note in Parsons and Shils 1951: 26–27.

ten, either by anthropologists insisting unilaterally on change, or by philosophers abstracting individual values from their social background. Saint Augustine said somewhere that a people is made up of men united in the love of something.

Second, the close link between ideas and values—here "cognitive" and "normative," or "existential" and "normative," aspects—is clearly acknowledged, as it was by Parsons and Shils (1951: 159–89), under the central concept of "value-orientation" as defined by Kluckhohn (Kluckhohn et al. 1951: 410–11). (The concept is open to criticism on another score, as was shrewdly noticed by an anthropologist.)[9] Thus the scheme for the classification of values used by Florence Kluckhohn includes by the side of values proper a minimum of ideas and beliefs. One may prefer the more ample treatment of the Navaho case by Ethel Albert, which includes not only the normally unverbalized "value-premises," but also a complete picture of the worldview as the "philosophical context" of the value system strictly defined (Albert 1956: 221).

The third point is the clear recognition of the fact that values are "hierarchically organized." Clyde Kluckhohn's programmatic article had a very lucid and sensitive page on the question (p. 420), but it is perhaps Florence Kluckhohn that developed this aspect most. Early in the research, she proposed a grid for the comparison of "value-orientations." It is a scheme of priorities distinguishing, in each instance under three terms, different stresses relative to relations between man and nature, to the conception of man, to relations between men, to time, and to action.[10] The author underlines the importance of hierarchy and of nuances in hierarchy. Each value system is seen as a hierarchical combination *sui generis* of elements which are universal in the sense of being found everywhere. This was a solution to a problem that much concerned Clyde Kluckhohn himself. He was reacting against an excessive stress on relativity in anthropological literature. He wanted to avoid falling into (absolute) relativism, and he tried to salvage a modicum of

9. "In the working out of the theory by far the major attention is paid to value-orientations (as against ideas and beliefs) because much of the theory is concerned with the selection by actors of objects and gratifications," writes Richard Sheldon in what is actually a minute of dissent (Sheldon 1951: 40). Sheldon went on to say that this stress on personality and on the "social system" resulted in cutting culture in two.

10. The reference is to a later version of Florence Kluckhohn (1961).

universal values.[11] Florence Kluckhohn found this universal basis in the very material which was elaborated into different value systems, in each case, by an original combination of particular value emphases.

Let me briefly articulate a double criticism. The scheme does not yet apply broadly enough to recognition of hierarchy, and therefore gets stuck in a measure of atomism: no relation is posited between the five subdivisions. What for instance about the relative stress between relations to nature, and relations between men (items 1 and 3)? A universal basis seems here to be unduly assumed. The scheme remains thus inevitably sociocentric. Indeed, it is actually centered on a White American and even a Puritan model. Other cultures may make different choices, but only in terms derived from the American choices.

A later text by Clyde Kluckhohn adds a new scheme of classification of his own to a presentation of those of Ethel Albert and Florence Kluckhohn. The paper,[12] apparently Kluckhohn's last word on the question, would deserve longer consideration than can be given to it here, less for the scheme itself than for the preoccupations that lead up to it. The general, universal bearing of the project is stressed, while the provisional character of the particular scheme is granted. The effort is to make the scheme purely relational: it consists of a series of qualitative, binary oppositions. What is more, it is supplemented by an effort to bring out, by tabulation, the associations between features and thus to reconstitute to some extent the systems analysed.

How is it, then, that a considerable effort containing so many correct perceptions leaves one finally unsatisfied? We are left, on the abstract side, with grids into the pigeon-holes of which we should be able to distribute the elements of any value system. It is clear that, notwithstanding Clyde Kluckhohn's last and pathetic effort to affirm a structural, or structuralist, approach and to recapture the living unity given at the start, the whole has vanished into its parts. Atomization has won the day. Why? Because, I submit,

11. Cf. especially Clyde Kluckhohn 1952. It must be added that Florence Kluckhohn was particularly keen on nuances in the hierarchical make-up, which enabled her to grasp variations not only between cultures but also within a given value system, thus securing an opening toward the question of changes in values.

12. Kluckhohn 1959. The text is apparently a part (pp. 25–54) of a volume of Installation Lectures, which I have not been able to identify. It would not have been earlier than 1959.

the attempt has been unwarily to unite fire and water, structure, hierarchical structure, and classification, that is, classification through individual features. The need for classification was certainly reinforced by the attempt to compare five cultures in one compass, and the most valuable products of the project are probably the monographic pictures in the manner of Albert that it produced. A somewhat unpalatable conclusion follows, namely that a solid and thorough comparison of values is possible only between two systems taken as wholes. If classification is to be introduced further on, it will have to start from wholes and not from itemized features. For the time being we are closer to Evans-Pritchard's "historiography" than to Radcliffe-Brown's "natural science of society."

Kluckhohn noticed that the term "value," chiefly used in the plural, had come recently into the social sciences from philosophy. He saw in it a kind of interdisciplinary concept[13] and, probably largely for this reason, mingled occasionally individual and group values. The term "value-orientation" itself is indicative of a commanding concern with the individual actor (see n. 9 above). Of course, all this tallies with a behavioral approach, but it is above all an index of the philosophical background of our anthropological problems. The philosophical debate is of intimidating dimension and complexity. Yet we cannot possibly leave it out entirely in an attempt to clarify the anthropological question. Fortunately, I believe that, conversely, an anthropological perspective can throw some light on the philosophical debate, and that it is thus possible to take a summary and yet no ineffectual view of it.

There are two kinds of philosophers or, rather, two kinds of philosophizing in the matter. One locates itself within modern culture and is careful to work in accordance with its constraints, its basic inspiration, its inner logic and its incompatibilities. From that point of view the conclusion follows that it is impossible to deduce what *ought to be* from what *is*. No transition is possible from facts to values. Judgments of fact and judgments of value are different in kind. It is enough to recall two or three major aspects of modern culture to show that the conclusion is inescapable. First, science is paramount in our world, and, as we recalled at the start, to make scientific knowledge possible the definition of being has been altered by excluding from it precisely the value dimension. Second,

13. See Kluckhohn 1959, sec. 2, and 1951: 389.

the stress on the individual has led to internalizing morality, to finding it exclusively within the individual's conscience while it is severed from the other ends of action and distinguished from religion. Individualism and the concomitant separation between man and nature have thus split the good, the true, and the beautiful and have produced a theoretically unbridgeable chasm between *is* and *ought to be*. This situation is our lot in the sense that it lies at the core of modern culture of civilization.

Now, whether this situation is comfortable or reasonable is quite another question. The history of thought seems to show that it is not, for no sooner had Kant proclaimed this fundamental split that his gifted successors, and the German intelligentsia as a whole, hastened in various attempts to reestablish unity. It is true that the social milieu was historically backward and that German intellectuals, while inspired by individualism, were still imbued with holism in the depth of their being. But the protest has continued down to the present day.

It must be admitted that, for one who turns away from the environment and attempts to reason from first principles, the idea that what man ought to do is, let us say, unrelated to the nature of things, to the universe and to his place in it, will appear queer, aberrant, incomprehensible. The same holds true of someone who would take into account what we know of other civilizations or cultures. I have said elsewhere that most societies have believed themselves to be based in the order of things, natural as well as social; they have thought they were copying or designing their very conventions after the principles of life and the world. Modern society wants to be "rational," to break away from nature and set up an autonomous human order (*HH*, App.A.: 261). We may thus be inclined at first flush to sympathize with those philosophers who have tried to restore unity between facts and values. Their attempts testify to the fact that we have not entirely broken away from the more common mould of mankind, that it is still in some manner present with us, underlying and perhaps modifying the yet compelling modern framework. But we should be on our guard.

The attempt can take different forms. One consists in annihilating values entirely. Either value judgments are declared meaningless, or the expression of mere whims or emotional states. Or, with some pragmatists, ends are reduced to means: having construed a category of "instrumental values," they proceed to deny the distinct existence of "intrinsic values," that is, of values proper.[14] Such attempts seem to be an index of the inability of some philosophical tendencies to take into account real human life, to mark a dead end of individualism. Another type can be taken as a desperate attempt at transcending individualism by resorting to a modern ersatz religion. In its Marxist form, and through it and somewhat similarly in totalitarian ideologies in general, this doctrine has proved fateful; it is sometimes regarded as sinister, at least in continental Europe, and rightly so. Here we must firmly side with Kolakowski in his impassioned condemnation of the trend, as against certain rambling intellectuals.[15]

We follow Kolakowski especially on one point; the danger does not arise only from the violent attempt to implement such doctrines, but is contained in the doctrine itself under the form of value incompatibilities that call for violence on the level of action. To confirm this point: in an article of 1922, which in retrospect appears prophetic of later developments in Germany, Karl Pribram has noted the parallel incongruity and structural similarity of Prussian nationalism and Marxist socialism. Both, Pribram pointed out, jumped from an individualistic basis to an illegitimate, holistic ("universalistic") construct, the State in the one case, the proletarian class in the other, which they endowed with qualities incompatible with their presuppositions. (Pribram 1922). Totalitarianism is present in germ in such encounters. Philosophers themselves are not always sensitive to such incompatibilities,[16] but their constructions are seldom applied to society. Here a question arises: it is convenient to link totalitarianism with such incompatibilities—yet there exist incompatibilities in societies without their developing into that scourge. Toennies insisted that both *Gemeinschaft* and *Gesellschaft* are present as principles in modern society. My provisional answer is that they are found on different levels of social life, while it is characteristic of modern artificialism to disregard such levels altogether and thus to make for collision between what it consciously introduces and the substratum which it does not really

---

14. It is the fulcrum of the discussion in the symposium edited by Lepley (1949). The pragmatists' attempt goes against the means/ends distinction, which is akin to the others we referred to and is as fundamental as they are to modern culture.

15. Kolakowski 1977. I alluded to the problem in *MM,*: 213, n. 3.

16. A caricatural example: according to Ritter, Hegel succeeded in building up an Aristotelian philosophy of the French Revolution (Ritter 1977).

know. There may well be, indeed there actually *is*, a need for reintroducing some measure of holism into our individualistic societies, but it can be done only on clearly articulated subordinate levels, so that major clashes with the predominant or primary value are prevented. It can be done, that is, at the price of introducing a highly complex hierarchical articulation, which can be imagined, *mutatis mutandis*, as a parallel to the highly elaborate Chinese etiquette.[17] This point will become clearer in what follows. At any rate, we should in the first place, as citizens of the world and of a particular state within it, abide with Kolakowski by the Kantian distinction as an integral part of the modern makeup.

Now, what are the consequences of the distinction for social science? Let us take as vanished the times when a behavioral science banned the study of social values together with that of conscious representations at large. We do study social representations as social facts of a particular kind. Here two remarks are called for. First, it is clear that we maintain this "value-free" attitude on the basis of the Kantian distinction, for otherwise our own native view of "facts" would command value judgments and we should remain locked up in our own system, sociocentric as all societies are except, in principle, our own. The point simply confirms the link between science in general and the *is/ought* separation. But then our approach is philosophically questionable. It may be argued that we should distinguish tyranny from legitimate rule. Leo Strauss maintained against Max Weber that social science could not escape evaluation,[18] and it is true that Weber was led by this "value-free" stand to undesirable admissions, such as his "ethic of conviction." More radically, one may contend that values cannot really be understood without our adhering to them (note the proximity to the Marxist plea), and that to relativize values is to kill them. In a discussion, A. K. Saran maintained the thesis in its full consequence.[19] According to this view, cultures cannot communicate, which means cultural solipsism, a return to sociocentrism. And yet, there is point in it in the sense that comparison implies a universal basis: it must appear in the end that cultures are not as independent

17. Dumont 1979: 796 (above, chap. 8). It goes without saying that, to be successful, such a distinction of levels should be present in the consciousness of the citizens.

18. Leo Strauss 1954, chap. 2 and p. 85.

19. Discussion and references in Dumont 1966: 25–27.

from each other as they would claim to be and as their internal consistency seems to warrant.

Stated otherwise, our problem is: how can we build a bridge between our modern ideology that separates values and "facts" and other ideologies that embed values in their world view?[20] Lest our quest should appear futile, let us not forget that the problem is in a way present in the world as it is. Cultures are in fact interacting, thus communicating in some mediocre manner. It behoves anthropology to give a conscious form to that groping and thus to answer a contemporary need. We are committed to reducing the distance between our two cases, to reintegrating the modern case within the general one. For the moment, we shall try to formulate more precisely and thoroughly the relation between them.

Values are in general intimately combined with other, non-normative representations. A "system of values" is thus an abstraction from a wider system of ideas-and-values.[21] This is true not only of nonmodern societies but also of modern societies, with one cardinal exception, namely that of (individual) *moral* values in their relation to scientific, "objective" knowledge. For all that we said previously about *ought* bears exclusively on individual, "subjective" morality. That this morality is, together with science, paramount in our modern consciousness does not hinder its cohabiting with other norms, or values of the common sort, namely traditional social ethics, even if some transition, some substitution of the former for the latter is taking place under our eyes. Thus the modern value of equality has spread in the last decades in European countries to domains where traditional ethics were still in force; from the French Revolution, in whose values it was implied, up to our days, the equality of women had not imposed itself against subordination as entailed by a whole nexus of institutions and representations. Now the struggle between the two "systems of values" has intensified, and the outcome has still to be seen: our individualist values are at loggerheads with the considerable inertia

20. As the reference to "embeddedness" may remind the reader, we have been following in the footsteps of Karl Polanyi and simply widening his thesis on the exceptional character of modern civilization.

21. We found the point stressed by Parsons and Shils 1951 as well as by Kluckhohn (above). The latter analyzed the interplay between normative and "existential" statements (1951: 392–94): he quoted (p. 422) Herskovits on "cultural focus" as linking the distribution of values and the configuration of ideas (see also *MM,*: 19–20, and Dumont 1979: 814 (see end of chap. 8 above).

of a battered social system that is gradually losing its own justification in consciousness.

A convenient example of the inseparability of ideas and values
is found in the distinction between right and left. It is widespread, if
not universal, and is still found with us in some manner, although
our attitude to it is highly consonant with modern ideology. We are
in the habit of analyzing it into two components. We see it essentially as a symmetrical opposition, where the two poles have equal
status. The fact that the two poles are unequally valued, that the
right hand is felt to be superior to the left hand, appears to us an
arbitrary, superadded feature, which we are at pains to explain.
Such was the frame of mind of Robert Hertz when he wrote his
classic essay, and it has prevailed ever since. It is wholly mistaken.
As I argued elsewhere, the reference to the body as to a *whole* to
which right and left hands belong is constitutive of the right, the left
and their distinction (see above, chap. 8, part 2). The contention
should be obvious: take a polar opposition at random, add to it a
difference in value, and you will not get right and left. Right and
left, having a different relation to the body (a right relation and a
left relation, so to speak) are different *in themselves*. (They are not
two identical entities situated in different places, as we know pretty
well from sensuous experience). Being different parts of a whole,
right and left differ in value as well as in nature, for the relation
between part and whole is hierarchical, and a different relation
means here a different place in the hierarchy. Thus the hands and
their tasks or functions are at one and the same time different and
ranked.[22]

There is something exemplary about this right/left relation. It is
perhaps the best example of a concrete relation indissolubly linked
to human life through the senses, which physical sciences have
neglected and which anthropology may presumably retrieve or
rehabilitate. I believe it teaches us in the first place that to say
"concrete" is to say "imbued with value." That is not all, for such a
difference in value is at the same time situational, and the point will
require attention. The fact is that, if certain functions are allotted to
the left hand, then, in relation to their performance, the right hand
will come second notwithstanding its being on the whole superior.

22. The relation between whole and part was previously defined as the hierarchical opposition, or the *encompassing of the contrary* (above chap. 8). For Thomas
Aquinas, difference by itself suggested hierarchy. So that "order is seen to consist
mainly in inequality (or difference: *disparitate*)," cf. Otto Gierke 1900, n. 88.

The right-and-left pair is indissolubly both an idea and a value, it is a value-idea or an idea-value. Thus at least some of the values of any given people are enmeshed in that people's conceptions. To discover them, it is not necessary to go about eliciting people's choices. These values have nothing to do with the preferable or the desirable—except in that they suppose that the naive perception of the relation between whole and parts, that is, of order as given in experience, has not been obliterated. The moderns tend to define value in relation to arbitrary will, Toennies's *Kürwille*, while we are here in the realm of *Naturwille* or natural, spontaneous will (Toennies 1971). The whole is not, strictly speaking, preferable to its parts, it is simply superior to them. Is the right "preferable" to the left? It is only apposite in some circumstances. What is "desirable," if one insists, is to act in accordance with the nature of things. As to the modern tendency to confuse hierarchy with power, who will pretend that the right hand has power over the left? Even its preeminence is, on the level of action, limited to the accomplishment of its proper functions.

The case also gives us a clue as to how we moderns manage to avoid the ranked nature of things, for we have not ceased to possess a right and a left hand and to deal with our body and with wholes in general. Not only have we developed permissivity in the matter in accordance with our devaluation of the hands and with our individualism. We also tend to *decompose* the original relation by separating value from idea, and in general from fact, which means separating ideas and facts from the whole(s) in which they are actually to be found. Rather than relating the level under consideration—right and left—to the upper level, that of the body, we restrict our attention to one level at a time, we suppress subordination by pulling apart its elements. This shunning of subordination, or, to call it by its true name, of transcendence, substitutes a flat view for a view in depth, and at the same time it is the root of the "atomization" so often complained of by romantic or nostalgic critics of modernity. The point holds in general: in modern ideology, the previous hierarchical universe has fanned out into a collection of flat views of this kind. But I am anticipating.[23]

23. To assert that the modern mode of thought is destructive of the wholes with which man had until then seen himself surrounded may seem excessive or incomprehensible. Yet I think it is true in the sense that each whole has ceased to be value-providing in the above sense. If one turns to our philosophies with the simple question: What is the difference between a whole and a collection, most of them are

In the nonmodern view that I here tried to retrieve, the value of the right or the left hand is rooted in their relation to the body, i.e. to a higher level of being: the value of an entity is dependent upon or intimately related to a hierarchy of levels of experience in which that entity is situated. Here is perhaps the main perception that the moderns miss, or ignore, or suppress without being fully conscious of so doing.[24]

---

silent, and when they give an answer, it is likely to be superficial or mystical as in Lukács, cf. Kolakowski 1977. I take it as exemplary that the constitution of Hegel's system results from a shift in the location of the Absolute, or of infinite value, from the Whole of Being (in the writings of his youth) to the Becoming of the individual entity—a point I intend to argue elsewhere. There is a small current of holistic thought, but it also bears the mark of the difficulty that modern minds experience in the matter, see Phillips 1976—the discussion is sometimes tendentious. A book of Alfred Koestler's (1967) represents an exception. To quote from a summary (p. 58): "Organisms and societies are multi-levelled hierarchies of semi-autonomous sub-wholes branching into sub-wholes of a lower order, and so on. The term "holon" has been introduced [by the author] to refer to these intermediary entities which, relative to their subordinates in the hierarchy, function as self-contained wholes; relative to their superordinates as dependent parts." Koestler is seen to stress hierarchy as a chain of levels, while I have insisted on the elementary relation between two successive levels. The definition of "holon" is valuable. I would only rank the two faces of this Janus in relation to each other: the integration of each subwhole as a unit in the next higher one is primary, its self-integration or "self-assertion" is secondary *HH,*: 245).

We have already noted Gregory Bateson's recognition of the hierarchy of levels (n. 5 above). A biologist, François Jacob, introduced the "integron" in a sense somewhat similar to Koestler's "holon" (Jacob 1970: 323).

24. Is is possible that what is true of particular entities or wholes (subwholes or "holons" in Koestler's terms) is true also of the great Whole, the universe or whole of wholes? Is it possible that the Whole in its turn needs a superior entity from which to derive its own value? That it can be self-integrative only by its subordination to something beyond itself? Clearly religions have a place here, and once could even try to deduce what the Beyond should be like in order to be final. Then we could say not only that men feel a need for a complement to the "empirically" given, as Durkheim supposed, but that the need bears on an apex of valuation. This speculation arises from an exactly opposite view put forward by Lovejoy. He begins his classical book *The Great Chain of Being* (1973, see below) by positing "otherworldliness" as a general attitude found in different forms in some of the world religions and consisting in taking refuge outside the world from its incoherence and wretchedness. Lovejoy states an absolute separation between this attitude and the world: it is only a place to get away from and about which otherworldliness has nothing to say (ibid: 28–30). Here we may wonder. Let us take, as Lovejoy tends to do, an extreme form of "otherworldliness" such as Buddhism. No doubt Buddha was not busy justifying the world. Yet he offers a kind of explanation of it, if a negative one. In general, the beyond is more than a refuge, it is a distant place from which, so to speak, one looks

The point has a bearing on the problem of evil. Two different conceptions are currently contrasted: for some, evil is only the absence or insufficiency of good, vice the limit or zero degree of virtue; for others evil is an independent principle pitched against its opposite as the will of Satan defying that of God (Lovejoy 1973, chap. 7). Yet if Leibniz's Theodicy is compared with Voltaire's discussion of the Lisbon earthquake, one senses a contrast of a perhaps different nature. Let me interpret freely. For Leibniz, the fact that there is evil *locally*, here and there, in the world does not prevent the world from being, *globally* considered, the best of all possible worlds. Voltaire concentrates on a massive example of evil and refuses to look elsewhere or beyond; or rather he simply cannot. Voltaire will not ask himself what are the conditions for a *real* world to exist. He might well say that it is a question beyond the reach of human reason. For Leibniz[25] good and evil are interdependent to begin with, the one inconceivable without the other. But that is not enough, for surely they are no more equal than are right and left. If I may make use of the definition I proposed of the hierarchical opposition, good must contain evil while still being its contrary. In other words, real perfection is not the absence of evil but its perfect subordination. A world without evil could not possibly be good. Of course we are free to call this a universe of faith as against a universe of common sense, of modern common sense. But it is also a universe of rich concreteness as against one of desiccated principle. More precisely, a universe thick with the different dimensions of concrete life, where they have not yet come apart. The

---

back with detachment upon human experience in the world; it is finally a transcendence that is posited and in relation to which the world is situated. Has not this transcendent glance been historically necessary to the understanding of the world as a whole? At any rate history shows abundantly, in India and perhaps in the West as well, that otherworldliness has powerfully acted on life in the world, and this process would be incomprehensible if an absolute heterogeneity was presupposed.

25. Cf. Michel Serres 1968. Leibniz's world should not be simply identified with the traditional world. Perhaps theodicies are an index of individualist questioning and an effort, more or less successful, to reassert the holistic view. On the other hand, the Voltairean mood has had to stomach certain lessons, to learn, for instance that one pole of a magnet could not be separated from the other as some would have wished. "Jadis, en brisant les aimants, on cherchait à isoler le magnétisme nord et le magnétisme sud. On espérait avoir deux principes différents d'attraction. Mais à chaque brisure, si subit, si hypocrite que fût le choc, on retrouvait, dans chacun des morceaux brisés, les deux pôles inséparables" (Bachelard in his preface to Buber 1938: 9).

different dimensions of life do of course exist for Voltaire, but his thought sorts them out, it cannot embrace them all at once. And no doubt we live in Voltaire's world, and not in Leibniz's. It is just a matter of advancing in the perception of the relation between them.

Now let us suppose that, enlightened by the right-and-left example, we agree not to separate an idea and its value but to consider instead as our object the configuration formed by *idea-values* or *value-ideas*. It may be objected that such complex entities will be difficult to handle. Can we really come to grips with such multidimensional objects in their interrelations? Certainly the task is not easy, as it goes against our most ingrained habits. Yet, we are not entirely deprived of clues to make a beginning. We start with three remarks. First the configuration is *sui generis*, value-ideas are ranked in a particular fashion. Second, this ranking includes reversal as one of its properties. Third, the configuration is thus normally segmented. I shall comment in turn on these three characteristics.

First about ranking. "High" ideas will both contradict and include "low" ideas. I called this peculiar relation "encompass-ment." An idea that grows in importance and status acquires the property of encompassing its contrary. Thus I found that in India purity encompasses power. Or, to take an example closer to us, from those that came up in the course of studying economic ideas: economists speak of "*goods and services*" as one overarching cate-gory comprising, on the one hand, commodities and, on the other, something quite different from commodities but assimilated to them, namely services.[26] This is incidentally an example of relations between men (services) being subordinated to relations to things (goods), and if we were to study, say, a Melanesian system of exchanges, it would come nearer to the mark to reverse the priority and speak of *prestations and goods*, I mean prestations (relations between men) including things or encompassing their contrary, things.

We have already alluded to the second characteristic, reversal. The logical relationship between priest and king, as found in India or, nearer to us, in Christianity itself, five centuries after Christ, under the pen of Pope Gelasius, is exemplary in this regard. In matters of religion, and hence absolutely, the priest is superior to the king or emperor to whom public order is entrusted. But *ipso facto* the priest will obey the king in matters of public order, that is,

26. Cf. *MM*, index, s.v. Hierarchy, instances.

in subordinate matters (above, chap. 1). This chiasmus is characteristic of hierarchy of the articulate type. It is obscured only when the
superior pole of the hierarchical opposition is coterminous with the
whole and the inferior pole is determined solely in relation to the
former, as in the instance of Adam and Eve, Eve being creatd from
a part of Adam's body. What happens here is that it is only on the
empirical level—and thus not within the ideology proper—that a
reversal can be detected, as when the mother comes to dominate in
fact the family in which she is in principle subordinate to her
husband. The reversal is built in: the moment the second function is
defined, it entails the reversal for the situations belonging to it. That
is to say, hierarchy is *bidimensional*, it bears not only on the entities
considered but also on the corresponding situations, and this
bidimensionality entails the reversal. As a consequence, it is not
enough here to speak of different "contexts" as distinguished by us,
for they are foreseen, inscribed or implied in the ideology itself. We
must speak of different "levels" hierarchized together with the
corresponding entities.

In the third place, values are often segmented or rather, I
should say, value is normally segmented in its application, except in
specifically modern representations. I shall give a few examples of a
striking contrast between nonmodern and modern cultures, which
bears on the way distinctions are organized or configurated. Im-
pressionistically, on one side, as I said of India, distinctions are
numerous, fluid, flexible, running independently of each other,
overlapping or intersecting; they are also variably stressed according to the situation at hand, now coming to the fore and now
receding. On the other side, we think mostly in black and white,
extending over a wide range clear either/or disjunctions and using
a small number of rigid, thick boundaries defining solid entities
(Dumont 1975*a*: 30). It is noteworthy that the same contrast was
recently found between early Christianity and the late Middle Ages
in political theology. According to Gerard Caspary, the "slow
growth of scholastic and legal modes of thinking," emphasizing
"clarity and distinctions rather than interelationships" has disembedded the political dimension while the "multifaceted and transparent symbols . . . have become one-dimensional and opaque
emblems."[27]

A similar contrast has been pointed out in modern psychology

27. Gerard Caspary 1979: 113–14, 189–91. The whole conclusion should be
read.

by Erik Erikson. Discussing the adolescent's identity formation he contrasts two possible outcomes of the process, which he calls "wholeness" and "totality," as two different forms or patterns of "entireness":

> As a *Gestalt*, then, wholeness emphasizes a sound, organic, progressive mutuality between diversified functions and parts within an entirety, the boundaries of which are open and fluent. [Note the plural!] Totality, on the contrary, evokes a *Gestalt* in which an absolute boundary is emphasized; given a certain arbitrary delineation, nothing that belongs inside must be left outside, nothing that must be outside can be tolerated inside. A totality is as absolutely inclusive as it is utterly exclusive: whether or not the category-to-be-made-absolute is a logical one, or whether the parts really have, so to speak, a yearning for one another. (Erikson 1964: 92)

We cannot at this point follow any further Erikson's fine discussion. We retain essentially the perception of two conceptions or definitions of a whole, one through a rigid boundary, the other through internal interdependence and consistency. From our point of view, the former is modern and arbitrary or somewhat mechanical, the second traditional and structural.[28]

It should be clear that such contrasts between segmented and unsegmented representations have not taken us away from values. In the first approximation the opposition is between holistic values in the former and individualistic values in the latter.

I owe to Robert Bellah a superb reference to hierarchy in Shakespeare. In the third scene of *Troilus and Cressida* Ulysses pronounces a long eulogy of order as *degree:*

> The heavens themselves, the planets, and this centre
> Observe degree, priority, and place,
> Insisture, course, proportion, season, form
> Office and custom, in all line of order. . .

There is one egregious example of the segmentation of value. It is the representation of the universe as a linear hierarchy of beings

28. Erikson takes both forms as normal, although one is obviously inferior ("more primitive"), to the other. At the same time he points out acutely the possible transition from the mechanical form to the totalitarian disease. In that regard the weakness or the very absence of the structural form in philosophical discourse is remarkable.

that is called the *Great Chain of Being*. It was influential all through our history from neoplatonism to the nineteenth century, as was shown in the well-known book which Arthur Lovejoy devoted to it (1973). It pictures the world as a continuous series of beings, from the greatest to the least. It combines, Lovejoy tells us, plenitude, continuity, and gradation. It is a kind of ladder with a secret. The rungs of the ladder are so multiplied that the distance between two successive rungs shades into insignificance and leaves no void; the discontinuity between different sorts of beings is thus seen as a continuity of Being as a whole. The hierarchical aspect is evident, yet it appears on reflection that Lovejoy did not do it full justice. As most moderns, he was unable to see the function of hierarchy in the scheme. He gave scant attention to the only treatise we have on hierarchy, that of the Pseudo-Dionysius Areopagitus, in fact a double treatise on celestial and on terrestrial hierarchy. Let us have a look at Dionysius's definition:[29]

> I mean by hierarchy a holy ordering, a knowledge, and an activity, which assimilates itself as closely as possible to the divine form, and which raises itself to the imitation of God in proportion to the lights which God has granted to it; the beauty which is worthy of God, being simple and good and the principle of initiation, is on the one hand absolutely pure of any dissimilarity, and on the other grants to each one, according to his desert, a share of its own light, while it initiates each one in the most divine initiation, forming them to an harmonious and indistinguishable likeness of itself. The aim of hierarchy is therefore the attainment, as far as possible, of likeness and of union with God.

It is worth stressing that in Dionysius the emphasis throughout is on communication if not on mobility (at least not in our sense of the term). The angels and other creatures situated between men and God are there to transmit or relay the word of God which men could not otherwise perceive, as well as to pave the way, as it were, for the ascent of the soul.[30]

29. Pseudo-Dionysius Areopagitus, *Celestial Hierarchy*, chap. 3, §§ 1–2, 164*d*–165*a*. The translation is by Jasper Griffin, Fellow of Balliol College, Oxford, to whom I am grateful, and who also provided the following translation.

30. Very similar is the function of Love (Eros) as defined in Plato's Symposium by Diotima: he is a daemon, that is, a being intermediary between gods and men: "He interprets and makes a communication between divine and human things, conveying the prayers and sacrifices of men to the Gods, and communicating the

It is not enough, then, to speak of a transformation of discontinuity into continuity. More widely and deeply, the Great Chain of Being appears as a form for acknowledging differences while at the same time subordinating them to and encompassing them in unity.

Nothing can be more remote from this grand scheme than the American "color bar." Of course there is no homology, for the latter representation is limited to men (in accordance with the modern split between man and nature). Yet it is as characteristic of the modern as the Great Chain is of the traditional mode of thought. All men, instead of being divided into a number of estates, conditions or statuses as previously, in harmony with a hierarchical cosmos, are now equal, but for one discrimination. It is as if a number of distinctions had coalesced into one absolute, impassable boundary. Characteristic is the absence of the shades still found elsewhere or previously: no half-breeds, mulattoes, or mestizos are recognized here; what is not pure white is black.

Clearly we reach here the perfect opposite of segmentation. The contrast is so decisive that one might as well speak of antisegmentation, and the similarity with the other examples adduced tends to show that this form is characteristic of modern ideology.

With ranking, reversal, and segmentation, we have gained some insight in the common, nonmodern, I am tempted to say "normal," configuration of value. Such a configuration is part and parcel of the system of representations (ideas-and-values) which I call, for the sake of brevity, ideology. This type of configuration appears very different from the modern type: more precisely, granted that it is not completely absent from modern society, but survives in it in parts and in some degree, it is a fact that modern ideology itself is of quite different type, is indeed as exceptional as Polanyi said of an aspect of it. Now, as we have seen, science has a predominant place and role in modern ideology. It follows that modern scientific, and to a large extent philosophic, ideas, linked as they are with the modern system of values, are often ill-fitted for anthropological study and sociological comparison. Actually it follows from the connection between ideas and values that, just as we must be "value-free" in our "laboratory," we should in principle at

---

commands and directions concerning the mode of worship most pleasing to them, from Gods to men. He fills up that intermediate space between these two classes of beings, so as to bind together, by his own power, the whole universe of things." (202e, Shelley's translation.)

the same time be wary of applying our own ideas, especially our most habitual and fundamental ideas to our subject matter. To do this is of course difficult, and at the limit impossible, for we cannot work "idea-free." We are caught between the Scylla of sociocentrism and the Charybdis of obscurity and incommunicability. All our basic intellectual tools cannot be replaced or modified at one stroke. We have to work piecemeal, and that is what anthropology has done, as its history shows. The reluctance one feels against putting oneself in question—for in the end this is precisely what the effort amounts to—inclines us to do too little, while self-aggrandizement to the neglect of the scientific community counsels to do too much.

Regarding our use of a given concept, it might be of some help to get a clearer view of its place among modern values. I shall take an example. Clearly the absolute distinction between subject and object is fundamental for us and we tend to apply it everywhere, even unknowingly. Its link with some of the ideas already mentioned is obvious, and it clearly bears a value stress.[31] At the same time, it has a bearing on a contemporary problem. We badly need a theory of exchanges, for they enshrine a good deal of the essence of certain societies, as in Melanesia. Now, judging from recent literature, we seem condemned either to subordinate exchanges to the social morphology, or the reverse. The two domains or aspects collide and we have no means of subsuming them under a unified framework. Have we not here a case where our absolute subject/object distinction obtrudes? When Lévy-Bruhl spoke of "participation" between men and objects, was he not trying to circumvent the distinction? Mauss's *Essay on Gift*, so celebrated nowadays, is largely busy acknowledging two facts, first that exchanges cannot be sliced up into economic, juridical, religious, and other aspects, but are all that at one and the same time (a point not irrelevant here, but one that is now widely admitted); and second that men do not exchange things as we would think but, inextricably and fluctuatingly mixed up with those "things," something of themselves.

I am not pleading for cancelling *all* distinction between subject and object; but only for releasing the value stress that bears on the

31. The distinction accompanies in particular the priority of the relation between man and nature, and on that account is already eccentric for a system stressing relations between men. The value stress is seen even in the contradictory valuations of subject and object in positivism and in idealism, of which Raymond Williams reminds us (1976: 259–60).

matter, thus suspending its *absolute* character and allowing the boundary to fluctuate as the case may be, and/or other distinctions to come into play in keeping with native values.[32]

But is such an approach practicable? It has been attempted. A young scholar, André Iteanu, has taken such a course in his reanalysis of the Orokaiva, a Papuan society, from Williams's and Schwimmer's writings. In my reading of his book (1983), he has found an alternative principle for ordering the data in an assumption that again contradicts our received conceptions, although it should not seem so surprising after all, namely that the society has to be thought of as including the dead, the relations with them being constitutive of it and offering the global framework within which not only all the detail of ritual and festive exchanges, but also what there is of social organization proper make sense.

The Orokaiva do not have moneys in the classical Melanesian sense. Yet, as Melanesian money has generally to do with life and the ancestors, the paramount place that the Orokaiva give to the dead reminds us of the cases where ceremonial exchanges do make use of institutional money. Here I am inclined to bring together two problems that can hardly be entirely left out of a discussion bearing on value. Those "primitive" moneys have to do with absolute value. Therefore their relation to money in the modern, restricted sense of the term is somehow homologous to the relation, among us, between value in the general, moral or metaphysical sense and value in the restricted economic sense. In the background of both lies the contrast between cultural forms that are essentially global and those in which the field is separated out or decomposed into particular domains or planes, that is, roughly speaking, between nonmodern and modern forms.

Perhaps two features of the contrast may prove significant. Is it a fact in tribal societies that, where we have elaborate systems of exchange making use of one or more traditional moneys—mostly shell-moneys—to express and seal a wide range of ceremonial transitions and important rituals, we do not have permanent elaborate chiefship or rulership, and conversely that where the latter is

32. There is a precedent in German philosophy in Schelling's philosophy of nature, where he wanted to transcend the Kantian duality, and downgraded this distinction to one of mere degree or complementarity within a class. I am not advocating Schelling's perhaps primitive and inefficient device. For us each particular context should be decisive.

found the former are absent? Melanesia and Polynesia seem clearly contrasted in that regard. If this were so, we might suppose that one thing can replace the other, that there is a certain equivalence of function between them. Now, in modern Europe the predominance of economic representations has resulted from the emancipation of economics from politics and has demanded, at some stage, the curtailment of political prerogatives (above, chap. 3). Is there here, despite the vast difference in the backgrounds, more than a chance parallelism, an index to a more general relation between two aspects of society?

Another feature drew the attention of Karl Polanyi. He contrasted the fixed "equivalencies" between objects of exchange in primitive or archaic societies with the fluctuating price of goods in market economies. Mainly in the former case, the sphere of equivalence and possibly of exchange may be restricted to a few types of objects, while in the second, money tends to be a universal equivalent. But the question I want to raise is about the contrast between fixed and fluctuating rates of exchange. Polanyi (1966) attributed the fixity encountered in Dahomey to royal regulation. But the phenomenon was probably widespread. In the Solomon Islands, where regulation by political authority was out of the question, the rate of exchange between native money and the Australian dollar remained unaltered over a long period, even though the devaluation of the dollar entailed very unpleasant consequences.[33] At the other end of the spectrum, in the case of a high civilization and a complex society, Byzantium offers a spectacular case of fixity. The purchasing power of gold money remained practically unchanged from the fifth to the eleventh century.[34] The fact seems unbelievable if one thinks of the vicissitudes of the Empire during that period, where it was repeatedly, in every century, threatened in its very existence. Given the circumstances, the admitted excellence of imperial revenue administration is perhaps not a sufficient explanation of this remarkable phenomenon. I propose a different hypothesis which may or may not be tested but which I see other reasons for putting forth. When the rate of exchange is seen as linked to the basic value(s) of the society it is stable, and it is allowed to fluctuate only when and where the link with the basic value and identity of the

33. Oral communication from Daniel de Coppet (about the 'Are 'Are on Malaita).

34. Ostrogorsky 1969: 68, 219n., 317, 371.

society is broken or is no longer perceived, when money ceases to be a "total social fact" and becomes a merely economic fact.[35]

It remains to recapitulate the foregoing and set in perspective the modern ideological framework and the anthropological predicament. The picture will be perforce incomplete and provisional, the language very approximate. The aim is to assemble a number of features, most of which have found stray recognition here or there, in order to perceive, or merely to sense, some of the relations between them. I insisted elsewhere on man as an individual as being probably the cardinal modern value, and on the concomitant emphasis on relations between men and things as against relations between men.[36] These two features have notable concomitants regarding value.

First, the conception of man as an individual entails the recognition of a wide freedom of choice. Some of the values, instead of emanating from the society, will be determined by the individual for his own use. In other words, the individual as (social) value demands that society should delegate to him a part of its value-setting capacity. Freedom of conscience is the standard example.[37] The absence of prescription which makes choice possible is actually commanded by a superior prescription. Let me say in passing that it is therefore idle to suppose that men must have in all societies a similar range of choices open to them. Contrariwise, and very generally, value is embedded in the configuration of ideas itself. As we saw with right and left, this condition prevails as long as the

35. Radcliffe-Brown had already attracted attention to fixed equivalences as against the action of supply and demand (1957: 112, 114, 138).—The hypothesis may seem unwarranted, coming after the careful and thoughtful study of Marshall Sahlins (1972, ch. 6). As formulated here, however, it is not straightforwardly contradicted by Sahlins's conclusion. We may read him as stating only that contact with a market economy and/or radical economic changes have directly or indirectly an action on fixed equivalences in the long run. Also there may be, between the two conditions that the hypothesis contrasts, intermediary transitional stages with a complex interaction between norm and fact.

36. Cf. above, chap. 3. Starting from these two kinds of relations and tracing their application and combinations, the German sociologist Johann Plenge developed a complete—hierarchical—and impeccable classification of relations in a brochure (Plenge 1930).

37. The individual's capacity is obviously limited. Analytically, *either* he exerts his choice between existing virtual values, or existing ideas, *or* he constructs a new idea-value (which must be rare).

relation between part and whole is effectively present, as long as experience is spontaneously referred to degrees of totality; and there is no place here for freedom of choice. We are faced, once again, with two alternative configurations; either value *attaches to the whole* in relation to its parts,[38] and value is embedded, prescribed, as it were, by the very system of representation, or value *attaches to the individual*, which results, as we have seen, in the separation between idea and value. The antithesis is economically seen in terms of Toennies's *Naturwille* and *Kürwille*, the crux of the matter being that freedom of choice or *Kürwille* is exercised in a world without wholes, or rather in a world where the assemblages, sets or empirical wholes that are still encountered are deprived of their orientating function or value function.

Let us turn to the complex link between the modern value configuration and the relation between man and nature. Relations between men have to be subordinated for the individual subject to be autonomous and "equal"; the relation of man to nature acquires primacy, but this relation is *sui generis*, for, whether or not the independence of the individual demands it, man is indeed separated from nature: the free agent is opposed to nature as determined,[39] *subject and object are absolutely distinguished*. Here we encounter science and its predominance in the culture as a whole. To cut the story short, let us say that the dualism in question is artificialist in essence: man has distanced himself from nature and the universe of which he was a part, and has asserted his capacity to remodel things according to his will. Again it makes full sense to say that *Naturwille* has been superseded by *Kürwille*, the latter being taken here less as arbitrary will than as detached, disembedded, independent will. Given the close link between the will and values, it is worthwhile asking whence came this unprecedented type of will.

I surmise that it was forged in the otherworldliness, or rather outworldliness of early Christianity, from which issues finally the figure of Calvin, a prototype of modern man, with his iron will rooted in predestination. Only this Christian gestation seems to me to make understandable the unique and strange "prometheism" of modern man (see above, chap. 1).

At any rate, with *Kürwille* as human will detached from nature

38. Koestler allows for more precision: "the whole" is mostly a subwhole or holon, itself part of a higher subwhole.
39. Descartes's *pensées et étendue*, etc.

and applied to its subjugation, we are in a position to appreciate the deep anchorage of the dichotomy between *is* and *ought* in modern ideology and life.

Finally, our two configurations embody two different relations between knowledge and action. In the one case, the agreement between the two is guaranteed on the level of the society:[40] ideas are in conformity with the nature and order of the world, and the subject can do no better than consciously insert himself in this order. In the other case, there is no humanly significant world order, and it is left to the individual subject to establish the relation between representations and action, that is to say broadly speaking, between social representations and his own action. In the latter case, this world devoid of values, to which values are superadded by human choice, is a subhuman world, a world of objects, of things. One can know it exactly and act on it on condition of abstaining from any value imputation. It is a world without man, a world from which man has deliberately removed himself and on which he is thus able to impose his will.

This transformation has been made possible only by the devaluation of relations between men, relations which generally commanded the relation to things. They have lost, in the predominant ideology, their concrete character; they are especially seen from the viewpoint of relations to things (remember the Parsonian variables) except for one residue, namely moral action. Hence the abstract universality of the Kantian imperative.

So much for the subject side of the matter. Despite our absolute distinction between subject and object, there is some homology between the ways we look at both sides. I wish to add a few notes on the object side to complete the picture and to draw attention to a few features of the modern configuration of knowledge. It is a commonplace to say that modern knowledge is distributed into a number of separate compartments, to speak of a high degree of division of labor, of scientific specialization. I shall try and characterize the modern model more precisely in contrast to the traditional one, of which we recalled some major aspects in the foregoing.

The modern configuration can be taken as resulting from the breakup of the value relation between element and whole. The

---

40. The relation is intrinsically problematic. To ensure it is the essential and distinctive function of religion (cf. the note in *MM*, 214).

whole has become a heap. It is as if a bag containing balls had volatilized: the balls have rolled away in all directions. This again is commonplace. The fact is that the objective world is made up of separate entities or substances in the image of the individual subject, whose empirically ascertained relations are taken as external to them.[41] Yet the image is poor. In the first place, it suggests that the final distribution of the elements is random. Actually a complex, multidimensional world of ordered and fluctuating relations has been analyzed, decomposed by the effort of (philosophical and) scientific reason into simpler components whose inner constitution and relations are quite peculiar. A somewhat better image is that of a multidimensional solid bursting out into a number of discrete, straight surfaces or planes that can accommodate only level linear figures and relations. Those planes have, I think, three characteristics: they are absolutely separate and independent, they are homologous to each other, and each of them is homogeneous throughout its extension.

The bursting out in general is relatively familiar: the history of modern painting from Impressionism onwards provides an example. The means that were until then subordinated to the descriptive reference were emancipated and each of them could in turn occupy the foreground. Nor is there any doubt as to the perfect separation of the "planes" of knowledge: do we speak of physics or chemistry, psychology or physiology, psychology or sociology? But what is it that determined the identity of each of the disciplines among which the constituents of the world have been distributed? The answer seems to be that the instrumental point of view is decisive.[42] Correlatively, we had occasion to point out the extreme and striking weakness of the notion of a "whole" in philosophical thought.

Secondly, the "planes" on which knowledge and progress are concentrated remain "homogeneous" throughout their extent. All the phenomena considered are of the same nature, have equal status, and are essentially simple. The paradigm here would be

41. Predominant at any rate. On "internal relations," see Philips 1976, cf. n. 23 above.

42. Radcliffe-Brown wrote of 'natural kinds of system' (1957: 23); thus implicitly admitting that the separation between scientific disciplines is grounded in nature. The relation with the predominance of nominalism in science is obvious. The Cartesian difficulty of conceiving the relations between soul and body is perhaps the archetype of such fission. Hence the surfeit of contradiction and of simple oppositions badly subsumed.

Galilei's model of rectilinear uniform motion: a single material point moving through empty space. As a consequence, the planes have a tendency to split when the development of science reveals an (instrumental) heterogeneity.

Yet all planes are homologous, at least in principle, in the sense that the methods applied to diverse kinds of phenomena are identical. There is only one model of the natural sciences. It is true that with time and experience the model may be altered, but only with difficulty (witness biology and psychology). The model is mechanistic, quantitative, it rests on cause and effect (one individual agent, one individual result).[43] It is essential to note that scientific *rationality* is present and at work only on each of these distinct planes, and that its exercise supposes that the whole has been put to pieces. It cannot reach beyond the relation of means to ends.

Successful as they have been in ensuring the mastery of man over the natural world, the sciences have had other results, one of which is to confront us with what Alexandre Koyré called "the enigma of man." If anthropology is dealing, in its own manner, with this "enigma," then it is both an integral part of the modern world, and in charge of transcending it, or rather of reintegrating it within the more common human world. I hope that our observations on value have pointed in that direction. There remains to face squarely the question of our relation to value: anthropology is poised between a "value-free" science and the necessity to restore value to its proper and universal place. The philosophical critic of social science demands that it should be evaluative. He may grant us the ability to go beyond mere neutrality in the matter and yet maintain that we are unable to get rid of it completely and to evaluate or prescribe.

That is true in practice. It is not quite so, I suggest, in principle, and the point is worth making. What happens in the anthropological view is that every ideology is relativized *in relation to others*. It is not a matter of absolute relativism. The unity of mankind, postulated and also verified (slowly and painfully) by anthropology, sets limits to the variation. Each particular configuration of ideas and values is contained with all others in a universal figure of which it is a partial expression (see chap. 8 above, first part). Yet this universal figure is so complex that it cannot be described, but only vaguely imagined as a kind of sum integral of all concrete configurations.

43. It is noteworthy that Radcliffe-Brown saw the incompatibility between a holistic or systemic approach and causal explanation and rejected causality from his "theoretical social science" (1957: 41).

It is thus impossible for us to grasp *directly* the universal matrix in which the coherence of each particular value system is rooted, but it is perceptible in another way: each society or culture carries the trace of the inscription of its ideology within the human predicament. It is a negative mark, carved below the surface, in intaglio. Just as an action has unforeseen consequences or "perverse effects," or as each individual choice in our societies is immersed in a milieu of greater complexity and thus brings forth involuntary effects, so each ideo-normative configuration has *its specific*, obscure yet compelling concomitants, which accompany it as its shadow and which manifest *the human condition* in relation to it. These concomitants are what I called in a somewhat different context the "nonideological features" that we find by comparison and which we see as nonconscious aspects, unsuspected by the people themselves (cf. *HH*, § 118).

There is thus in each concrete society the imprint of this universal model, which becomes perceptible to some degree as soon as comparison begins. It is a negative imprint, which authenticates, so to speak, the society as human, and whose precision increases when comparison proceeds. It is true that we cannot derive a prescription from this imprint, but it represents the reverse side of the prescription, or its limit. In principle, anthropology is thus fraught with progress in the knowledge of value, and hence of prescription itself, and this should lead in the end to a reformulation of the philosopher's problem.

But what about here and now? Granted that the meaning of "prescription" is made more complex in our perspective, to the extent that we should prefer to speak of counsel rather than injunction, can we not offer something of the sort on the basis of our factual conclusions? We found that the modern configuration, however opposed to the traditional, is still located within it: the modern model is an exceptional variant of the general model and remains encased, or encompassed, within it. Hierarchy is universal; at the same time it is here partially but effectively contradicted. What is it, then, that is necessary in it? A first and approximate answer is that there are things that equality can and things that it cannot do. A contemporary trend in public opinion, in France and elsewhere, suggests an example.

There is much talk round about of "difference," the rehabilitation of those that are in one way or an other "different," the recognition of *alter*. This may mean two things. In so far as it is a matter of enfranchisement in general, equal rights and opportunities, equal treatment of women or of homosexuals, etc.—and such seems to be the main import of the claims put forward on behalf of such categories—there is no theoretical problem. It should only be pointed out that in such equalitarian treatment difference is disregarded, neglected, or subordinated, and not "recognized." Given the easy transition from equality to identity, the long-range outcome is likely to be in the direction of the erasing of distinctive characteristics in the sense of a loss of the meaning or value previously attributed to the corresponding distinctions.

But there may be more in these claims. The impression is that another meaning is also subtly present in them, namely the recognition of *alter qua alter*. I submit that such recognition can only be hierarchical—as was keenly perceived by Burke in his *Reflections on the Revolution in France*. Here, to recognize is the same as to value or to integrate (remember the Great Chain of Being). This statement flies in the face of our stereotypes or prejudices, for nothing is more remote from our common sense than Thomas Aquinas's dictum that "order is seen to consist mainly in inequality (or difference: *disparitate*)" (above, n.22). Yet it is only by a perversion or impoverishment of the notion of order that we may believe contrariwise that equality can by itself constitute an order. To be explicit: *alter* will then be thought of as superior or inferior to Ego, with the important qualification of reversal (which is not present in the Great Chain as such). That is to say that, if *alter* was taken as globally inferior, he would turn out as superior on secondary levels of consideration.[44]

What I maintain is that, if the advocates of difference claim for it both equality and recognition, they claim the impossible. Here we

44. For the application to societies, see the first part of chapter 8 above. If we suppose the levels to be numerous, and the reversal multiplied, then we have a fluctuating dyadic relationship which may statistically give the impression of equality. In a quite different context, Sahlins' analysis of exchange in the Huon Gulf is pregnant with meaning (Sahlins 1976: 322 ff.). Briefly: (1) between two commercial partners, each of the exchanges in a series is unbalanced, alternatively in one and the other direction, in approximation to a balance reached in the end, i.e. for the series as a whole; equality is thus reached through a succession of somewhat unequal exchanges; (2) each particular exchange is thus not closed but remains open and calls for the next one: the stress is on the continuing relationship more than on instantaneous equivalence between goods. All aspects of our problems are here contained in a nutshell: the difference between hierarchy and equality is not at all what we are wont to suppose.

are reminded of the American slogan "separate but equal" which marked the transition from slavery to racism.

To be more accurate, however, I should say that the above is true on the level of pure representation—equality *or* hierarchy—and thus make room for an alternative of a different kind. As to the *practical* forms of integration, most of those we can think of either assemble equal, principally identical agents, as in cooperation, or refer to a whole and are implicitly hierarchical, as the division of labor. Only conflict qualifies, as Max Gluckman has shown, as integrator. We should then say, speaking roughly, that there are two ways of somehow recognizing *alter:* hierarchy and conflict. Now, that conflict is inevitable and perhaps necessary is one thing, and to posit it as an ideal, or as an "operative value," is quite another[45]—although it is in keeping with the modern trend. Did not Max Weber himself grant more credibility to war than to peace? Conflict has the merit of simplicity while hierarchy entails a complication similar to that of Chinese etiquette. The more so, as it would here have to be encompassed within the paramount value of individualism and equality. Yet I must confess my irenic preference for the latter.

Postscript (1983). A footnote is perhaps required. It may be thought with some reason that the above comparison proposes too narrow a view of modern culture, a picture so incomplete that it might apply for some time in the past but does not fit the present anymore. Thus, it will be argued, the type of science presented or implied above has long been superseded as theory, in philosophy the separation between "is" and "ought to be" is far from being generally admitted nowadays, etc.

This kind of criticism can be met in two stages. First, the endeavor was to lay bare a general configuration that underlies the common way of thinking as well as specialized knowledge. By "common way of thinking" is meant not only that of the man in the street, but that presupposed by political institutions as well, or, again, the predominant assumptions in the study of society. In such a consideration all existing features do not weigh equally: that a new feature appears in a speciality does not give it the same weight as any other in the global configuration. For instance, it would seem

45. This is what, in my view, Marcel Gauchet (1980) does in a thoughtful reappraisal of Tocqueville (see esp. pp. 90–116).

that relativity theory, though not so recent, has not to this day conquered a place of the same order as Newtonian physics in the common representations.

Second, there is a problem of vocabulary, and it overlies a problem of method. The configuration which it was the aim of the whole research to isolate was called modern in the sense of being *characteristic* of modern societies as opposed to nonmodern ones. Individualism is so fundamental therein that we may call it, altogether, an individualist configuration. On the other hand, if one speaks of modernity in a merely chronological sense, then it is found to contain, not only on the level of social practice, but even on that of ideology itself, much more than the individualist configuration which characterizes it comparatively. (By the way, this is not true only in view of the most recent, properly "contemporary" developments, but much earlier.) In the light of the results we have attained, this situation is seen as highly meaningful, and as liable in its turn to an analysis in renewed terms.*

*See Introduction to this volume, *in fine*.

Works Cited

Albert, Ethel M. 1956. "The Classification of Values: A Method and Illustration." *American Anthropologist* 58: 221–48.

Arendt, Hannah. 1958. *The Origins of Totalitarianism*. London.

Augustine, Saint. 1972. *The City of God*. Penguin Books.

Ayçoberry, Pierre. 1982. "Franz Neumann, *Behemoth*." *Le Débat* 21 (September): 178–91.

Barker, Ernest. 1934. See Gierke 1957.

———. 1947. "Introduction," in Barker, ed., *Social Contract: Essays by Locke, Hume and Rousseau*. The World Classics, 511. London.

Bateson, Gregory. 1972. *Steps to an Ecology of Mind*. Ballantine Books.

Beck, Brenda E. F. 1972. *Peasant Society in Konku: A Study of Right and Left Subcastes in South India*. Vancouver.

———. 1973. "The Right-Left Division of South Indian Society." In Needham 1973: 391–426.

Belaval, Y., and others. 1978. *La révolution kantienne*. Paris.

Berlin, Isaiah. 1976. *Vico and Herder: Two Studies in the History of Ideas*. London.

Bevan, Edwyn. 1927. *Stoïciens et sceptiques*. (Translated from the English.) Paris.

Bidez, J. 1932. "La Cité du monde et la Cité du soleil chez les Stoïciens." *Bulletin de l'Académie Royale de Belgique*, Lettres, série V, vols. 18–19: 244–94.

Bosanquet, Bernard. 1910. *The Philosophical Theories of the State*. 2d ed. London.

Bouglé C., and E. Halévy, eds. 1931. *La doctrine de Saint-Simon, Exposition, Première année, 1829*. Paris.

Bourdieu, Pierre. 1972. *Esquisse d'une théorie de la pratique*, précédée de *Trois études d'ethnologie Kabyle*. Paris.

Bracher, Karl Dietrich. 1972. *Die deutsche Diktatur*. Cologne.

Brésard, Marcel. 1962. "La 'volonté générale' selon Simone Weil." *Le Contrat Social* 7, no. 6: 358–62.

Brown, Peter. 1971. *La vie de saint Augustin*. Paris. (Translated from *Augustine of Hippo: A Biography*, Berkeley, Calif, 1967.)

Bruford, W. H. 1975. *The German Tradition of Self-Cultivation*. Cambridge.

Buber, Martin. 1938. *Je et Tu*. Paris.

Buchheim, Hans. 1962. *Totalitäre Herrschaft, Wesen und Merkmale*. Munich.

Bullock, Alan. 1963. *Hitler*. Verviers. (French translation of *Hitler, A Study in Tyranny*, London, 1952.)

Burke, Edmund. 1968. *Reflections on the Revolution in France*. Penguin Books.

Burridge, Kenelm. 1979. *Someone, No One: An Essay on Individuality*. Princeton.

Cahnman, Werner J. 1970. "Toennies und Durkheim: Eine dokumentarische Gegenüberstellung." *Archiv für Rechts- und Sozialphilosophie* 56, no. 2: 189–208.

———. 1973. *Ferdinand Toennies: A New Evaluation*. Leiden.

Carlyle, A. J. 1903. *The Second Century to the Ninth*. Vol. 1 of R. W. and A. J. Carlyle, *A History of Medieval Political Theory in the West*. 2 vols. Edinburgh and London.

Caspary, Gerard E. 1979. *Politics and Exegesis: Origen and the Two Swords*. Berkeley, Calif.

Cassirer, Ernst. 1946. *The Myth of the State*. New Haven.

Chronicles of the Pilgrim Fathers. n.d. New York.

Coleman, D. C., ed. 1969. *Revisions in Mercantilism*. London.

Condorcet, Antoine de Caritat, Marquis de. 1933. *Esquisse d'un tableau historique des progrès de l'esprit humain*. Paris. (Originally published 1795.)

Congar, Yves M. J. 1968. *L'Ecclésiologie du haut moyen âge*. Paris.

Conze, Edward. 1967. "Buddhism and Gnosis." In *Le origini dello gnosticismo*. Colloquio di Messina, 13–18 April 1966. Leiden.

Crocker, Christopher. 1977. "Les réflexions du soi." In *L'identité: Séminaire interdisciplinaire dirigé par Claude Lévi-Strauss, 1974–75*, edited by J. M. Benoist, 157–84. Paris.

Daraki, Maria. 1981. "L'émergence du sujet singulier dans les Confessions d'Augustin." *Esprit*, February: 95–115.

Déclaration des droits de l'homme et du citoyen. 1900. Paris.

Derathé, Robert. 1950. *Jean-Jacques Rousseau et la science politique de son temps*. Paris.

Descombes, Vincent. 1977. "Pour elle un Français doit mourir." *Critique* 366 (November 1977): 998–1027.

Douglas, Mary. 1978. "Judgments on James Frazer." *Daedalus* (Fall): 151–64.

Dumont, Louis. 1953*a*. "The Dravidian Kinship Terminology as an Expression of Marriage." *Man*, no. 54 (March). Reprinted in: Dumont 1983*a*.

———. 1953*b*. "Dravidian Kinship Terminology." *Man*, no. 224 (September 1953). Reprinted in Dumont 1983*a*.

———. 1960. "World Renunciation in Indian Religions." (Reprinted in Dumont 1980, App. B.)

———. 1962. "The Conception of Kingship in ancient India." (Reprinted in Dumont 1980, App. C.)

———. 1966. "A Fundamental Problem in the Sociology of Caste." *Contributions to Indian Sociology* 9: 17–32.

———. 1970. "A Structural Definition of a Folk Deity." In Dumont, *Religion, Politics and History in India*. Paris and The Hague. (Written in 1953).

———. 1971*a*. "Religion, Politics and Society in the Individualistic Universe." *Proceedings of the Royal Anthropological Institute for 1970*, pp. 33–41.

———. 1971*b*. "On Putative Hierarchy." *Contributions to Indian Sociology*, n.s. 5: 61–81.

———. 1975*a*. *La civilisation indienne et nous*. 2d ed. Collection U Prisme. Paris.

———. 1975*b*. "On the Comparative Understanding of Non-Modern Civilizations." *Daedalus* (Spring).

———. 1977. *From Mandeville to Marx: The Genesis and Triumph of Economic Ideology*. Chicago.

———. 1979. "The Anthropological Community and Ideology." *Social Science Information* 18, no. 6.

———. 1980. *Homo Hierarchicus: The Caste System and Its Implications*. Complete Revised English edition. Chicago.

———. 1982. "Totalité et hiérarchie dans l'esthétique de K. P. Moritz." In *Les Fantaisies du Voyageur*, pp. 64–76. *Revue de Musicologie*, numéro spécial André Schaeffner.

———. 1983*a*. *Affinity as a Value: Marriage Alliance in South India, with Comparative Essays on Australia*. Chicago.

———. 1983*b*. *Essais sur l'individualisme: Une perspective anthropologique sur l'idéologie moderne*. Paris.

———. 1983*c*. Preface to Karl Polanyi, *La Grande Transformation*, French translation, pp. 1–19. Paris.

———. 1985*a*. "Identités collectives et idéologie universaliste; leur interaction de fait." *Critique* 456 (May): 506–18.

———. 1985*b*. "L'idée allemande de liberté selon Ernst Troeltsch." *Le Débat* 35 (May): 40–50.

Durkheim, Emile. 1953. *Montesquieu et Rousseau précurseurs de la sociologie*. Paris.

Dvornik, F. 1966. *Early Christian and Byzantine Political Philosophy: Origins and Background.* 2 vols. Washington, D.C.

Ehrhardt, Arnold A. T. 1959–69. *Politische Metaphysik von Solon bis Augustus.* 3 vols. Tübingen.

Erikson, Erik H. 1964. *Insight and Responsibility.* New York.

Faye, Jean-Pierre. 1972. *Langages totalitaires: Critique de la raison / l'économie narrative.* Paris.

Fichte, J. G. 1845–46. *Sämmtliche Werke.* Edited by J. H. Fichte. 8 vols. Berlin.

Figgis, John Neville. 1914. *The Divine Right of Kings.* 2d ed. Cambridge.

———. 1960. *Political Thought from Gerson to Grotius, 1414–1625.* New York. Harper Torchbooks. (Originally published 1907.)

Friedländer, Saul. 1982. "De l'antisémitisme à l'extermination." *Le Débat* 21 (September): 131–50.

Friedrich, C. J., M. Curtis, and B. R. Barber. 1969. *Totalitarianism in Perspective: Three Views.* New York.

Gauchet, Marcel 1980. "Tocqueville, l'Amérique et nous." *Libre* 7: 43–120.

Gierke, Otto. 1900. *Political Theories of the Middle Age.* Translated by F. W. Maitland. Cambridge. (Quotations are from the Beacon paperback edition, 1958.)

———. 1913. *Das deutsche Genossenschaftsrecht.* 4 vols. Berlin.

———. 1957. *Natural Law and the Theory of Society, 1500 to 1800.* Translated by Ernest Barker. Boston. (Originally published in 2 vols., Cambridge, 1934.)

Gilson, Etienne. 1938. *Héloïse et Abélard.* Paris.

———. 1969. *Introduction à l'étude de saint Augustin.* Paris.

Goodenough, E. R. 1940. *An Introduction to Philo Judaeus.* New Haven.

Guéroult, Martial. 1974. *Etudes sur Fichte.* Paris.

Halévy, Elie. 1900–1904. *La formation du radicalisme philosophique.* Paris. 3 vols. (English translation: *The Growth of Philosophic Radicalism*, 1 vol., London, 1928).

Haller, William. 1956. "The Levellers." In Lyman Bryson and others, eds., *Aspects of Human Equality.* New York.

Heckscher, Eli F. 1955. *Mercantilism.* Rev. ed. 2 vols. London.

Hegel, G. W. F. 1907. *Hegels theologische Jugendsschriften.* Edited by H. Nohl. Tübingen. (Translated by T. M. Knox as *Early Theological Writings*, Philadelphia, 1971.)

———. 1942. *Philosophy of Right.* Translated by T. M. Knox. Oxford.

———. 1964. *Political Writings.* Oxford.

———. 1966. *Politische Schriften.* Frankfurt.

Herder, J. G. 1964. *Une autre philosophie de l'histoire.* Translated and with an introduction by Max Rouché. Paris.

———. 1968. *Werke.* Edited by Suphan. 33 vols.

Hertz, Robert. 1960. *Death and the Right Hand*. Translated by R. and C. Needham. London.

HH. See Dumont 1980.

Hill, Christopher. 1961. *The Century of Revolution, 1603–1714*. Edinburgh.

Himmler, Heinrich. 1978. *Discours secrets*. Paris. (French translation of *Geheimreden*.)

Hitler, Adolf. 1933. *Mein Kampf*. Munich. (Translated by Ralph Manheim, Boston, 1971.)

Hobbes, Thomas. 1929. *Leviathan*. Edited by W. G. Pogson Smith. Oxford.

Hsu, Francis L. 1961. "American Core Value and National Character." In Hsu, ed., *Psychological Anthropology*, pp. 209–30. Homewood, Ill.

Iselin, Isaac. 1764. *Über die Geschichte der Menscheit*. (5th ed., Basel 1786.)

Iteanu, André. 1983. *La ronde des échanges: De la circulation aux valeurs chez les Orokaiva*. Cambridge and Paris.

Jäckel, Eberhard. 1973. *Hitler idéologue*. Paris. (French translation of *Hitlers Weltanschauung*, 1969.)

Jacob, François. 1970. *La logique du vivant: Une histoire de l'hérédité*. Paris.

Jellinek, Georg. 1902. *La Déclaration des Droits de l'Homme et du Citoyen*. Paris. (Originally published in German, 1895.)

Kaiser, Gerhard. 1973. *Pietismus und Patriotismus im literarichen Deutschland*. Frankfurt. (Originally published 1961.)

Kluckhohn, Clyde. 1952. "Categories of Universal Culture." Draft, Wenner-Gren Symposium, June 1952. Kluckhohn file, Tozzer Library, Harvard University.

———. 1959. "The Scientific Study of Values." Offprint, Kluckhohn file, Tozzer Library, Harvard University.

Kluckhohn, Clyde, and others. 1951. "Values and Value-Orientation in the Theory of Action." In Talcott Parsons and Edward A. Shils, eds., *Toward a General Theory of Action*, pp. 388–433. Cambridge, Mass.

Kluckhohn, Florence. 1961. "Dominant and Variant Value Orientations." In F. Kluckhohn and F. L. Strodtbeck, eds. *Variations in Value Orientations*. Evanston, Ill.

Koestler, Arthur. 1967. *The Ghost in the Machine*. London.

Kolakowski, Leszek. 1977. "The Persistence of the Sein-Sollen Dilemma." *Man and World* 10, no. 2.

Koyré, Alexandre. 1958. *From the Closed World to the Infinite Universe*. Harper Torchbooks.

Lakoff, Sanford A. 1964. *Equality in Political Philosophy*. Harvard.

Lalande, André. 1968. *Vocabulaire technique et critique de la philosophie*. Paris.

Landes, David S. 1969. *Unbound Prometheus*. Cambridge.

Leach, Sir Edmund. 1961. *Rethinking Anthropology*. London.

———. 1973. "Melchisedech and the Emperor: Icons of Subversion and Orthodoxy." *Proceedings of the Royal Anthropological Institute for 1972*, pp. 5–14. London.

———. 1976. *Social Anthropology: A Natural Science of Society?* Radcliffe-Brown Lecture 1976. Offprint from *Proceedings of the British Academy*, vol. 62. Oxford.

Léon, Xavier. 1954–59. *Fichte et son temps*. 2 books in 3 vols. Paris.

Lepley, Ray, ed. 1949. *Value: A Co-operative Inquiry*. New York.

Leroy, Maxime. 1946–62. *Histoire des idées sociales en France*. 3 vols. Paris.

Lévi-Strauss, Claude. 1947. "La sociologie française." In G. Gurvitch and W. E. Moore, eds., *La sociologie au XXe siècle*, 2: 513–45. Paris.

Lovejoy, Arthur D. 1941. "The Meaning of Romanticism for the Historian of Ideas." *Journal of the History of Ideas* 2, no. 3 (June): 257–78.

———. 1973. *The Great Chain of Being*. Oxford. (Originally published 1933.)

Lukács, Georg. 1955. *Die Zerstörung der Vernunft*. 2 vols. Berlin.

Lukes, Steven. 1973. *Emile Durkheim*. Penguin Books.

Macpherson, C. B. 1962. *The Political Theory of Possessive Individualism: Hobbes to Locke*. Oxford.

Maine, Sir Henry Sumner. 1887. *Ancient Law*. London.

Mann, Thomas. 1922. *Betrachtungen eines Unpolitischen*. Berlin. (Originally published 1918. Translation: *Reflections of a Nonpolitical Man*, New York, 1983.)

Marcaggi, V. 1904. *Les origines de la Déclaration des Droits de l'Homme*. Paris.

Marcuse, Herbert. 1960. *Reason and Revolution*. Boston.

Marx, Karl. 1953. *Grundrisse der Kritik der politischen Oekonomie*. Berlin. (Extracts translated by David McLellan as *Grundrisse*, Harper Torchbooks, New York, 1983.)

Maser, Werner. 1970. *Hitler's Mein Kampf: An Analysis*. London.

Mason, Tim. 1982. "Banalisation du nazisme." *Le Débat* 21 (September): 151–66.

Mauss, Marcel. 1922. Introduction to Robert Hertz, "Le péché et l'expiation." *Revue de l'Histoire des Religions* 86: 1–4, 54–60.

———. 1925. *Essai sur le don: Forme et raison de l'échange dans les sociétés archaïques*. (Reprinted in Mauss 1950. Translated by I. Cunnison as *The Gift*, Aberdeen, 1954.)

———. 1947. *Manuel d'ethnographie*. Edited by Denise Paulme. Paris.

———. 1950. *Sociologie et anthropologie*. Introduction by Claude Lévi-Strauss. Paris.

———. 1968–69. *Oeuvres*. Edited by V. Karady. 3 vols. Paris.

Mauss, Marcel, and Henri Hubert. 1899. "Essai sur le sacrifice." *Année*

Sociologique 2. (Reprinted in Mauss 1968–69, vol. 2. Translated by W. D. Halls as *Sacrifice, Its Nature and Function*, London, 1954.)

Meinecke, Friedrich. 1915. *Weltbürgertum und Nationalstaat*. 3d ed. Munich.

Michel, Henry. 1895. *L'idée de l'Etat*. Paris.

Mill, James. 1808. *Commerce Defended*. 2d ed. London. (Reprinted New York, 1965.)

Minder, Robert. 1962. *Kultur und Literatur in Deutschland und Frankreich*. Frankfurt-am-Main.

MM. See Dumont 1977.

Mol, Hans. 1976. *Identity and the Sacred: A Sketch for a New Social Scientific Theory of Religion*. Agincourt, Canada.

Morris, Charles. 1956. *Varieties of Human Value*. Chicago.

Morris, Colin. 1972. *The Discovery of the Individual, 1050–1200*. London.

Morrison, Karl F. 1969. *Tradition and Authority in the Western Church, 300–1140*. Princeton.

Needham, Rodney, ed. 1973. *Right and Left: Essays on Dual Symbolic Classification*. Foreword by E. E. Evans-Pritchard. Chicago.

Nelson, Benjamin. 1973. "Max Weber on Church, Sect and Mysticism." *Sociological Analysis* 34, no. 2.

―――. 1975. "Weber, Troeltsch, Jellinek as Comparative Historical Sociologists." *Sociological Analysis* 36, no. 3.

Neumann, Franz. 1942. *Behemoth: The Structure and Practice of National-Socialism*. New York.

Nolte, Ernst, 1963. *Der Faschismus in seiner Epoche: Die Action Française, der Italienische Faschismus, der Nationalsozialismus*. Munich.

Northrop, F. S. C. 1946. *The Meeting of East and West*. New York.

Ostrogorsky, Georges. 1969. *Histoire de l'Etat byzantin*. Paris.

Parsons, Talcott, and Edward A. Shils, eds. 1951. *Toward a General Theory of Action*. Cambridge, Mass. Harper Torchbook, 1962.

Partner, Peter. 1972. *The Lands of St. Peter*. London.

Peterson, Erik. 1951. "Der Monotheismus als politisches Problem." In *Theologische Traktate*, pp. 25–147. Munich.

Phillips, D. C. 1976. *Holistic Thought in Social Sciences*. Stanford.

Philonenko, Alexis. 1968. *Théorie et praxis dans la pensée morale et politique de Kant et de Fichte en 1793*. Paris.

Pinson, Koppels. 1934. *Pietism as a Factor in the Rise of German Nationalism*. Reprinted New York, 1968.

Plass, Ewald. 1969. *What Luther Said or Says*. St. Louis.

Plenge, Johann. 1916. *1789 und 1914*. Berlin.

―――. 1930. *Zur Ontologie der Beziehung (Allgemeine Relationstheorie)*. Münster in Westphalen.

Polanyi, Karl. 1957a. *The Great Transformation*. Boston (Originally published 1944.)

―――. 1957b. "The Economy as an Instituted Process." In *Trade and*

Market in the Early Empires, edited by Karl Polanyi, Conrad M. Arensberg, and Harry W. Pearson. Glencoe, Ill.

Polanyi, Karl, and Abraham Rotstein. 1966. *Dahomey and the Slave Trade: An Analysis of an Archaic Economy*. Seattle and London.

Polin, Raymond. 1953. *Politique et philosophie chez Thomas Hobbes*. Paris.

Popper, Karl. 1945. *The Open Society and Its Enemies*. London.

Prange, G. W., ed. 1944. *Hitler's Words*. Washington, D. C.

Pribram, Karl. 1912. *Die Entstehung der individualistischen Sozialphilosophie*. Leipzig.

———. 1922. "Deutscher Nationalismus und deutscher Sozialismus." *Archiv für Sozialwissenschaft und Sozialpolitik* 49: 248–376.

Radcliffe–Brown, A. R. 1953. "Dravidian Kinship Terminology." *Man*, no. 169 (July).

———. 1957. *A Natural Science of Society*. Glencoe, Ill.

———. 1958. *Method in Social Anthropology*. Edited. by M. N. Srinivas. Chicago.

RAIN. 1976. "Schools Anthropology: Exorcising Misconceptions." *Royal Anthropological Institute News* 12, no. 2 (January–February).

Rauschning, Hermann. 1939. *La Révolution du nihilisme*. Paris. (French translation of *Die Revolution der Nihilismus*, Zurich and New York, 1938.)

Ritter, Joachim. 1977. "Hegel und die französische Revolution." In *Metaphysik und Politik*. Frankfurt. (Originally published 1957.)

Rivière, Jean. 1962. *Le problème de l'Eglise et de l'Etat au temps de Philippe le Bel*. Louvain.

Robertson, Roland. 1982. "Response to Louis Dumont." *Religion* 12: 86–88.

Rousseau, Jean-Jacques. 1856. *Oeuvres complètes*. Paris.

———. 1861. *Oeuvres et correspondance inédites*. Edited by Streckeisen-Moultou. Paris.

———. 1964. *Oeuvres complètes, vol. 3: Du Contrat Social; Ecrits politiques*. Bibliothèque de la Pléiade. Paris.

Sabine, George H. 1963. *A History of Political Thought*. 3d. ed. London.

Sahlins, Marshall. 1972. *Stone Age Economics*. Chicago.

———. 1977*a*. *Culture and Practical Reason*. Chicago.

———. 1977*b*. *The Use and Abuse of Biology: An Anthropological Critique of Biosociology*. London.

Salomon, Ernst von. 1953. *Le Questionnaire*. Paris. (Translated from *Der Fragebogen*, Hamburg 1951.)

Schiller, Friedrich. 1967. *On the Aesthetic Education of Man*. Translated by E. M. Wilkinson and L. A. Willoughby. Oxford.

Schumpeter, Joseph A. 1954. *History of Economic Analysis*. Oxford. (Reprinted London, 1967.)

Schwartz, E. 1934. "Publizistische Sammlungen." *Abhandlungen der*

Bayerischen Akademie, Philologische-Historische Abteilung, n.s. 10. Munich.

Serres, Michel. 1968. *Le système de Leibniz et ses modèles mathématiques*. 2 vols. Paris.

Sheldon, Richard C. 1951. "Some Observations on Theory in Social Science." In Talcott Parsons and Edward A Shils, eds. *Toward a General Theory of Action*. Cambridge

Sieburg, Friedrich. 1930. *Dieu est-il français?* Paris

Smith, Adam. 1904. *An Inquiry into the Nature and Causes of the Wealth of Nations*. Edited by Edwin Cannan. 2 vols. London.

Southern, R. 1970. *Western Society and the Church in the Middle Ages*. Penguin Books.

Spitzer, Leo. 1944. Rejoinder to Lovejoy 1941. *Journal of the History of Ideas* 5, no. 2: 191–203.

Stern, Fritz. 1965. *The Politics of Cultural Despair: A Study in the Rise of the Germanic Ideology*. Anchor Books. (Originally published 1961.)

Strauss, Léo. 1954. *Droit naturel et Histoire*. Paris. Originally published as *Natural Right and History*, Chicago, 1953.

Talmon, J. L. 1952. *The Origins of Totalitarian Democracy*. London. (Reprint: Mercury Books, 1961).

Taminiaux, Jacques. 1967. *La Nostalgie de la Grèce à l'aube de l'idéalisme allemand*. The Hague.

Taylor, Charles. 1975. *Hegel*. Cambridge.

————. Unpubl. "Normative criteria of distributive Justice." 43 pp., mimeo.

Tcherkézoff, Serge. 1983. *Le Roi Nyamwezi, la Droite et la Gauche: Révision comparative des classifications dualistes*. Cambridge.

Theunissen, Michael. 1970. *Hegels Lehre vom absoluten Geist als theologisch-politischer Traktat*. Berlin.

Tocqueville, Alexis de. 1961. *De la démocratie en Amérique*. 2 vols. Paris.

Toennies, Ferdinand. 1971. *Ferdinand Toennies on Sociology: Pure, Applied, and Empirical*. Selected writings, edited and with an Introduction by Werner J. Cahnman and Rudolph Heberle. Chicago.

Trevor-Roper, Hughes, ed. 1973. *Hitler's Table Talk, 1941–1944*. London. (Originally published 1953.)

Troeltsch, Ernst. 1916*a*. "Die deutsche Idee von der Freiheit." *Neue Rundschau* 1916, no. 1: 50–75. (Reprinted in Troeltsch 1925*b*, pp. 80–107.)

————. 1916*b*. "Die Ideen von 1914." *Neue Rundschau* 1916, no. 1: 605 ff. (Reprinted in Troeltsch 1925*b*, pp. 31–58.)

————. 1922. *Die Soziallehren der christlichen Kirchen und Gruppen*. Vol. 1 of *Gesammelte Schriften*. Tübingen. (Originally published 1911. Translated by O. Wyon as *The Social Teaching of the Christian Churches and Groups*, 2 vols., New York, 1960.)

———. 1925*a*. "Das stoisch-christliche Naturrecht und das moderne profane Naturrecht." In *Gesammelte Schriften*, vol. 4. Tübingen.

———. 1925*b*. *Deutscher Geist und Westeuropa*. Tübingen. (Reprinted Aalen, 1966.)

———. 1960. *See* Troeltsch 1922.

Turner, Henry A. 1975. *Reappraisals of Fascism*. New York.

Ullmann, Walter. 1955. *The Growth of Papal Government in the Middle Ages*. London.

Vaughan, C. E. 1962. *The Political Writings of Jean-Jacques Rousseau*. 2 vols. Oxford. (1st ed., Cambridge, 1915).

Vichniac, Isabelle. 1977. "Des millions de fillettes et d'adolescentes sont victimes de mutilations sexuelles." *Le Monde* (28 April).

Villey, Michel. 1963. *La formation de la pensée juridique moderne: Le Franciscanisme et le droit*. Cours d'Histoire et de la philosophie du Droit. Paris.

Viner, Jacob. 1958. *The Long View and the Short*. Glencoe, Ill.

Weber, Max. 1920. *Die protestantische Ethik und der Geist des Kapitalismus*. Vol. 1 of *Gesammelte Aufsätze zur Religionssoziologie*. Tübingen. (Translated by Talcott Parsons as *The Protestant Ethic and the Spirit of Capitalism*, New York, 1958.)

Weldon, T. D. 1946. *States and Morals*. London.

Williams, Raymond. 1976. *Keywords*. New York.

Glossary

This glossary includes only a handful of basic terms as used in this book. The asterisk (*) signals another entry in the glossary. The reader is referred to passages within the book for explanations, exceptionally to other works for longer developments.

Hierarchy: To be distinguished from power, or command: order resulting from the consideration of value. The elementary hierarchical relation (or hierarchical *opposition) is that between a whole (or a set) and an element of that whole (or set)—or else that between two parts with reference to the whole. It can be analyzed into two contradictory aspects belonging to different levels: it is a distinction within an identity, an *encompassing of the contrary* (p. 227). Hierarchy is thus bi-dimensional (p. 253). In general, see the Postface to *HH*.

Holism: We call holist (holistic) an *ideology that valorizes the social whole and neglects or subordinates the human individual; see the opposite: *individualism. By extension, a sociology is holistic if it starts from the global society and not from the individual supposed to be given independently.

Ideology: Social set of representations; the set of ideas and values that are common in a society (= global ideology); a specified part of the global ideology: economic ideology. (Cf. *MM*, 7, 17 ff., etc.)

Individual: Regarding the human individual, or "the individual," we must distinguish:
   (1) the *empirical* subject, indivisible sample of the human species, as encountered in all societies;
   (2) The independent, autonomous *moral* and, thus, essentially nonsocial being, as encountered first of all in our modern ideology of man and society. The distinction is indispensable in sociology (p. 16).

Individualism: (1) By opposition to *holism, we call individualist an ideology which valorizes the individual (= which has the individual in sense (2) of *individual, and neglects or subordinates the social whole). On the relation of this *opposition to that between *inworldly individual/outworldly individual, see p. 56, n. 23.
(2) Having found that individualism in this sense is a major feature in the configuration of features that constitutes *modern ideology, we designate this *configuration* itself as individualistic, or as "individualist ideology," "individualism" (p. 17 ff.).
279   See *Relations.

Inworldly individual / outworldly individual: The individual in sense (2) of *individual, if "nonsocial" in principle, in thought, is social in fact: he lives in society, "in the world." In contrast, the Indian renouncer becomes independent, autonomous, i.e. an individual, by leaving the society properly called; he is an "outworldly individual" (*HH*, App. B).

Modern ideology: The set of common representations that are *characteristic* of modern civilization (pp. 17, 268, etc.). See *Individualism.

Opposition: The term designates solely an intellectual distinction and not a factual relation, like conflict, etc. We distinguish the symmetric or equistatutory opposition (= where the two terms have equal status, as the distinctive opposition in phonemics) and the asymmetric hierarchical opposition, whose inversion is meaningful (p. 230). See *Hierarchy.

Outworldly: See Inworldly individual

Relations: In the individualistic ideological configuration, the relation between man and things (or nature, or the object) is valorized as against the relation between men (*MM.*). The contrary is true of holistic ideologies. (See pp. 36, 106–7, 166, 260 n. 36.)

Value: Under this term, often in the plural, the anthropological literature refers to some extent to what we prefer to call *hierarchy. Value is segregated in *modern, individualistic ideology; in contrast it is an integral part of representations in holistic ideologies (chap. 9).

Value-ideas: As it is impossible to separate ideas and values in nonmodern forms of thought, one is led to speak of value-ideas, or idea-values (pp. 249 ff.).

Index

Italicized page numbers refer to direct quotations; boldfaced page numbers refer to continuous discussions.